The Problems
of the Philosophy
of History

The Problems
of the Philosophy
# of History
An Epistemological Essay

GEORG SIMMEL

Translated and Edited, with an Introduction,
by Guy Oakes

THE FREE PRESS
A Division of Macmillan Publishing Co., Inc.
NEW YORK

The research on which this translation is based was supported by a grant from Monmouth College.

The Free Press
A Division of Macmillan Publishing Co., Inc.
866 Third Avenue, New York, N.Y. 10022

Library of Congress Catalog Card Number: 76-51588.

Printed in the United States of America

printing number
1   2   3   4   5   6   7   8   9   10

Library of Congress Cataloging in Publication Data

Simmel, Georg, 1858-1918.
   The problems of the philosophy of history.

   Translation of Die Probleme der Geschichtspil-
osophie, 2d ed.
   Includes bibliographical references and index.
   1. History--Philosophy. 2. Knowledge, Theory
of. I. Title.
D16.8.S613   901   76-51588
ISBN 0-02-928890-8

Contents

✂✂✂✂✂✂✂✂✂

V

Preface to the
Second Edition (1905)

How does the theoretical construct that we call history develop from the material of immediate, experienced reality? That question is the subject of this book. It will establish that this transformation of immediate, experienced reality is more radical than the naive consciousness usually supposes. In this sense, the book is a critique of historical realism: the view according to which historical science is simply a mirror image of the event "as it really happened." The error committed here seems to be no less significant than the error of aesthetic realism. According to the latter thesis, the purpose of art is to copy or reproduce reality. This thesis fails to recognize how completely any "reproduction" actually forms the contents of reality. The constitutive power of the intellect in relation to nature is generally acknowledged. However the point that the intellect has the same constitutive power in relation to history is obviously more difficult to grasp. This is because mind is the material of history. Consider the formative categories of the mind, their general autonomy, and the sense in which the material of history satisfies the requirements of these categories. Consider also the distinction between these categories and the material of history itself. If mind constitutes history, then this distinction is not so clear as it is in the case of the natural sciences. The purpose of this book, therefore, is to establish—not in detail, but only in principle—the a priori of historical knowledge. For historical realism, history is a simple reproduction of the event. Any discrepancy between history and the event is merely the result of an abridgment that is purely quantitative. In opposition to this standpoint, we shall establish the legitimacy of the Kantian question: how is history possible?

Consider *Kant's* question: how is nature possible? As a contribution to our weltanschauung, the value of Kant's answer to this question lies in the freedom which the self or ego achieves in its relationship to everything that falls within the domain of mere nature. The self produces nature as its own idea. The general, constitutive laws of nature are simply the forms of our mind. Nature is thereby subjected to the sovereign self; not, of course, to the capriciousness of the self and its concrete vacillations, but rather to the *existence* of the self and the conditions necessary for its existence. The origin of these conditions is not independent of the self. On the contrary, they constitute its own immediate life. Consider the two forces which threaten modern man: nature and history. In Kant's work, the first of these forces is destroyed. Both seem to suffocate the free, autonomous personality. Nature has this property because mechanism subjects the psyche—like the falling stone and the budding plant—to blind necessity. History has this property because it reduces the psyche to a mere point where the social threads woven throughout history interlace. The entire productivity of the psyche is analyzed as a product of evolution. In the work of Kant, the autonomous mind escapes the imprisonment of our empirical existence by nature. The concept of nature formed by consciousness, the intelligibility of the forces of nature, what nature can be in relation to the psyche—all this is an achievement of the psyche itself. The mind frees the self from enslavement by nature. But this enslavement is now transformed into another: the mind enslaves itself. On the one hand, the personality is analyzed as an historical phenomenon. History, on the other hand, is the history of mind. In consequence, the personality seems to remain free from the tyranny of historical inevitability. But actually, history as a brute fact, a reality, and a superpersonal force threatens the integrity of the self quite as much as nature. In reality, therefore, history represents constraint or coercion by a force alien to the self. In this case, however, the temptation to conceive necessity as freedom is much more subtle. This is because the force which constrains us has the same essential nature that we have. It is necessary to emancipate the self from historicism in the same way that Kant freed it from naturalism. Perhaps the same epistemological critique will succeed here too: namely, to establish that the sovereign intellect also forms the construct of *mental existence* which we call history only by means of its own special categories. Man as an object of knowledge is a product of nature and history. But man as a knowing subject produces both nature and history. Consider the form of all mental reality which acquires consciousness and can be derived from every self as history. This form is a product of the constitutive ego. Consider the stream of existence in which the mind discovers itself. It is the mind itself which maps out the shores of this stream and determines the rhythm of its waves. Only under these conditions does the mind constitute itself as "history." The definitive purpose of the ensuing investigations may, therefore, be described as follows: they attempt to emancipate the mind—its formative power—from historicism in the same way that Kant freed it from nature.

In the first edition of the book, this basic problem was not yet sufficiently clear to me. While the second edition is constructed around this basic problem, the sense in which this can be said of the first edition is obviously very limited. In consequence, the present text must be regarded as a completely new book. Even the pages that were taken from the first edition now have a meaning that is more or less different from the original. This is a consequence of the change in the basic purpose of the book.

Preface to the
First Edition (1892)

The introduction to these investigations may be restricted to the following point of emphasis: this inquiry is purely epistemological. Any theory that is concerned with human beings must be rigorously distinguished from the promulgation of norms. For the same reason, the task of the theory of knowledge is limited to an immanent analysis of knowledge. In the analysis of any theory, the purpose of epistemology is to identify the basic theoretical elements, the relationship between the theory and its immanent aims, and the status of the theory in relation to other theories. The ensuing reflections may be represented as a preliminary epistemological critique of historical empiricism and as an exercise in the philosophy of history. They should not be misunderstood as an attempt to alter the facts of historical knowledge. Just to the contrary. Their only purpose is to identify these facts.

The Problems
of the Philosophy
# of History

Introduction:
Simmel's Problematic

Simmel's Refutation of Historical Realism

The fundamental problem of this book, Simmel tells us, is the refutation of historical realism. As Simmel conceives it, historical realism is a theory of historical knowledge which offers an answer to the question: under what conditions is historical knowledge possible? It is also a theory of historical reality insofar as it supplies an answer to the question: under what conditions is the process of history possible? Or, as Simmel poses this latter question: under what conditions does an event become history? Simmel reminds us that the concept of history is ambiguous in the following respect. On the one hand, history is a mode of experience, an inquiry that has its source in this mode of experience, and a type of knowledge that this sort of inquiry generates. In this sense of history, Thucydides's view of the Peloponnesian War is historical, and his investigation of the war is a history. Thucydides experiences the war historically; he sees it as having a history, and this leads him to pose certain kinds of questions and attempt to answer them. On the other hand, history is the object of historical experience; an historical investigation is an inquiry into the properties of this object. History is the object of historical knowledge. In this sense of history, the Peloponnesian War

1

itself is history. Put another way, it has a history, or it falls within the domain of history. "History," therefore, identifies an experience and the object of this experience, an investigation and the subject matter of this investigation, a kind of knowledge and the object of this kind of knowledge. As Simmel represents it, historical realism is a philosophy of history in both of these senses of the term "history." It makes a claim about the conditions under which historical knowledge and experience are possible: therefore it is an epistemological thesis. And it makes a claim about the conditions for the existence of the object of this sort of knowledge: therefore it is also an ontological thesis.

Historical realism claims that historical knowledge is possible insofar as it constitutes a mirror image of the event as it actually happened. On this view, the ideal history is a copy or reproduction of its subject matter. It follows that there is a sense in which the historian is comparable to the photographer: his purpose is to reproduce the features of his subject. History resembles a documentary film: its purpose is faithful reproduction. Consider descriptions of historical events as they actually happened or descriptions of the acts and artifacts of historical actors as they actually experienced them. If these propositions are the protocol sentences or the basic observation statements of history—the foundations of historical inquiry—then it seems to follow that only two sorts of propositions fall within the domain of historical knowledge: the protocol sentences of history and their logical consequences. The ideal biography of Luther, for example, would be a certain kind of autobiography: Luther's account of the events of his life as he actually experienced them. The ideal history of the Reformation would be a collection of such autobiographies, a series of reports by the historical actors describing the events as they really happened. There is only one true history of the Reformation: the account that approximates a complete reproduction most closely. To the extent that any history deviates from this sort of ideal description, it is defective. There are various possible sources of error in history. An historical account can go wrong by omission, condensation, deletion, or addition; by a shift in emphasis; by failing to pose questions about the event that were important to the actors who actually experienced it; by posing novel questions that the historical actors did not ask; or by imposing a novel structure or framework upon the event. There is only one source or criterion for historical truth: faithfulness of reproduction. In this light, consider two different but mutually consistent accounts of Luther's famous encounter with Zwingli. From the standpoint of historical realism, it is impossible for both accounts to satisfy the criteria for historical truth. Only one account can be true: the version that most closely approximates a description of the event as it actually happened. This is a consequence of the criterion for historical truth that historical realism requires: correspondence with the facts. An historical account is successful to the extent that it is a successful reproduction. It is a failure to the extent that it is a poor reproduction.

In Simmel's analysis of the doctrine, this is the principal epistemological thesis to which historical realism is committed. Historical realism is also committed to a metaphysical thesis, a theory of historical reality. This thesis provides an answer to a question which Simmel usually poses in the following terms. Under what conditions does an event become history? Under what conditions does any event, experience, act, or artifact fall within the domain of history? Under what conditions is historical reality possible? In other words, what are the conditions under which the predicate "historical" may be ascribed to any item? By what criterion can the events which fall within the domain of historical reality be distinguished from the events which do not? Historical realism claims that historical reality is constituted by the events as they actually happened, experiences as they were actually experienced, actions as they were actually performed. An event becomes history simply because it is an event, because it happened. Simmel also articulates this thesis in language that will be analyzed in the next section of this essay. The metaphysics of historical realism, as Simmel sees it, may be reduced to the following proposition: an event is constituted by the form of history because it is constituted by the form of reality. The categories of history and reality are coextensive. It follows that all the human experiences, events, actions, and artifacts that really existed qualify as historical.

As Simmel conceives it, therefore, historical realism may be analyzed as a metaphysical thesis and an epistemological thesis. Historical reality is the fabric or web (Simmel favors metaphors taken from the textile industry) of all autobiographies, their relationships, and their products. Historical knowledge is an attempt to recreate or reproduce this fabric. In principle—although this is never possible in practice—historical knowledge should be a copy of historical reality. Simmel also calls this doctrine "naturalism" or "historical empiricism." This seems to be an appropriate label. Historical realism, as Simmel characterizes it, is a logical consequence of any epistemology which situates the foundations of empirical knowledge in sensations, sense-impressions, sense-data, protocol sentences, or observation statements untainted by theory. In other words, Simmel's account of historical realism can easily be translated into the language of empiricism, either the older empiricism of Locke, Hume, or Mill or the more recent logical positivism of the members of the Vienna Circle and their epigones. Stated in the language of the older empiricism, historical realism claims that historical knowledge is ultimately a copy or reproduction of sense impressions. Stated in the language of logical positivism, a philosophical vocabulary which varied as the positivists altered their views, the propositions which constitute historical knowledge are either protocol sentences— theory-free observation statements that describe sense-data—or their logical consequences.

In the essay, Simmel's account of the relationship between historical realism and historical empiricism is confusing. This relationship is not clarified when Simmel introduces the concept of historicism, a doctrine which he apparently sees as intimately related to both historical realism and historical empiricism. For any attempt to understand the basic problematic of the essay, this confusion is interesting, but extremely troublesome and apparently unresolvable. In some contexts, we are led to believe that historical realism is equivalent to historical empiricism. In other contexts, we are led to believe that historical empiricism is only one among several different and mutually inconsistent types of historical realism. Simmel himself identifies another type of historical realism: historical idealism. Historical idealism, he says, is a form of epistemological realism. Like historical empiricism, it also conceives history as a reproduction of the event as it really happened. From the perspective of historical idealism, however, what is "real" is a metaphysical idea. In other words, the ultimate constituents of historical reality are metaphysical ideas, not sense impressions, sense data, or some other referent of pure observation statements. Therefore historical empiricism and historical idealism, two mutually inconsistent theories of historical reality, are both forms of historical realism.

The concept of historicism enters the essay in a curious way. Simmel's work antedates the protracted controversies over this idea that developed within the German sociohistorical sciences. The concept of historicism is notoriously ambiguous: its content varies unexpectedly and obscurely from one historicist and anti-historicist writer to another. The concept may remain an interesting artifact for historians of ideas. For analytical purposes, however, it is utterly worthless. In other publications, Simmel criticizes a thesis that he calls "historicism." Although we never learn the exact import of this thesis, it seems to reduce to the following claim. An historical phenomenon can be understood only by reference to its origins. Consider a given historical interpretandum, a description of an event. Historicism, as Simmel conceives it, claims that the only possible interpretans from which this interpretandum can be deduced is a description of the genesis and development of the event in question. All historical interpretations, therefore, must be genetic interpretations. To understand an historical phenomenon is to identify the conditions for its development.[1] In the preface to the second edition of the essay, Simmel suggests that his main purpose is the refutation of historicism. He tells us that it is necessary to emancipate the self from historicism in the same way that Kant freed it from naturalism. This, he says, is "the definitive purpose" of the essay: to emancipate the mind—its formative power—from historicism in the same way that Kant freed it from nature. Therefore it is paradoxical that historicism is never again mentioned in the second edition. It is mentioned only once in the third edition, in a note in which Simmel criticizes a view that he calls "empiricist historicism" (see the fifth note in Simmel's notes to this volume). What are we to make of this? Does Simmel entertain some idiosyncratic view of historicism according to which historicism is indistinguishable from historical realism, or perhaps indistinguishable from historical empiricism? Recall that Simmel has also identified the fundamental problem of the book as the refutation of historical realism. Or does the essay perhaps have two fundamental problems: the refutation of historical realism and the refutation of historicism? Or—even as he summarizes the basic problematic of the essay—is Simmel still uncertain about the fundamental purpose of the book? Simmel admits that when he published the first edition of the essay (1892), the "basic problem" of the book was not yet sufficiently clear to him. Does this confession also hold for the second edition? Does the basic problematic of the essay remain obscure? Or perhaps Simmel began the book as a critique of historicism and then shifted to a critique of realism. The arguments which Simmel employs in the essay to refute historical realism are not refutations of historicism as Simmel conceives it. In other words, the book is not, in fact, a critique of historicism. But did Simmel intend the essay as such a critique? Or did he work out the arguments first and then vacillate over the question of which doctrine they refuted: historicism or historical realism? Unless more material from Simmel's correspondence and diaries is discovered and published, these questions can only provide subject matter for speculation.

Although Simmel's intentions concerning the basic purpose of the book remain somewhat inarticulate, at least the following facts are indisputable. Simmel does indeed claim that the purpose of the book is to refute historical realism. And the book actually contains several arguments which, if sound, constitute a refutation of this doctrine. Therefore it is not an exaggeration to say that Simmel's intention is to refute historical realism. This is one demonstrable and definitive purpose of the book. Why does Simmel attempt to refute historical realism? Why does he think that historical realism is a doctrine that should be attacked? In Simmel's view, historical realism is not a patently absurd thesis which no one would be inclined to accept. It is not a position which rests on premises that are obviously false—just to the contrary. As Simmel sees it, there is a sense in which historical realism is true.

Suppose, Simmel suggests, we consider the subject matter of the historical sciences. In other words, suppose we examine human experience: "the ephemeral event as such, the purely atemporal significance of experience, the subjective consciousness of human agents." From the perspective of historical inquiry, Simmel claims, this subject matter is already "constituted by a priori forms of comprehension. The categories which constitute this material as history are already present in the material itself, at least in an embryonic or modified form." According to Simmel, this is one basic difference between the natural sciences and the sociohistorical sciences. As Kant established in the *Critique of Pure Reason,* the basic categories of the natural sciences—the apriorities of nature—are dictates of the intellect that are imposed upon nature. They have no exact counterpart in the given phenomenon itself. Consider, for example, the category of causality. It cannot be deduced from observations of temporal succession. Even if an event x is invariably followed by the event y, this does not establish that x is the cause of y. Causality is an a priori category of the intellect, a constitutive concept, one of the conditions for the intelligibility of natural phenomena. It cannot be deduced from any description of observations, no matter how exhaustive. However, Simmel claims, the question of the apriorities of history cannot be resolved so precisely and definitively. Why not? In order to answer this question, Simmel suggests that we examine the categories that are employed to distinguish the historical event from the event that does not fall within the domain of history. What will this examination reveal? "We will find a counterpart for these categories in the material of history itself more often than we will find a counterpart for the categories of the intellect in the material of sense perception" (Simmel, p. 63, below).

Simmel returns to the problem of the relationship between the sociohistorical sciences and the material of history in one of his most brilliant studies: "The Constitutive Concepts of History." In this essay, Simmel is interested in a distinction which may be explained in the following way. Consider any phenomenon. This phenomenon conceived as an object of historical knowledge can be distinguished from the same phenomenon conceived as an object of human experience. Put another way, a distinction can be made between a description of this phenomenon insofar as it falls within the domain of history and a description of the same phenomenon insofar as it falls within the domain of human experience. Another distinction can also be made. The phenomenon conceived as an object of historical knowledge can be differentiated from the same phenomenon conceived as the object of a purely "objective, systematic knowledge." The phenomenon as an object of human experience is completely irrelevant to this latter sort of knowledge (Simmel, 1967, p. 161).

Perhaps the following approximates an account of the sort of distinction Simmel has in mind. Reconsider the case of Martin Luther. Simmel thinks that it is possible to distinguish Luther's life as he experienced it from Luther's life as an object of historical investigation. Luther's experience of his own life can be distinguished from Luther's biography, an object of historical knowledge. Also, Simmel thinks, we can distinguish Luther's life as an object of historical knowledge from Luther's life as the object of a different kind of knowledge. Simmel calls this sort of knowledge "systematic" and "objective." It is not a form of historical knowledge, and Luther's experience of his own life is irrelevant to the criteria for this sort of knowledge. Suppose that Luther is described insofar as he represents a novel type of religiosity or a new kind of revolutionary who plays a crucial role in the process of modernization, the prophet who is also a charismatic politician. There is a sense in which these descriptions might be called objective. Luther's life is represented as an object of a certain type: it is described only insofar as it falls under certain categories of which Luther may have been utterly unaware. The question of whether these descriptions are appropriate is independent of Luther's experience of his own life. There is also a sense in which these descriptions might be called systematic. The type of revolutionary or religiosity Luther is said to represent is not peculiar to sixteenth-century Germany, nor to the kinds of societies that are indigenous to what is conventionally called "Western culture" or "Western civilization." From the standpoint of this sort of description, therefore, Luther could be compared to other putative instances of the same types that are identifiable at other times and in other societies. Again, in Simmel's view, the question of how Luther may have experienced his own life is irrelevant to the question of whether he falls under one of these systematic types.

How can these distinctions be made? How is an historical description of an event different from a description of that event as an object of human experience. How is it different from the sort of description that Simmel calls objective and systematic? History, Simmel tells us, focuses upon certain contents of life and places them in relief. They are arranged in novel sequences and subsumed under the technical concepts that are peculiar to historical inquiry. Nevertheless, Simmel claims, these contents remain the products or "offspring" of human life, "documents" of human experience. Unlike the objective, systematic sciences, history does not cut "the umbilical cord that connects it to the blood stream of human life" as it is actually experienced. History is the only form of conceptualization in which the meaning and the dynamics, the motivation and the development of human experience are preserved. History may translate the objects of human experience into novel constructs and syntheses. Nevertheless, Simmel claims, human experience remains indispensable to the forms and contents of history. "This is because they are necessarily forms and contents of objects of human experience" (Simmel, 1967, p. 163). According to Simmel, this is "the definitive property of historical knowledge" (Simmel, 1967, p. 161). An item is an object of historical knowledge only if it is an object of human experience. Historical inquiry may categorize and classify these objects in schema that were never dreamt of by the historical actors, but they remain objects of human experience. According to Simmel, this is the reason it is possible to identify a counterpart for the categories of history in the material of history itself—human experience and its artifacts.

Suppose that an event is an object of historical investigation only if it is an object of human experience. Suppose that a description of the properties of an event insofar as it is an object of human experience is essential to history. Suppose that a counterpart for the categories of historical inquiry can be identified in the subject matter of history itself. Suppose, as Simmel puts it, that there is an "essential identity" between historical knowledge and its object. What conclusion will we draw? A mistaken conclusion, according to Simmel. We will be inclined to accept "that form of naturalism which holds that knowledge is possible as a simple reproduction of its object and conceives the faithfulness of this reproduction as the criterion for knowledge itself." In other words, historical realism seems to be a logical consequence of the "definitive property of historical knowledge." This is why Simmel thinks that there is a sense in which historical realism is true.

The language that Simmel employs in his discussion of historical realism is, of course, archaic. However this should not lead us to conclude that the thesis itself is an anachronism. Although fashions in scholarly vocabulary—both in the sociohistorical sciences and in philosophy—have obviously changed considerably since Simmel wrote the essay, the thesis that he calls historical realism remains one of the most influential metatheoretical assumptions of the sociohistorical sciences. Historical realism has been stated in many ways, in more ways than can be surveyed here. Often we are told that there is an essential difference between the subject matter of the sociohistorical sciences and nature. The subject matter of the sociohistorical sciences is already defined as such by the historical actor himself. Put another way, the contents of any culture are already defined as such by the natives who participate in it. Therefore the historian—and much of what now passes for sociology, ethnography, ethnology, and cultural or social anthropology falls within the domain of history as Simmel conceives it—finds himself in a peculiar epistemological predicament. He is obliged to investigate phenomena for which an essential and incorrigible account is already available. This is the account of the historical actor himself, the native's view of his own experience, his own actions and their products. Any social world, past or present, is constituted as such by the native's definitions of its properties. It follows that the first step in any sociohistorical investigation is to discover how the native experiences his own social world. If the investigation is successful, there is a sense in which it should mirror or reproduce the native's own experience.

Is it surprising that we owe one of the most influential and widely imitated versions of historical realism to Max Weber? In articulating his version of historical realism, Weber uses the expressions "meaning," "understanding," and "interpretation." In Weber's view, any sociohistorical phenomenon is identifiable as such only by reference to its meaning, as this meaning is defined or understood by the historical actor himself. An event becomes history only if a meaning of this sort can be ascribed to it. To identify an historical phenomenon, therefore, it is necessary to identify the meaning of some object of human experience. In order to interpret an object of human experience historically, there is a sense in which it is necessary to understand it in the same way the historical actor understood it. Or, to employ Simmel's language, there is a sense in which historical interpretation is a reproduction of the historical actor's understanding of the objects of his own experience. Weber's initial sketch of this thesis is contained in the Roscher-Knies monograph (Weber, 1975, pp. 154, 157-158, 185-186). It reappears in both the 1904 essay on the objectivity of the social sciences (Weber, 1968, pp. 170, 175, 177-178, 180-181, 200-201) and the Eduard Meyer monograph (Weber, 1968, p. 262). Weber's most extensive analysis of this thesis is contained in his critique of Stammler. Among several other examples that Weber uses to illustrate its import, he considers the conditions under which two persons can be identified as performing an act of exchange.

> Let us suppose that two men who otherwise engage in no social relation—for example, two uncivilized men of different races, or a European who encounters a native in darkest Africa—meet and exchange two objects. We are inclined to think that a mere description of what can be observed during this exchange—muscular movements and, if some words were spoken, the sounds which, so to say, constitute the material of the behavior—would in no sense comprehend the essence of what happens. This is quite correct. The essence of what happens is constituted by the meaning which the two parties ascribe to their observable behavior, a meaning which regulates the course of their future conduct. Without this meaning, we are inclined to say, an exchange is neither empirically possible nor conceptually imaginable (Weber, 1968, pp. 331-332).

Weber does not claim that the student of the sociohistorical sciences is obliged to reproduce the meaning of an historical phenomenon as it was experienced by the historical actor. According to Weber, this is impossible (Weber, 1975, pp. 165-166, 169, 177-179, 181). Historical interpretation does not qualify as a unique kind of "intuition," a "recreation" of the "immediate experience" of some sociohistorical phenomenon. Nor does it express a diffuse, unanalyzable feeling which is the result of the investigator's gift for "sympathetic" or "empathetic" participation in the actions of others. In Weber's view, the essential purpose of historical interpretation is to reproduce the meaning of the phenomenon as it was understood—but not as it was experienced—by the historical actor. From the standpoint of Simmel's essay, it is this methodological requirement that qualifies Weber as an historical realist. There is a sense, a subtle sense, in which Weber commits the historian to the project of understanding the historical phenomenon "as it really happened." From Weber's perspective, "as it really happened" should not be read "as the meaning of the event was actually experienced," but rather "as the meaning of the event was actually understood."

Historical realism has been stated in many other ways. Sometimes the student of the sociohistorical sciences is instructed to share the mental life of the historical actor: his purposes, beliefs, feelings, and intentions. There is a sense in which he is invited or required to become the person he is investigating.[2] Sometimes he is only advised to discover how the historical actor sees his own experience so that it can be described from the actor's point of view.[3] Sometimes he is told to adopt the native's pretheoretical definition of the properties of his social world. This pretheoretical definition is said to constitute social reality. It supposedly identifies the social world as lived and taken for granted by the native. It articulates his experience of his own social world. As this is sometimes put, it comprises his situational knowledge of his life-world, a variety of knowledge that is limited by the native's zones of relevance.[4] There are many variations in the language used to state this thesis, variations which reflect contemporary fashions in philosophy and the social sciences: phenomenological social science, ethnomethodology, the sociology of everyday life, and what might be called "Wittgensteinian"—or perhaps "Oxford"—social science.[5]

So much for the doctrine of historical realism, its import, its influence, and its variations. What are the defects of historical realism? On what grounds does Simmel reject this view of the foundations of the sociohistorical sciences? The essay contains several closely related arguments which attack the soundness of this doctrine; however Simmel does not give equal weight to each argument.

The first argument begins with the premise that reality is infinitely complex. Every event is constituted by an infinite profusion of qualities that cannot be reduced to any finite set of descriptions, no matter how exhaustive. Since "no science can express the qualitatively infinite profusion of real existence," it follows that historical realism—which conceives knowledge as a "mirror image of reality"—must be false. Simmel does not take this argument very seriously. He says that it does not refute historical realism "in principle." Why not?

> Even under these ideal conditions—even if a qualitatively and quantitatively complete description of reality were actually possible—the discipline of history would still be different from a mirror image of reality. Just as a portrait would retain its peculiar nature and value if color photography could reproduce a phenomenon with absolute accuracy (Simmel, p. 80, below).

Suppose that reality were not infinitely complex. Or suppose that a complete representation of infinitely complex reality were possible— historical realism would still be false. Historical knowledge is not even a putative copy of historical reality: the purposes of historical knowledge are not the purposes of a photographic reproduction. Even if such a reproduction were possible, it would still fail to qualify as historical knowledge. That is why this argument, in Simmel's view, does not refute historical realism in principle; it assumes that there are conditions under which historical knowledge could qualify as a copy of historical reality. But this is impossible. Under what conditions can historical realism be refuted in principle?

The second argument attacks the epistemological thesis of historical realism. According to Simmel, knowledge which qualifies as a reproduction of reality is impossible. "Every form of knowledge represents a translation of the immediately given data into a new language, a language with its own intrinsic forms, categories, and requirements." Historical knowledge cannot qualify as a copy of reality because it represents a "translation" of reality into another language, the language of historical inquiry. The grammar of this language—its "intrinsic forms, categories, and requirements"—does not conform to the grammar of the language of the immediately given.

> In order to qualify as a science, the facts—inner, unobservable facts as well as external, observable facts—must answer questions which they never confront in reality and in their form as brute data. In order to qualify as objects of knowledge, certain aspects of the facts are thrown into relief, and others are relegated to the background. Certain specific features are emphasized. Certain immanent relations are established on

the basis of ideas and values. All this—as we might put it—transcends reality. The facts as objects of knowledge are formed into new constructs that have their own laws and their own peculiar qualities (Simmel, p. 77, below).

Consider, for example, a biography of Luther. It cannot possibly qualify as a reproduction of Luther's life as he actually experienced it. The historian poses questions about Luther's life that Luther himself did not pose. He employs categories that were unavailable to Luther. He makes distinctions that Luther did not make and could not have made. He also glosses over distinctions that were important to Luther. Certain aspects of Luther's life are stressed as significant. Other questions are omitted or neglected as insignificant. However the criterion for distinguishing aspects that are important and significant from aspects that are unimportant and insignificant does not lie in "the brute facts." As Simmel puts it, the criteria on which these distinctions are based "transcend reality." Independent of these distinctions, historical knowledge is impossible. But these distinctions cannot be deduced from any description of reality. Therefore history cannot possibly qualify as a reproduction of reality.

> History proceeds by posing questions to its raw material and ascribing meaning to singular phenomena. The result is often not what the "heroes" of history meant or intended at all. History reveals meanings and values in its raw material. These meanings and values structure the past in such a way that a new construct is produced, a construct which satisfies the criteria that *we* impose (Simmel, p. 78, below).

But why is this the case? Why does historical knowledge rest on criteria, distinctions, questions, discriminations, metatheoretical and axiological assumptions that cannot be identified in the raw material of history?

Simmel's third argument answers this question. Consider, he suggests, the relationship between an historical interpretation and a portrait. Physiognomy as such—a face as it really appears—cannot be captured in any portrait: a portrait is possible only insofar as certain aspects of the face can be discriminated. This process of discrimination excludes other aspects from the representation. In addition, what constitutes a representation of a face varies from one style to another: commitment to a given style allows certain possibilities of representation and excludes others. Also a portrait is possible only insofar as certain aspects of the face are discriminated by the use of a certain technique: the use of a given technique excludes possibilities of representation offered by other techniques. This is why a portrait in oil by a Dutch master cannot be said to reproduce the real face more or less faithfully than a charcoal sketch by Ernst Barlach. In the sense of reality that is at stake here—reproduction of all the characteristics of the physiognomy—neither is more or less "realistic" than the other. It follows that no portrait can qualify as an exact reproduction of the face as such. A portrait is possible only on the basis of the criteria for representation that constitute a certain style and the methods of representation that are required by certain standards of technique. In this respect, Simmel tells us, an historical description resembles a portrait.

> It is impossible to describe the single event as it really was because it is impossible to describe the event as a whole. A science of the total event is not only impossible for reasons of unmanageable quantity. It is also impossible because it would lack a *point of view* or *problematic*. Such a problematic is necessary in order to produce a construct that would satisfy our criteria for knowledge. A science of the total event would lack the category that is necessary for the identification and coherence of the elements of the event (Simmel, p. 82, below).

What follows? There is no knowledge of reality as such. "Given a criterion for knowledge that is perfectly general"—given a criterion of knowledge that would require an exhaustive representation of reality—it would be impossible to identify or distinguish any aspect of reality.

It follows that a description of historical reality as such is logically impossible. Any description of historical reality is a putative answer to a certain historical question. Such a question is possible only if certain aspects of reality can be discriminated and distinguished from other aspects. It follows that an historical question is logically dependent upon criteria for the identification and categorization of kinds of events and experiences and also criteria for the identification and individuation of specific events and experiences. Independent of criteria for the categorization, identification, and discrimination of events and types of event, experiences and types of experience, historical reality is incoherent. Since these criteria only identify specific aspects of events and experiences and not the event or experience as such, it follows that history as a representation of the event as it really occurred is logically impossible. This is because the event as it really occurred—as opposed to certain aspects of the event—is not a logically possible object of any question. There is no history: there are only histories. Since no history qualifies as a reproduction, a history can only represent one instance of the application of one differential problematic to the raw material of reality. Suppose we consider two different accounts of the same historical phenomenon. Put another way, suppose we consider one historical phenomenon represented from the standpoint of two different problematics. What is the relationship between these two accounts?

Simmel's answer to this question provides a fourth argument against historical realism. "If we are sufficiently careful about how the import of this remark should be understood," Simmel cautions us, "we can say that each history—each individual branch of historical science—has its own peculiar criterion of truth." In what sense is this the case? How could this thesis be established? Suppose we consider two different histories of the same phenomenon. Compare Martin Luther as the subject of a political history with Martin Luther as the subject of a psychohistory. What is the relationship between these two accounts?

> In the same way that objective differences in their subject matter are identifiable, so we can also identify logical differences between their theoretical ideals or criteria for knowledge. Consider the differences between these problematics. It follows that the kinds of propositions which satisfy abstract criteria for truth within these different branches of historical science will also be different. Therefore it also follows that these propositions cannot possibly be exact mirror images of reality (Simmel, p. 83, below).

Psychohistory and political history represent two different, but not necessarily alternative or mutually inconsistent, historical problematics. A biography of Martin Luther from the perspective of psychohistory is not concerned with the same historical phenomenon as a biography of Luther from the perspective of a history of politics. These two kinds of history discriminate different aspects of Luther's career as objects of investigation. They represent his life by reference to different sets of concepts. They also raise different kinds of questions about the aspects of Luther's life that they identify as deserving investigation. Because of the differences in the logical properties of the kinds of questions they pose, these two problematics have different theoretical purposes; it follows that the truth conditions for the answers to these questions are also different. As Simmel sees it, the conditions for the adequacy of a psychoanalytical study of Luther's career are not the same as the criteria for the adequacy of a political history of his life.

Consider, for example, the problem of explaining the fateful result of the encounter with Zwingli. A psychohistorian will pose one set of questions about this event. A political historian employs a different problematic; he poses a different set of questions, and his interpretations are appraised by reference to the criteria required by his problematic. But, Simmel warns, it does not follow that one of these accounts must be false—there is a sense in which they are not even alternatives. Historical truth, as Simmel conceives it, can be ascribed to both varieties of history. "It obviously follows that the criteria for truth in these two disciplines—and not merely their special, technical criteria—are completely different. The conditions under which a proposition is true in these two disciplines are simply not the same." Within each historical problematic, Simmel tells us, truth can be ascribed to "the propositions which satisfy *its own* immanent criteria for truth." In the essay, Simmel compares the criteria for historical interpretation or historical truth employed in various problematics: philological history and the history of ethics, the history of technology and domestic political history, the history of art and church history. Each of these problematics, Simmel claims, has its own distinctive criteria for truth. What follows as regards the status of historical realism? It is clear that "there is no sense in which historical truth qualifies as a mirror image of reality."[6]

In Simmel's view, therefore, historical realism is conclusively refuted.[7] Historical knowledge is not possible as a reproduction of reality: an event does not become history simply because it happened. If historical realism is false, under what conditions is history possible?

Simmel's Kantian Turn: Under What Conditions Is History Possible?

The Kantian turn of Simmel's problematic is unmistakable. Simmel himself repeatedly stresses the relationship between his essay and the *Critique of Pure Reason.* In view of the radical defects of historical realism, what follows? A Kantian question. In opposition to historical realism, Simmel claims, "we shall establish the legitimacy of the Kantian question: how is history possible?" In other words, Simmel thinks that the principal question of his essay has the same source as the main question of the *Critique of Pure Reason.* Kant provides a refutation of an empiricist theory of knowledge. Knowledge of nature is not possible on the grounds that the empiricists think: it is not a copy or a reproduction of sense impressions. If experience does not constitute a sufficient foundation for knowledge, then the following question, the principal problem of Kant's first critique, obviously arises: under what conditions is knowledge of nature possible? Simmel's own reasoning retraces these steps. He provides a refutation of historical realism. Historical knowledge is not possible on the grounds that the historical realists suppose: it is not a reproduction of the event as it actually happened. If historical realism fails to provide a foundation for historical knowledge, then what follows? The principal question of the essay: under what conditions is historical knowledge possible?

Simmel thinks that the strategy he employs to answer this question can also be described as Kantian. He tells us that "it is necessary to emancipate the self from historicism in the same way that Kant freed it from naturalism." And how did Kant achieve the emancipation from naturalism? By means of an *Erkenntniskritik:* an epistemological critique, an inquiry into the presuppositions of knowledge. Kant, in Simmel's view, attempts to answer the main question of the *Critique of Pure Reason* by posing the question: on what presuppositions does knowledge of nature rest? What are the a priori conditions for the possibility of knowledge of this sort? "Perhaps," Simmel suggests, "the same epistemological critique will succeed here too." Simmel proposes to deal with the main question of the essay by posing the problem: what are the presuppositions of historical knowledge? If historical knowledge is possible, on what grounds must it be based? Or, as Simmel also puts it, what are the a priori conditions for the possibility of history?

As Simmel sees it, the import of his answer to this question could also be described as Kantian. Man as an object of knowledge may be "a product of both nature and history." But consider man as "the cognitive subject," the investigator who raises questions about nature and history. From this perspective, man "produces both nature and history." History is possible only as a "form" of experience, knowledge, and reality; the constitutive properties of this form are products of the categories or a prioris of the human mind. These categories constitute the conditions for the possibility of history. In other words, there are a priori presuppositions which state the conditions under which it is possible to experience reality historically and think historically. These presuppositions define the sense in which historical experience and knowledge are possible, and they determine the limits of history as a form of experience and knowledge.

Consider Kant's claim about natural science. We have knowledge of an
object when we have produced a unity in the manifold of its perception. In the most general sense, this thesis also holds true for historical
knowledge. The unity of the Kantian object is only the unity of an
apperception. Apperception is the source of the unity of the multiplicity and heterogeneity of sense perceptions, the ground of their coherence and order. In historical inquiry, the unity of the consciousness of
the knowing subject—the historian—is the source of the unity of the
historical person— the object of the inquiry (Simmel, p. 98, below).

In the essay, therefore, Simmel sees himself as extending the
Kantian concept of an a priori presupposition in order to deal with a
question that Kant did not take up. Simmel employs the Kantian
problematic in order to resolve the question of the possibility of
history. How does Simmel manage this? Under what conditions is
historical knowledge possible? What are the a priori conditions for
the possibility of history? What are the constitutive categories of
historical inquiry? Simmel's answer runs as follows. An event becomes history only if it falls under the form or category of history; it
is possible to experience an event historically only if it falls under
this form. An event becomes a possible object of historical knowledge only under the same condition. Simmel also states this thesis in
the following way. An event becomes history only if it satisfies the a
priori conditions of history. Put another way, the predicate "historical" can be ascribed to an event only if certain a priori conditions
are satisfied. But what does this mean? In what sense is history a
form? What are the a prioris that constitute history as a form?

Form is the axiomatic concept of Simmel's thought. All of the
works for which he is remembered—in sociology, aesthetics, the
history of philosophy, the philosophy of the sociohistorical sciences,
epistemology, and metaphysics—rest on the assumption that the
world as a whole and aspects of it become possible objects of
knowledge and experience only if they are constituted by some form
or forms. Simmel is the great pyrotechnist of modern sociohistorical
thought. By present standards, the scope of his work is astonishing:
sociological theory; sociologies of various aspects of modernity—
money, the city, the role of numbers in modern life, the intellectualization of the world, secrecy, the stranger; Kant scholarship;
comparative studies of Goethe and Kant, Schopenhauer and Nietzsche; an aesthetic and philosophical study of Rembrandt's art, one of
his most provocative and enigmatical works; works on metaphysics
and what would now be called metaphilosophy; and many occasional
essays on an incredible range of subjects—death, fate, love, meals,

tact, women, the Alps, the actor, sexuality, expressionism, Rodin's sculpture. This unlikely assortment of scholarly and quasi-scholarly work appears to be unsystematic, inchoate, and—as it would probably be put today—unprofessional. Simmel's peers took or mistook appearance for reality and interpreted the scope of his work as evidence of dilettantism. It is not necessary to convict the Berlin mandarins of anti-Semitism in order to explain why they persistently denied Simmel the professorship to which he thought he was entitled. In their view, he was not a serious scholar. Another, more charitable view of the scope of Simmel's writings runs as follows. The apparently unsystematic character of Simmel's work is only appearance. All of his mature works are produced by the use of the same basic conceptual tool, the concept of form. It is his fundamental methodological principle. Therefore an examination of Simmel's concept of form will reveal order in apparent chaos and establish that the many fragments of his work are intimately connected. On the other hand, it is difficult to resist the conclusion that this fundamental concept is obscure. Simmel's own remarks on his idea of form are metaphorical, illustrative rather than analytical. Form is perhaps the most perplexing and inaccessible concept in Simmel's thought: vague, ambiguous, and elusive, but also axiomatic.[8]

A form, Simmel tells us, is a category or a collection of categories. He also describes forms as languages into which the world or aspects of it may be translated (Simmel, 1911, p. 17; 1922a, p. 29; 1922b, p. 7). These languages may be conceived as general schemata which constitute conditions for the intelligibility of the world as a whole or aspects of it. A form is a taxonomy, a system of classification, or a conceptual scheme. A form has both an epistemological and an ontological status. It constitutes the conditions under which the world can be experienced and conceived in a certain way, the conditions under which it can become the object of a certain kind of knowledge. Any such conceptual scheme contains categories, criteria, principles, distinctions, and requirements that are immanent and peculiar to the form itself. These properties of the form cannot be derived from reality as such; they cannot be deduced from any description of the contents on which the form is imposed. A form, therefore, supplies the conditions for a certain kind of experience and a certain kind of knowledge: this is why it is an epistemological category. However a form is also a condition for the existence of a certain kind of object, an object insofar as it is formed or constituted in a certain way, an object insofar as it falls under a given form. Therefore form is also an ontological category. Economics and painting, sexuality and marriage, prostitution and the drama, flirtation and the bourgeois household, Simmel tells us, are all forms. However law, society, morality, history, philosophy, art, science, religion, fate, love, and death are also forms. The same holds for reality, knowledge, existence, and value. Simmel even says that form itself is a form. In his major book on metaphysics, the fragmentary work called *Lebensanschauung,* life and form are described as "the ultimate constitutive principles of the world" (Simmel, 1922a, p. 16). Simmel makes the same claim in his book on Rembrandt. Form and life are the "ultimate" or "final categories of a weltanschauung" (Simmel, 1919, p. 67). If prostitution, morality, and value are all forms, then there must be hierarchical relationships between forms. An item can fall within the conceptual scheme of one form— painting, for example—only if it falls under the conceptual scheme of another form, art. An item can fall within the conceptual scheme of history only if it falls under the form of existence or reality.

Simmel claims that no form is exhaustive (Simmel, 1907, p. 57; 1922a, pp. 32-34). No conceptual scheme can provide a complete classification of reality. The language of every form is incomplete. Why is this the case? Simmel answers this question in his paper "On Aesthetic Qualities" (Simmel, 1968, pp. 81-85). Employing aesthetic realism as one of his foils, Simmel defends the thesis that art cannot represent all contents. In support of this thesis, he employs two arguments. "Art and artistic media have grown historically." At different points in history, therefore, "art must have different relationships to objective being" (Simmel, 1968, p. 81). Because of the historicity of all artistic activity and every object of art, it follows that there are contents that cannot be embraced by the form of art as it is constituted at a given stage of history.

Simmel's second argument is more interesting conceptually. Certain contents do not seem to be possible objects of art. "Certain objects are a priori excluded from works of art. It seems that some objects are withheld from artistic reproduction in the same measure in which interest in their *reality* dominates the imagination associatively" (Simmel, 1968, p. 83). As examples of items that interest us only because they fall under the form of reality, Simmel mentions the routine objects of everyday life. In Simmel's view, the objects of the quotidian world which are of interest to us only because they exist do not seem to be possible objects of aesthetic representation. If our interest in an item is exclusively determined by the fact that it falls under the form of reality, then it cannot fall under the form of art. As an illustration of what he regards as the mutual exclusiveness of art and reality, Simmel offers the rider on horseback. A representation of the rider "produces a contradiction if he is rendered in natural size, since his life-size representation will have realistic effects" (Simmel, 1968, p. 83). Exactly what is the contradiction? Simmel does not say. Perhaps he has the following point in mind. Reality as a form represents the world in one way; art represents it in another way. Compared with reality, art is an alternative language with different principles, criteria, distinctions, and requirements. Therefore a putatively artistic life-size representation of a man on horseback would appear to be inconsistent with the immanent conditions of art as a form. The contradiction—if the point that Simmel wants to make here has been correctly identified—is a case of internal consistency. A putative object of art that represents a rider on horseback in life-size is inconsistent with the conditions for the possibility of art itself.[9]

Simmel's view of the incompleteness of forms is more complicated than the foregoing paragraph suggests. Is the incompleteness of any form a consequence of the historicity of forms, a contingent matter of fact, a consequence of the dialectical interplay between form and life? On this view, forms are incomplete for the following reason. Life generates forms that transform the contents of life within new conceptual schemes, schemes which are inevitably shattered by the inexorable process of life itself. Or is the incompleteness of any form an essential aspect of the concept of form? Independent of the fact that forms vary historically, does every form have logical properties which entail that an exhaustive taxonomy of reality is impossible? Are forms not only incomplete for empirical, historical, or evolutionary reasons, but also for logical, conceptual, or immanent reasons? In the important first chapter of his book on the nature of philosophy, Simmel provides a typically Simmelian answer to this question: seminal, provocative, ambiguous, and inconclusive. A form, we learn, can embrace all contents. At least this holds for the "great" or "principal" forms. Because of their immanent properties, Simmel claims, "every given content can fall under one of these forms" (Simmel, 1911, p. 16). As illustrations of forms of this sort, he mentions knowledge and art. In the paper "The Conflict in Modern Culture" Simmel suggests that all forms are, in principle, exhaustive. This status is not reserved for the "great" or "universal" forms. "In principle, it is completely possible that a form which is perfect and meaningful purely as a form will represent a fully adequate expression of immediate life, clinging to reality as if it were an organically grown skin. This is undoubtedly the case of the great works of art" (Simmel, 1968, p. 17).

Art, in other words, is a form which, at least in principle, can provide an exhaustive representation of life. In the essay "On Aesthetic Qualities," however, Simmel argues that art is both empirically and logically incomplete. Should we conclude that the forms of painting and economics are incomplete, and the higher forms of art and science are not? Or should we conclude that the forms of art and science are incomplete, and the still more universal forms of knowledge and value are not? Simmel does not instruct us concerning what conclusion, if any, we should draw. Although it is in principle possible for each of these "great forms"—in the *Lebensanschauung,* they are called *"Weltformen"* or "universal forms"—to "translate the entire world into its language," in fact this does not happen. This is because—and here he repeats the first of the two arguments contained in the paper "On Aesthetic Qualities"—forms are subject to variations. Consider, Simmel suggests, conceptual schemes and the criteria for observation and the classification of observations; the translation of perceptual data into the constructs of the natural or socio-historical sciences; criteria for truth and falsity. In other words, consider all of the forms in which the world and its aspects become constituted as objects of knowledge. All of these forms, Simmel claims, have evolved in the course of intellectual history. This is a process that "will undoubtedly continue" (Simmel, 1911, p. 18). Because of this perpetual historical process of variation and transformation, the constitution of reality within the limits of any given form is incomplete, fragmentary, and impermanent. Recalling Fichte's remark that the kind of philosophy one has depends upon the kind of man he is, Simmel claims that the same point holds much more generally. "The kind of knowledge that humanity has at any given moment is dependent upon what humanity is in this moment" (Simmel, 1911, p. 18).

Finally, forms are not only impermanent and incomplete: they are also incomparable or incommensurable. A portrait cannot be evaluated by employing the criteria appropriate to the evaluation of a theory in small particle physics. Nor can an historical interpretation. Simmel's most complete analyses of the incommensurability of forms are contained in this volume and in *The Main Problems of Philosophy.* [10] In the first chapter of the latter volume—"On the Nature of Philosophy"—Simmel considers the relationship between the forms of philosophy, science, and art. This discussion focuses upon the problematical status of criteria for truth in philosophy.

As Simmel sees it, philosophy is not a system of doctrines: it is a form of life or a way of experiencing the world. The results of philosophical activity are not propositions that have truth value in some straightforward sense, nor even in some very extended sense. The results of philosophizing are not propositions at all. They are expressions or responses of a typical kind of human being to the world. The philosophy of Kant, for example, is not a collection of doctrines contained in his books. It is the systematic response of a certain type of human being to the world, a response which Kant's books express. It follows that criteria for the evaluation of the products of philosophical activity—expressions of forms of life—are not comparable to criteria for the evaluation of the products of scientific research—empirically verifiable propositions. In this respect, philosophy as an activity which expresses a certain view of the world is comparable to art. "If art is a world view as experienced by a certain temperament, then a philosophy could be called the temperament expressed by a certain world view" (Simmel, 1911, pp. 23- 24). It follows that there is a sense in which the results of philosophy are incommensurable with the results of science. There is also a sense in which the component expressions of different philosophies are incommensurable. Each philosophy contains its own criteria for adequacy of expression. Favorite Simmelian examples of incommensurable philosophical types are Plato, Meister Eckhardt, Spinoza, Kant, Schopenhauer, and Nietzsche. As Simmel puts it in his lectures on Schopenhauer and Nietzsche, metaphysical value and empirical truth value, philosophy and science, and even individual philosophies are all "incommensurable" (Simmel, 1923, pp. 12- 13, 42, 59, 191- 192). The products of any given kind of philosophical activity, therefore, can only be appraised by reference to its own immanent criteria for truth, adequacy, or appropriateness. The result appears to be a total relativization of philosophy: the elimination of truth from philosophical inquiry, or perhaps the elimination of philosophy as an inquiry. As Simmel sees it, however, this is only appearance. In reality, philosophy replaces one criterion for truth— truth as correspondence with an object—with another—truth as the coherence of expressions.[11]

The following, therefore, appear to be the definitive properties of forms as Simmel conceives them. (1) A form is a collection of categories, a language, a taxonomy, or a conceptual scheme which makes it possible to represent the world in a certain way. (2) This conceptual scheme has an epistemological status. It is a logical condition—a transcendental presupposition, as Simmel sometimes puts it—for the possibility of a certain kind of knowledge and experience. (3) A form also has a metaphysical status. It is an ontological condition for the existence of certain kinds of things: aspects of the world, *Weltinhalte,* insofar as they are constituted by this form. (4) The criteria, principles, categories, distinctions, and requirements that define any form are immanent to the form itself. They cannot be deduced from any description of unformed contents. (5) Nor can the definitive properties of one form be deduced from the properties of any other form. Forms are incommensurable. It follows that the products of any form—contents formed in a certain way—cannot be explained, understood, judged, or evaluated by reference to the criteria of other forms. (6) No form is complete. No form can provide an exhaustive taxonomy of the world and its contents. (7) There are hierarchical relationships between forms. In other words, there are forms that have the following property: a given content can be constituted by the form in question only if it is also constituted by some other form. If these are the essential properties of forms as Simmel conceives them, then it should not be difficult to understand his answer to the following question. Under what conditions is history possible?

In order for contents to fall within the domain of history, "it is necessary to conceive these contents from the perspective of the peculiar category of the historical." Historical knowledge amounts to a "transformation of experienced reality." In this respect, history is no different from the natural sciences. Both are "dependent upon the formative purposes of knowledge and the a priori categories which constitute the form or nature of knowledge as a product of our synthetic activities." An event or an experience, therefore, becomes history only if it is constituted by the form of history. It is a possible object of historical knowledge only if it has been translated into the language of the categories of history. In order to understand this point, Simmel suggests that we consider a province of history in which "the immediate reconstruction of the object of knowledge seems to be very easily possible," a province of history that "even seems to require the sort of account that would qualify as an exact and exhaustive recreation of the object itself." The history of philosophy, Simmel claims, is such a province. Under what conditions can the work of a philosopher be experienced historically?

Under what conditions is it a possible object of historical knowledge? Not under the conditions that the historical realist supposes. "A forming or structuring of the data is necessary."

> The intellectual contents which were created and directly experienced by the philosopher must be reconstructed by his historian. It is necessary to provide an interpretation of the data that satisfies the a priori requirements of knowledge. Only under these conditions can the raw material—philosophy—become a new construct—the history of philosophy (Simmel, p. 77–78, below).

Or, Simmel suggests, consider a person who experiences his own life historically and views it as an object of historical knowledge. Consider the autobiography. "Here the relationship between knowledge and its object seems to be even more intimate. Here it seems to be even more plausible to suppose that the forms of being and knowledge are simply one and the same melody played in two different keys." In this case, the historian has a privileged and unique access to the events and experiences that provide the subject matter of the history. No translation or transformation of the raw material would seem to be necessary or desirable in order to produce the autobiography. It is only necessary for the historian to allow his own memory to speak and reconstruct the past as it was actually experienced.

But, according to Simmel, this is only appearance. Autobiography is "the very case in which the following point can be made most clearly: knowledge—the synthesis of the original data—is a consequence of a priori forms. Although they hold for this material, they are not deducible from it." Life and history, experience and historical knowledge are not identical forms. An event insofar as it is an object of human experience does not have the same properties as this same event insofar as it is an object of historical knowledge. History and experience translate the event into two different languages. Each of these two languages has its own distinctive categories, criteria, and principles. Luther's encounter with Zwingli as an object of Luther's own experience does not have the same properties as this meeting conceived as an object of historical knowledge. This holds true even if the form·of historical knowledge at stake is autobiography. However there is an intimate relationship between the properties of a phenomenon as constituted by the form of history and the properties of that phenomenon as constituted by the forms of experience and reality.

The categories of history, Simmel tells us, "are exponents of a second power. They can only comprehend material which already falls under the category of direct experience." An event that does not fall within the domain of human experience is not a possible object of historical knowledge. If an event is not an object of experience, then it cannot become history. From the fact that an item is constituted as an object of human experience, however, it does not follow that it falls within the domain of history. The constitution of a given event as an object of human experience, therefore, is a necessary condition for the constitution of this same event as an object of historical knowledge. But it is not a sufficient condition.

Simmel claims that the same relationship obtains between the form of history and the form of existence or reality. An experience can become history only if it really existed. An event can become history only if it really happened. The play *Hamlet* satisfies this condition for historicity. However the character in the play of the same name does not, assuming that this particular Hamlet is not numbered among the real princes of Denmark. According to Simmel, Hamlet can still be the object of other kinds of knowledge and experience. Most obviously, he falls under the forms of the drama, art, morals, philosophy, and psychoanalysis, assuming that Simmel would admit psychoanalysis into the kingdom of forms. If Hamlet did not exist, however, he is not a possible object of historical knowledge. From the fact that an item falls under the form of existence or reality, however, it does not follow that it also falls under the form of history (see this volume, Chapter Three, section 8). The same relationship obtains between the form of history and the form of meaning or significance (see this volume, Chapter Three, section 5). Simmel's view of the necessary and sufficient conditions which must be satisfied for any item to qualify as historical seems to be the following: any item falls under the form of history if and only if it falls under the forms of existence or reality and significance or meaning. This condition—if it is a correct analysis of Simmel's position—identifies what he calls "the threshold of historical consciousness," a concept crucial to the essay (see this volume, Chapter Three, sections 3- 8). "This threshold is located where the existential interest intersects with the interest in the significance of content." "Where these two criteria mesh," Simmel tells us, "we find the specific interest in the facticity of certain distinctive sequences of events, persons, circumstances, and states that provides the foundation for history." It is this relationship between history and other forms presupposed by history that is at stake when Simmel claims that the subject matter of history is a "half-formed" or "proto-product."

The events and experiences that fall under the form of history are already constituted by a priori forms. Recall that "the categories which constitute this material as history are already present in the material itself, at least in an embryonic or modified form." This does not mean that there is any sense in which the sociohistorical sciences even approximate a reproduction of their subject matter. Or does it? Ironically and paradoxically, Simmel comes precipitously close to accepting historical realism. As we have seen, he claims that there is a very intimate relationship between the meaning of an event as the historical actor experienced or understood it and a historical inter-pretation of that event. The relationship is not exact reproduction. But precisely what is it? Simmel claims that the definitive purposes of historical knowledge often "only oblige us to emphasize, system-atize, and—from the standpoint of logic—complete elements that are already present in the object prior to its historical analysis." Suppose, as Simmel claims, that there is a sense in which the definitive properties of the object of historical knowledge are already preformed or prefigured in the raw material of history. Then it seems that there is also a sense in which historical interpretation should reproduce or recreate the properties of this raw material. Simmel admits as much himself. Historical interpretation rests upon the possibility of recreating the properties of events and experiences. Therefore how does historical knowledge differ from a reproduction of events as they really happened or a recreation of experiences as they were actually experienced?

Simmel struggles with this problem in Chapter One of this volume. The following, Simmel tells us, is one of the necessary conditions for the possibility of history: it must be psychologically possible to recreate the mental acts of historical persons. Unless this condition is satisfied, "the observable acts of historical persons would simply be unintelligible motions of physical objects." In other words, historical knowledge would be impossible. But, Simmel warns us, the historian's reproduction of the "mental act" of the historical person is not sufficient to constitute historical understanding. Suppose that it were possible for the historian to reproduce the knowledge that Galileo had at the time he made the crucial move from dynamics to kinematics, Luther's beliefs at the time he wrote the ninety-five theses, or Goethe's feelings as they are expressed in his letters to Frau von Stein. None of these acts or instances of recreation, according to Simmel, qualifies as an historical interpretation. "On the contrary, it is necessary to conceive these contents from the perspective of the peculiar category of the historical." In other words, it is necessary to conceive them by reference to the principles, criteria, distinctions, and questions that the historian himself imposes upon the raw material of history. They must satisfy the a priori conditions of history.

As Simmel describes them, the a prioris of history are the categories that define history as a form. If history is a language, then the a prioris of history constitute its grammar. Like the form of history itself, the a prioris have both an epistemological and an ontological status. They are propositions which state logically necessary conditions for the possibility of historical experience and historical knowledge. And they are also propositions which state ontological conditions for the possibility of historical events and experiences. Like the form of history, the a priori categories that constitute it cannot be derived from the raw material of history.[12] Like forms, the a prioris that constitute a given form are related hierarchically. The following, according to Simmel, is an example of an a priori presupposition of history. Certain physical movements of every individual—he mentions gestures, expressions, and sounds—are based on mental processes. This proposition, Simmel says, "can never be more than a hypothesis." In other words, it cannot be derived from any description of observations, no matter how complete. "However it functions as an a priori of all practical and theoretical relations between one subject and another."[13]

Although Simmel claims that historical knowledge, a product of the constitutive categories of the human mind insofar as it experiences the world historically, cannot be derived from the raw material of history, some sort of recreation of this material is a necessary condition for the possibility of history. "Each time a psychological entity is recreated and understood, this signifies that the historian makes this process his own. And—insofar as the person can be identified with his mental states—it can be said that at this moment he really *is* this psychological process" (Simmel, p. 92-93, below).

Does this mean that it is a necessary or sufficient condition for historical interpretation that the historian of science should in some sense "become" Galileo? Simmel repeatedly denies that this is the case. "The identity that is at stake here"—between the mental states of the historian and the mental states of the historical person—"is not a mechanical copy of the primary event." The historian only reproduces "the content or meaning of the event insofar as it is intelligible." Although Simmel's text remains obscure on this point, perhaps his intentions could be expressed in the following way. The interpretations produced by the historian of science do not rest on his ability to recreate Galileo's cognitive acts—although Simmel, unlike Weber, never argues that this is logically impossible. These interpretations rest on the historian's discovery of the propositions that Galileo knew. The historian of religion is not obliged to recreate Luther's mental acts of believing. But he is required to discover what Luther believed. The literary historian or biographer is not required to reenact Goethe's passions. But he is obliged to identify them.[14]

The foregoing account is only a sketch of the problematic on which *The Problems of the Philosophy of History* is based. This problematic commits Simmel to the pursuit of the following strategy. First, he tries to prove that historical realism is false. If historical realism is false, then a certain kind of question arises. What are the conditions for the possibility of history? Under what conditions does an event become history? In response to this question, Simmel offers a certain kind of answer. He describes both the question and the answer as Kantian. History is possible only as a form, a product of the constitutive activities of the mind. An event or an experience can become history only if it satisfies the a priori conditions that constitute history as a form. By employing the same *Erkenntniskritik* that Kant used in order to free the mind from nature, Simmel proposed to liberate it from history.

In pursuing this strategy, Simmel is led to take up many questions: the concepts of personal and group identity; the concept of historical interpretation; the question of the relationship between history, art, science, and philosophy; the problematical status of criteria for truth in history; the concept of an historical law; the sense in which meaning or significance can be ascribed to historical events; the question of the relationship between meaning and value, teleology and axiology; the concept of progress in history; the critique of historical materialism; and the idea that there are non-cognitive, extra-theoretical interests that are not a priori or logical conditions for the possibility of history, but rather substantive, axiological conditions. This bewildering variety of problems may give some indication of the intellectual riches of the book. However it is likely to confuse the reader who does not keep the following point in mind. Each of these issues is stated, scrutinized, analyzed, and—with varying degrees of care and detail—resolved within the limits of the basic problematic of the essay. Simmel's critique of historical materialism, for example, is an aspect of his critique of historical realism: he attacks historical materialism on the ground that it pretends to reproduce the properties of events as they actually occurred. His discussion of the idea of progress in history is also tied to the critique of historical realism. Simmel's purpose here is to establish that no form of progressive historical development can be deduced from any description of the events themselves: historical realism cannot make sense of the idea of historical development. Simmel discusses the concepts of personal and group identity, meaning, significance, and interpretation because he thinks that they are all constitutive categories of history as a form. His account of the complex relations between history, the sciences, art, and philosophy is a consequence of his interest in the definitive properties of history as a form.

This essay is not intended to provide an exposition and an analysis of each of the major questions of the book, Simmel's responses to them, and the reasoning on which these responses are based. That would require several volumes, each longer than Simmel's own essay. The purpose of this discussion, described in Simmelian language, is to reproduce the constitutive presuppositions of Simmel's reasoning. It is an account of the conceptual framework within which Simmel introduces the themes that make up this complex and inconclusive essay. Sometimes Simmel only presents his ideas in a dilatory fashion, on other occasions only by hints, speculations, and allusions, never in close analytical detail, and always with the suggestion that there is more here than meets the eye, perhaps even more than is dreamt of in the philosophy of the neo-Kantian epistemologist of the sociohistorical sciences.

Simmel's Text

The text translated below is the "second edition, completely revised" of Simmel's *Die Probleme der Geschichtsphilosophie*. The book was published in Leipzig in 1905 by Duncker and Humblodt, Simmel's principal publisher. Simmel's division of the book into chapters and sections and his use of italics and quotation marks have been followed scrupulously. The table of contents of the 1905 edition is also reproduced above.

The first edition of the essay appeared in 1892; in the preface to the second edition, Simmel tells us that the basic problematic of the work was not sufficiently clear to him at that point. This is why he calls the second edition a completely new book. "Even the pages that were taken from the first edition now have a meaning that is more or less·different from the original. This is a consequence of the change in the basic purpose of the book." This is a good description of the relationship between the two editions. The problematic of the second edition never appears clearly in the first—the essay of 1892 may be compared to a set of notes from which the essay of 1905 was written. The main themes and problems of the 1905 version are contained in the original text, and some of the solutions to these problems are also present; however the analysis of 1905 is obviously more subtle, refined, and carefully executed. In the 1892 version, Simmel never follows the logic of any problem with care or pursues any line of investigation to its conclusion. The first edition is an essay in the pejorative sense of being essayistic: a set of fragmentary remarks vaguely related by Simmel's neo-Kantian mode of analysis. The 1892 essay would make an excellent syllabus for a seminar on the philosophical questions of the sociohistorical sciences as they were conceived at the time. The principal difference between the two editions of the essay could be described in the following way. The first edition has its source in a collection of problems that are never connected in any systematic fashion; the second edition has its source in a problematic that is constructed carefully and pursued systematically.[15]

In the third edition of 1907, Simmel adds a number of notes and appendices which, he tells us, are intended to clarify the basic problematic of the essay. The material from the third edition which serves this purpose is included in the Notes of this volume. The source of this material is identified by references in brackets. For convenience, Simmel's notes, several of which run to an inordinate length, have been numbered serially and placed at the end of the text.

Notes

1. Simmel criticizes this thesis—"a superficial doctrine which leads to the most perplexing errors"—in an essay called "On the Nature of Historical Understanding" (see Simmel, 1957, pp. 72-73, 76-77). On p. 77, we find the following argument:

   > We would never be able to understand the what—the essence or import—of a thing as a consequence of its historical genesis unless there were some sense in which we could understand this essence itself, independent of its historical genesis. If this latter sort of understanding were not possible, then the attempt to understand anything in terms of its historical development would obviously be an utterly absurd undertaking.

   In other words, a genetic interpretation cannot be a sufficient condition for historical interpretation. See also Simmel's critique of historicism in his paper "On the History of Philosophy." Among other criticisms that he raises against the "excesses" of historicism—which "sets up the concept of history as an idol, a status formerly occupied by the concept of nature"—Simmel argues that this doctrine confuses the development of a given subject with the subject itself (Simmel, 1957, pp. 38-39). See also the essay "The Problem of Historical Time" (Simmel, 1957, pp. 43-58). This essay is not an explicit criticism of historicism, nor is it an immanent critique, an argument which deduces unacceptable consequences from the premises of the historicist position. It might be called an implicit critique of historicism. In this paper, Simmel sketches and defends a theory of historical interpretation that is obviously inconsistent with historicism. Finally, for some brief but illuminating remarks on historicism, see the first lecture in Simmel's series of sixteen lectures on Kant. Here he introduces a distinction between the "ideal construct" of the philosopher's personality and "the real historical man" (Simmel, 1921, pp. 3-4).

2. We owe an early statement of this view, and presumably one of the earliest manuals on what is now called methodology, to Joseph-Marie Degérando. In his advice to the principals of an expedition to Australia, an abortive voyage which was undertaken at the beginning of the nineteenth century, Degérando offers the following instructions concerning the importance of learning native languages.

   > It is a delusion to suppose that one can properly observe a people whom one cannot understand and with whom one cannot converse. The first means to the proper knowledge of the Savages, is to become after a fashion like one of them; and it is by learning their language that we shall become their fellow citizens (Degérando, 1969, p. 29).

3. This thesis is favored by British social anthropologists. See, for example, J. M. Beattie, 1964, pp. x, 83-84. The ethnographer is instructed to see the

native's social relations in the same way the native sees them. The purpose of this transposition in perspective is to enable the ethnographer to approximate what Simmel calls "reproduction."

4. This is, of course, the language of Alfred Schutz. See Schutz, 1962, 1964, 1967. See also Schutz and Luckmann, 1973.

5. See the foregoing references to Schutz and to Schutz and Luckmann. See also Garfinkel, 1967; Filmer *et. al,* 1973; Douglas, 1970; Winch, 1963; Louch, 1966; MacIntyre, 1962. And perhaps even Wittgenstein himself. It is always dangerous to attribute a thesis to Wittgenstein, who shares more common ground with Simmel than has ever been acknowledged. See Wittgenstein, 1967.

6. Simmel's discussion of these examples comes dangerously close to the sort of historical relativism or skepticism with which he has repeatedly been reproached. This is a criticism which Simmel both rejects and resents. See, for example, the final section of the essay: "Historical skepticism and idealism." In taking a summary view of the essay, Simmel says, "there is a temptation to conclude that its principal tendency is skeptical." This is certainly true. Are there conditions under which the theses of one historical problematic can be evaluated by reference to the criteria of another problematic? Are there conditions under which the results of applying two different problematics could be mutually inconsistent? Or are historical problematics simply incommensurable? They certainly seem to be. Simmel compares differences between historical problematics with the differences between portraits of the same model by different artists. Each portrait represents the same model. And each can be a valuable—even an equally valuable—work of art. From the fact that Rembrandt represents himself in one way and David Levine represents him in another way it does not follow that one of these representations must be false. Is there a sense in which both representations can be true? Simmel seems to think so. The fact that neither of two alternative representations must be false proves that "in the solution of the objective aesthetic problem it is the personal or subjective factor that is decisive." "The same proof," Simmel claims, "holds for history." What conclusion should we draw from these remarks? That criteria for the evaluation of historical interpretations are like criteria for the evaluation of portraits? That criteria for historical interpretation are essentially no different from aesthetic criteria? If that is the case, then the evaluation of two alternative accounts of the same historical phenomenon would be comparable to the evaluation of two alternative portraits of the same subject. A portrait may be flattering or unflattering. It may represent the subject as naive or cynical, honest or devious, chaste or lascivious. But suppose that this portrait satisfies the criteria for representation and the technical standards for execution required by a given style of portraiture. Could such a portrait be false? Simmel consistently leads us to conclude that there is no sense in which this could be the case. It is, of course, this

conclusion which is responsible for the doubt that falsity could be ascribed to any historical interpretation. And if there are no conditions under which one of two alternative historical interpretations must be false, we might be inclined to conclude that there are no conditions under which either interpretation can be true. But, Simmel warns us, this is not the conclusion we should draw from his essay. The skeptical tendency of the book is only apparent. For Simmel's argument on this point, see the concluding section of the essay.

7. Simmel's arguments attack the epistemological thesis of historical realism, not the ontological thesis. Why does Simmel fail to attack the ontological thesis directly? The text provides no conclusive answer to this question. Simmel himself does not distinguish the epistemological and ontological claims of the doctrine. The following hypothesis, however, would explain why Simmel limits his arguments to an attack on the epistemological thesis. If an event becomes history simply because it is an event, simply because it happened—the ontological thesis—then under ideal conditions historical knowledge should constitute a reproduction of the properties of the event as it actually happened—the epistemological thesis. But, Simmel argues, the epistemological thesis is false. Therefore it follows that the ontological thesis is also false, in which case, Simmel does not require independent arguments to refute the ontological thesis.

8. For a useful analysis of Simmel's concept of form based on a careful reading of many of Simmel's most opaque texts, see Weingartner, 1960.

9. Compare this discussion of the conditions under which an item can become an object of art with Simmel's account of the conditions under which an event can become history. See especially his analysis of the concept of the "threshold of historical consciousness" in Chapter 3, sections 7 and 8 of this volume.

10. See Simmel, this volume, Chapters One and Two; 1911, pp. 8-43; 1922a, pp. 29-31; and 1923, pp. 12-13, 42-59. Simmel's thesis that forms are incommensurable is closely related to a thesis discussed in the previous section of this essay. Not only are criteria for truth, validity, soundness, adequacy, or appropriateness "relative" in the sense that they are immanent properties of specific forms that vary from one form to another: these criteria also vary from one problematic to another within the same form. As we have seen, criteria for historical interpretation vary from one historical problematic or branch of history to another. Simmel claims that the criteria for the appraisal of a painting are not the same as the criteria for the appraisal of a photograph. Presumably criteria for the evaluation of a painting are not the same as the criteria for the evaluation of a sculpture. Does it follow that criteria for the evaluation of a gothic representation are different from the criteria for the evaluation of a baroque representation? And if this is the case, should we conclude that criteria for the truth of Aristotelian mechanics are not the same as the criteria for the truth of

Newtonian mechanics? This would entail that Aristotelian mechanics could not be criticized on the grounds of Newtonian mechanics. In other words, does Simmel's theory of knowledge—his theory of the logic of forms—belie his own repeated and emphatic denials? Does it lead to skepticism, the relativity of all axiological criteria—including criteria for empirical truth and logical validity—and a solipsism of forms and their component problematics? The problems which these questions raise constitute one of Simmel's principal concerns in this volume.

11. On the problematical status of criteria for truth in philosophy and the question of whether there is any sense in which truth can be ascribed to the products of philosophical activity, see Simmel, 1911, pp. 27–29.

12. But they can be—and, according to Simmel, there are instances in which they must be—derived from the categories of other forms; specifically, the a prioris of the forms of human experience and existence or reality. The presuppositions for the possibility of understanding everyday life—the a priori conditions under which it is possible to understand the quotidian world—"are reproduced more completely in historical research than in any other discipline." Again, Simmel comes dangerously close to the doctrine of historical realism that he wants to refute. The a prioris of historical interpretation are in part derived from the a prioris of everyday life. Does it follow that historical interpretation reproduces the properties of its subject matter? This issue troubles Simmel, and he attempts to resolve it. With what success, see Simmel, this volume, Chapter One.

13. For other examples of a priori presuppositions of history, see Simmel, this volume, Chapter One.

14. This interpretation of Simmel's intentions absolves him of the charge that he is committed to the same doctrine of historical realism that he proposes to refute. But is it consistent with Simmel's text? See especially Simmel's remarks in Chapter One on the sense in which recreation or reproduction is a necessary condition for historical interpretation.

15. The most obvious difference between the texts of 1892 and 1905 is the disparity in length: 109 pages in 1892 and 169 pages in 1905. Much of what Simmel has to say in 1905 simply does not appear in any form in 1892. The following material from the second edition is not contained in the first: Chapter One, sections 5, 8, and 9; Chapter Two, section 6 and most of sections 10 and 11; Chapter Three, section 12. Much of the material which is only sketched in 1892 is completely rewritten in a more careful and systematic fashion in 1905. Compare, for example, the cursory discussion of the concept of historical interpretation in the first edition (Simmel, 1892, pp. 16–20) with Chapter One, section 8 of the second. Compare also Chapter One, section 11 of the second edition with the corresponding material in the first (Simmel, 1892, pp. 24–26). The material presented in pp. 30–33 of the first edition is completely rewritten in Chapter One, section 12 of the second. Chapter Three of the second edition

contains an analysis of the relationship between the axiological and the teleological presuppositions of historical research, an analysis of the relationship between the concepts of value and significance, and an analysis of the extra-theoretical and axiological interests on which historical knowledge is based—in the first edition, there is only a crude sketch of this material. The crucial concept of a threshold of historical consciousness that Simmel introduces and analyzes in Chapter Three of the second edition cannot be identified in the text of 1892.

References

Beattie, J.M.
   1964   *Other Cultures*, New York
Degérando, Joseph-Marie
   1969   *The Observation of Savage Peoples*, Berkeley and Los Angeles
Douglas, Jack (ed.)
   1970   *Understanding Everyday Life*, Chicago
Filmer, Paul, et al.
   1973   *New Directions in Sociological Theory*, Cambridge, Mass.
Garfinkel, Harold
   1967   *Studies in Ethnomethodology*, Englewood Cliffs, N.J.
Louch, A.R.
   1966   *Explanation and Human Action*, Berkeley and Los Angeles
MacIntyre, A.D.
   1962   "A Mistake about Causality in Social Science," in P. Laslett and W.G. Runciman (eds.) *Philosophy, Politics, and Society*, Second Series, Oxford
Schutz, Alfred
   1962   *Collected Papers*, Volume I, The Hague
   1964   *Collected Papers*, Volume II, The Hague
   1967   *The Phenomenology of the Social World*, Evanston
Schutz, Alfred, and Thomas Luckmann
   1973   *The Structures of the Life-World*, Evanston
Simmel, Georg
   1892   *Die Probleme der Geschichtsphilosophie*, Leipzig
   1905   *Die Probleme der Geschichtsphilosophie*, second edition, completely revised, Leipzig (third edition, 1907)
   1911   *Hauptprobleme der Philosophie*, second edition, Leipzig
   1919   *Rembrandt: ein kunstphilosophischer Versuch*, second edition, Leipzig
   1921   *Kant. Sechzehn Vorlesungen gehalten an der Berliner Universität*, fifth edition, Berlin and Leipzig

1922a	*Lebensanschauung, Vier metaphysische Kapitel*, second edition, Munich and Leipzig
1922b	*Philosophie des Geldes*, fourth edition, Munich and Leipzig
1923	*Schopenhauer und Nietzsche*, third edition, Munich and Leipzig
1957	*Brücke und Tür*, Stuttgart
1967	*Fragmente und Aufsätze*, Hildesheim
1968	*The Conflict in Modern Culture and other Essays* (translated with an introduction by K. Peter Etzkorn), New York

Weber, Max
1968	*Gesammelte Aufsätze zur Wissenschaftslehre*, third edition, Tübingen
1975	*Roscher and Knies: The Logical Problems of Historical Economics*, New York

Weingartner, Rudolph H.
1960	*Experience and Culture: The Philosophy of Georg Simmel*, Middletown, Conn.

Winch, Peter
1963	*The Idea of a Social Science*, London

Wittgenstein, Ludwig
1967	"Bemerkungen über Frazer's *The Golden Bough*," *Synthese*, volume 17

Chapter One

On the Immanent Limits
of Historical Inquiry

ᨏᨏᨏᨏᨏᨏᨏ

1. The Psychological Status of History

The theory of knowledge in general begins with the fact that
knowing is a kind of conceiving, the conception of a knowing
subject, a person, or a psyche. The theory of historical knowledge,
therefore, may be defined as follows: the *objects* of its inquiries are
also the conceptions, intentions, desires, and feelings of personalities.
In other words, persons are its subject matter. All observable or
external events and processes—political and social, economic and
religious, legal and technological—would be both uninteresting and
unintelligible if they were not causes and effects of mental processes.
If history is not a mere puppet show, then it must be the history of
mental processes. So the observable events which history describes
are merely bridges that link impulses and volitional acts, on the one
hand, and the emotional reactions which these external events
produce, on the other. The various attempts to reconstruct the
physical conditions responsible for the peculiarities of historical
events do not alter this fact. The properties of soil and climate would
have no more bearing upon the course of history than the climate
and soil of Sirius if they did not influence—directly or indirectly—the
psychological constitution of nations. The *mental* status of historical

processes, therefore, seems to require the following ideal for historical inquiry: history should be a form of applied psychology. If there
were a nomological science of psychology, then the relationship
between history and psychology would be the same as the relationship between astronomy and mathematics.

2. *Nomological Regularity and Individuality*

On the other hand, the following difficulty immediately arises. A
law can only comprehend the general properties of objects of knowledge. This is a consequence of the import of a law: every phenomenon which satisfies certain conditions will have certain consequences—consequences that are totally independent of the individuality of the phenomenon. At least in part, however, history is
concerned with the individual, with absolutely unique personalities;
the question of whether history is exclusively concerned with the
individual is not at issue here. Consider the attempt to understand an
historical individual merely as the point at which general psychological laws intersect—laws which would produce another individual if
they were combined differently. Of course the relationship between
different physical phenomena can be understood in this way. However the idea that an historical individual could be understood in this
fashion seems to be not only utopian, but clearly erroneous.

This antithesis, however, may not be irresolvable. Consider those
relations the formulation of which we call laws of nature. They only
hold for certain aspects of a phenomenon—the phenomenon itself is
a given fact. In other words, its existence cannot be deduced from a
law of nature. Imagine an ideally complete natural science which
would establish that all qualitative differences between bodies could
be deduced from laws concerning modifications in the same basic
material. This basic material would be respresented in a nonqualita-
tive fashion. The reason for this is as follows. For the pragmatics of
knowledge, quality is intelligible only if a distinction can be established between some given quality and other qualities. In a strict
sense, however, even this primary material must be "produced" in
some fashion or other; otherwise it would be impossible for one
specific set of laws to acquire the force it has. Moreover it is always
possible to imagine another basic material for which the same complex of laws would be valid, even though a completely different
world would be the result. Consider this impenetrable, unanalyzable

residue of given fact. It is a presupposition and a definitive condition for the possibility of an analysis of real, material phenomena, the sort of analysis that is undertaken by employing laws of nature. Perhaps the same sort of residue exists is precisely the same fashion within the domain of mental phenomena, only with this difference: it is not one and the same for every sequence of phenomena. On the contrary, each phenomenon has its own characteristic residue.

Consider the fact that matter as such has certain definitive, primary properties. These properties—as we might put it—constitute the material world as a total entity. There is no sense in which this fact contradicts the universality of the laws of matter. On the contrary, it is a condition for their actual, empirical efficacy. In the same way, each mind could possess an original, primary quality. Like the material residue of matter, this quality could not be conceived as a nomological modification of some other quality this is even more primary: it would be a presupposition for the possibility of generally valid laws that apply to every mind in the same way. These laws would form the empirical domain of the mental. Clearly, these qualities could vary from one individual to another, but this variation would not affect the universality of the *laws*. Each *individual* mind would simply be an analog of the *entire* material world. Under these conditions, there would be no reason to doubt that the same laws governing the association and reproduction of ideas, differences in sensibility, the development of volition, apperception and suggestibility would apply with equal validity to Nero and Luther and to Jesus and Bismarck. Without a foundation or a basic point of reference, however, these laws are mere abstractions. This foundation would not lie in some material that is constituted by the laws themselves. On the contrary, it would lie in some antecedent material that is presupposed by the laws, a material that would constitute—as we might put it—the actual a priori of these laws. It is obvious that the nature of this material will determine the nature of the structures it produces. Of course our capacity to acquire knowledge of the structure of the mental beyond the limits of immediate consciousness is limited by a system of symbols that is quite tentative. Perhaps that is because the categories available for this purpose are constituted for objects of knowledge that are totally different from mental phenomena.

Consider, however, the following view of individual existence. On the one hand, general laws govern each and every case; on the other, the purely empirical material determines—as this might be expressed—the selection and combination of these laws, the kinds of effects they have, and the limits of these effects. A conception of existence which employs these two categories seems to me to be logically unobjectionable. Moreover, this conception makes it possible to provide a consistent account of the relationship between the validity of psychological laws and the uniqueness of historical individuals. Suppose that knowledge of the material world were complete. What would it provide? A unique representation of the definitive features of a material world which—as the original, primary matter of fact—both makes possible and defines the real limits within which general laws hold. In the domain of the mental, the same sort of logic would be reproduced with an unlimited number of variations. History would remain an instance of the "application" of psychological laws that are unconditionally universal. Consider, however, the material of history. It can never be derived from these laws. On the contrary, it is a condition for their application. This material would remain infinitely diverse. Therefore it would produce realities of incomparable and irreducible individuality.[1]

3. The Psychological a priori and Its Polar Antitheses

Let us put aside the question of the theoretical category to which knowledge of the immanent features of historical processes belongs. Consider the following fact. These features provide both the beginning point and the ultimate goal for every description of the observable features of historical processes. This fact rests on a series of special presuppositions. It is the purpose of the theory of historical knowledge to provide an account of these presuppositions.

In the work of Kant, the formative power of mental activity—in opposition to the given "material" of ideation—acquires an unprecedentedly enlarged domain. On the naive view, we are passive recipients of knowledge, which is transmitted to us from the things that are the objects of knowledge. Kant established that all knowledge is a function of the intellect. The intellect, by means of its own a priori forms, structures the entire domain of knowledge. This formal extension of the domain of mental activity can easily become a substantive restriction if the following point is forgotten: the mental functions which Kant describes as the a priori of knowledge are only supposed to be valid for existing knowledge of *natural science.* Consider the following issue. Is the experience of the *mental* only "possible" given a priori presuppositions which are not contained within the Kantian system? For example, is the causality by means of which we comprehend the appearance of one idea as the consequence of another different in principle from the causation of one physical movement by another? This issue is certainly open to question.

However the following point is much more essential. The Kantian a priori, which is "a general condition for the possibility of experience," is only the most highly abstract stage in a sequence of a priori propositions, the less abstract members of which penetrate much deeper into single regions of experience. Consider propositions insofar as they are—as we might put it—seen from the top of this sequence, its most abstract level. They are empirical in the sense that they represent an application of the most general forms of thought to specific material. However these same propositions can function in an a priori fashion for entire provinces of knowledge. They function as relational forms, serviceable to that peculiar capacity of the mind which classifies, defines, and stresses each given mental content in such a way that it can be molded to fit the most diverse constitutive forms. Considered as propositions, these relational forms appear as a priori statements. They remain relatively unconscious, depending upon the extent to which consciousness is in general focused more on the given and the relatively external, rather than on its own immanent function. Because these relational forms invariably present the most diverse contents in the same way, and because they are innate and essentially universal, a certain disposition is produced: in our consciousness, they appear as absolutely self-evident. The point that those matters which come first in the rational order of things— the cognitive functions of the mind—come last from the standpoint of our awareness and our observation is also valid in this context. Consider the extent to which the unconscious power of these relational forms governs matters of fact. Kant, because of his rigorous distinction between the a priori and the empirical, did not grasp this point in its full significance. This distinction, as a matter of method, principle, and category, remains completely absolute. What is at issue here only concerns the *contents* which function in an a priori fashion. It can be established that, within special branches of knowledge, these contents have the complete constitutive power of the a priori. This is the case even though—when viewed from the more abstract perspective that is the exclusive problematic of Kant's work—they are actually empirical.

Compared with the work of Kant, contemporary thought includes more abstractions within the domain of experience. However the a priori also extends much deeper in our thinking. Consider the most general forms to which every single experience is subordinated, forms that embrace every material. Consider also the more special forms that are established empirically and function in an a priori fashion only for certain contents. From the standpoint of content and praxis—but, of course, not from the standpoint of the system of categories—there are innumerable intermediate cases between these two kinds of forms. As an illustration, consider the relationship between the law of causality or the comprehension of identical elements from different objects under a single concept, on the one hand, and the methodological or other presuppositions of a given form of life or a specific science, on the other. Every legal system, for example, presupposes the desirability of a certain state of affairs. The presupposition that human relations can realize this state of affairs only through established norms and penal regulations governing their violation is a very general a priori. One of its consequences is a certain formation: the establishment of certain relations between preexisting ideas. However this relational form governing the making of laws is not so general as, for example, the causal relationship between internal motive and external action. This relationship is also a necessary condition for legislation. Although it holds for phenomena, it cannot be deduced directly from them. Consider also the a priori that constitutes the form of law as such. It is more general than those presuppositions on which the details of legal practice rest. For example, the principle that the burden of proof rests upon the plaintiff or the varying validity of rights sanctioned by custom structures the facts in the interest of knowledge of what is right. However this structure does not lie in the factual material itself; on the contrary, it requires an interpretation of these facts.

All human intercourse invariably rests on the assumption that certain physical movements of every individual—gestures, expressions, and sounds—are grounded on mental processes which may be cognitive, affective, or volitional. We understand the unobservable only by analogy to the observable. Language itself is an indication of this: all mental processes are designated by words which are taken from the world of external perception. On the other hand, we understand the observable aspects of human conduct only by reference to underlying immanent features. A certain relationship between experience and its spontaneous extension is a necessary condition for this process. This relationship is quite transparent: first-person experience establishes the connection between inner processes and their expressions. Because of this connection, we conclude that the same process which we observe in the case of another person is also associated with a mental process that is analogous to our own. Consider the proposition that the mental life of other persons, at least insofar as it is associated with their observable behavior, corresponds to our own. This proposition can never be more than a hypothesis; however it functions as an a priori of all practical and theoretical relations between one subject and another. Suppose one were inclined to say that it is only experience which shows us that this assumption is correct: in every case, we can observe the kind of external conduct which we attribute to the other person on these analogical grounds. This reasoning is circular. In the first place, we would never be able to make an inference of this sort unless the equivalence of mental processes were presupposed. In the second place, experience as such only leads to increasing increments of certainty concerning the following proposition: it can be observed that certain *expressions* of some other person are invariably consequences of certain other expressions. Given the nature of the intervening mental process which links one expression with another, this process can never be observed. Not only do we interpret single observed actions or forms of words by reference to a corresponding mental basis. We also construct a sequence of mental processes which has innumerable components and is in principle continuous and which has no direct counterpart in the external world. Underpinning this sequence, or these many sequences, is the total character of the personality. We interpret observable processes that are experientially indistinguishable by reference to very diverse and often antithetical mental processes. And it is by no means the case that this sort of interpretation is confined to situations where we suspect lying or dissimulation. Without these additional psychological presuppositions, by means of which we complete or supplement the primary perceptions which are associated with immediate ones, the conduct of every other person would remain nothing but a meaningless and incoherent chaos of disconnected impulses.

In discussing a priori ideas, it is tempting to ascribe the following import to them: they are correlated in complete experience and juxtaposed to the contents of the perceptually given. This view overlooks the following point. Linguistically, the a priori is only the formulation of mental energies that transform the given material of perception into objects of knowledge. The a priori plays a dynamic role in our thought. It is a real function which is precipitated or crystallized in its final, objective results: knowledge. Its meaning is not exhausted by the logical import of the concepts in which it may be expressed. On the contrary, the significance of the a priori is determined by its efficacy in producing the world of our knowledge.[2] In this sense of a priori, the following is an a priori proposition. The personality of every other person is an entity for us. In other words, it is an intelligible nexus of processes. We acquire *knowledge* of another person by means of this structure, or insofar as he is constituted by this structure. The function which corresponds to this concept complements or supplements the mental facts which lie behind the observable facts.

However this function also extrapolates beyond these facts in the following way. We also complete or supplement the *external* or *observable* process in such a way that it corresponds to the mental structure of it, a structure we take for granted; for example, in such a way that such an internal or mental structure is actually produced. Consider a reporter who witnesses the occurrence of a certain event. We are inclined to think that it is almost impossible for him to describe exactly what he saw. Every legal deposition or any report of a street fight confirms this. Even if he makes the best efforts to adhere to the truth, the narrator adds elements to what he directly observes, aspects which complete the event in the following sense: they identify what he infers from what is really given. In the same way, the listener, given the range of *his* experience and its effect on his fantasy, must always imagine more than what is in fact reported to him. The psychology of perception has established innumerable cases in which we unconsciously complete fragmentary impressions of single objects and movements in such a way that they conform to our previous experience. Exactly the same point holds for events which are interconnected. In its essentials, this completion or supplementation of the observable process is determined by psychological assumptions and our experience of the following: the continuity and development of mental life, the correlation of mental energies, and the content of teleological processes. This all depends upon external stimulation. However, given this stimulation, the external processes are also supplemented in the following respect. In accordance with experiential laws governing the relation between the mental and the physical, the external processes produce a continuous, parallel series of mental processes. Precisely this spontaneous supplementation is one of the strongest proofs of the following proposition: these mental processes are not simply deduced from the facts either. On the contrary, they are correlated with the facts on the basis of general presuppositions. In any case, everyday life provides enough opportunities to confirm the validity of this a priori and the specific consequences that it entails. Actually, our conduct invariably counts upon a response: the observable behavior of some other person. In the case of more abstract and complex mental processes, however, these consequences immediately become uncertain and produce innumerable errors. This shows that, even in the more unambiguous cases, these consequences only qualify as presuppositions of the following sort: they are trustworthy in the sense that they are useful for the purposes of both theory and practice. But they are not certain in the sense that they can be deduced, with logical necessity, from what is actually and empirically given.

These presuppositions of everyday life are reproduced more completely in historical research than in any other discipline. Their influence upon history is also greater than their influence upon any other discipline. In general, history employs these presuppositions uncritically, without making any attempt to verify them. Suppose that every interpretation and extrapolation were so completely self-evident that each observed fact could be classified exactly and unambiguously under the presupposition appropriate to it. Even in this case, the identification of these presuppositions would still be an important task, albeit an extraordinarily subtle and difficult one. That is because we sometimes correlate very different external consequences with the same inner process. This is comprehensible only because of the diversity of the mental correlates or consequences that can be associated with the same external process. Sometimes we think that the process must fall under one psychological norm; in other cases we think that it must fall under a completely antithetical one.

As an illustration, consider Sybel's account of the relationship between the Committee of Public Safety and the Hebertists during the year 1793 (*History of the Revolutionary Era,* volume II, p. 364).

> Formerly they (the Hebertists) enjoyed excellent relations with Robespierre. This was because he relied on their forces and, accordingly, promoted their interests. However what irrevocably estranged them from Robespierre was the simple fact that he had become the leader of

the most powerful force in the state. The Hebertists, on the other hand, remained in a subordinate position.

Consider the following observable facts. Robespierre promotes the interests of the Hebertists: they form an alliance with him. Now Robespierre wins the dominant political position: they break off the alliance. Given certain underlying psychological presuppositions, these facts qualify as a thoroughly intelligible sequence. But the presuppositions in question are certainly not so conclusive or unambiguous as they might initially appear. It happens often enough that someone who promotes the interests of another gains his favor and practical devotion through manifest good deeds. However precisely the contrary can also happen.

Consider, for example, the following anecdote from the bloody family wars of the Trecento. A Ravenna aristocrat had all of his enemies together in one house and could have killed them very easily: instead he let them go and treated them liberally. In consequence, they attacked him with redoubled force and cunning and could not rest until he had been killed. The anecdote goes on to make the reason for this clear: they could not endure the shame produced by this act of charity. Here too the sequence of external events is quite intelligible. We only need to interpolate and supplement these events with the following psychological presupposition: the devaluation of the sense of personal integrity which so often makes charity a consuming worm for the recipient and converts him into an enemy of his benefactor. In this example, it makes no difference for our purposes whether the historical evidence includes explicit claims by the participants themselves, claims which express their putative psychological states in such a way that the historian is not obliged to employ descriptions of these states as assumptions. In the first place, there are innumerable similar cases in which it would be necessary to employ these assumptions because of the modest historical data available concerning the external processes themselves. Moreover, the historian could accept this immediate data—the participant's claims about his psychological state—only under the following condition. He recognizes it as a possible psychological state, and he can reconstruct it in the light of his own experience. We can understand that the elevation of Robespierre to the position of head of the government produced hostile actions on the part of the Hebertists only because of the hatred and envy this aroused in them. On the other hand, we would have no difficulty in accepting the plausibility of a report that contradicts this view: the full development of the powerful personality of Robespierre and the dominant position which he achieved broke the resistance—even the inner resistance—of the Hebertists. In view of this, the Hebertists knew that they were powerless to do anything. But at least they might have wanted to maintain some degree of participation in political power by being submissive and subordinate. If we presuppose certain psychological norms, this form of behavior becomes completely intelligible. Consider, for example, the Senate of Rome in the era of the military dictatorship. In the one case, we are satisfied with the thesis that charity or the attainment of political domination was correlated with a certain psychological effect. In the other case, we are satisfied with the thesis that these acts excluded this psychological effect and produced another. However we do not discover the reason for this difference in the observable act itself. On the contrary, we acquire knowledge of the psychological state responsible for this difference only through the consequences it produces. These consequences, on the other hand, are intelligible only if we presuppose a certain state of mind as their antecedent.

Consider democratic constitutions in which a government is formed by one of two major political parties and is subject to electoral recall on short notice. We are told that abuse of power by the governing party is out of the question. This is because the governing party surely fears that it will shortly become the oppressed party itself and suffer the revenge of the oppressor. In reality, nevertheless, this situation just as often exhibits the most ruthless and imprudent exploitation of ephemeral political power. Given the equivalence of the external facts, how is this difference in the effect to be explained? In practice, by reference to differences in internal factors: the "character" of the personalities or parties determines which of these two antithetical consequences will ensue. However knowledge of this "character"—whatever it may be—is possible only through knowledge of its observable expressions: the mental cause of the difference can never be immediately grasped. On the contrary, it invariably remains a hypothesis which underpins the empirical phenomenon. However the necessity of this hypothesis for understanding the phenomena is established by the following consideration. The obvious unavoidability of inferring the mental cause only from these empirical phenomena and the necessity of carefully investigating all its contradictions does not cast any doubt at all upon the application and the adequacy of the hypothesis itself.

I shall adduce only one more example. Knapp (*Agricultural Labor,* p. 82) makes the following claims concerning the circumstances of Russian agricultural workers after the abolition of serfdom.

> The peasants obligated themselves to perform certain services for the lord in exchange for wages. However they were not happy with this situation. This was because the new laws did not guarantee permanent employment with the lord. These circumstances did not help the lord much either. The peasant work, performed by agreement rather than by compulsion, was badly done in spite of the wages.

The first thesis presupposes as self-evident—or at least as requiring no further discussion—that the affective response to a certain situation will not change as long as the external properties of the situation remain the same. This holds even if the inner factors which were originally responsible for that affective response change completely. The second thesis makes it appear perfectly obvious that the peasant, over whom the lord could no longer exercise complete domination and with whom he was now obliged to negotiate, worked less industriously than before. Suppose the facts showed that economic productivity in Russia constantly increased after 1864. If that were the case, then a set of psychological premises contrary to those presupposed in Knapp's account would not have made the relationship between cause and effect any less plausible. We would see right away that it is not observable conduct, but rather the ethical basis and motive from which conduct proceeds, which determines whether work is done with pleasure and affection rather than with the contrary feelings. And, as regards compulsory peasant labor, the data on Prussia before the abolition of serfdom indicate the contrary of the foregoing. We hear the constant complaint that serfs make the poorest, most indolent and dishonest workers.[3]

Examples of this sort appear repeatedly in every work of history. On the one hand, these illustrations should not be misused in the interests of a cheap and unjustified skepticism concerning psychological interpretation in general. On the other hand, the differences between possible interpretations should be sufficient to show that psychological interpretation cannot be regarded as an unambiguous concept that requires no further analysis. These presuppositions and the importance of choosing between them are most crucial in the numerous cases in which the observable facts have not been established clearly and unambiguously, cases in which the identification and classification of facts is dependent upon psychological probability. Even in the most obvious cases, it is not "the plain fact" that resolves the question of the intelligibility of the consequences of a phenomenon. On the contrary, psychological major premises—in relation to which "the plain fact" serves as a minor premise—are responsible for the fact that the consequence of a phenomenon seems to be possible and intelligible. We subsume observable human actions under the unobservable purposes and feelings which are necessary in order to fit these actions into an intelligible scheme. Suppose, however, that we could not proceed beyond the actually verifiable material of history. Then the prospects for establishing any kind of historical development or for understanding one historical detail as a consequence of another would be very bad indeed. Somewhere Helmholtz says that the proof of the law of causality would be very weak if it were necessary to deduce this law from experience. Cases in which it holds without exception are very infrequent in comparison with the enormous number of cases in which a complete causal account is lacking. Suppose that this point holds for processes in the submental world of natural objects. In that case, proof of causality would be even more problematical where the issue concerns the causal relationship between visible processes and the obscure and complex brain processes that link these observable processes.

Given the thesis of psycho-physical correspondence—which we shall not discuss here—we could have complete knowledge of an historical personality only under the following conditions. First, all the observable and bodily influences and changes which obtain between the single acts of an historical personality would be completely transparent. Second, we would have knowledge of the psychic meaning or value of every cerebral process that is located in this sequence. However this ideal is unattainable; perhaps it is even self-contradictory. Therefore we must be satisfied with the attempt to underpin and interpolate observable processes with mental processes.

4. Conscious and Unconscious Motives

Consider the hypothetical status of every explanation of an observable historical event. It is a consequence of the fact that these explanations rest on psychological premises. This hypothetical status is not only a result of the questionable import of processes of consciousness and the fact that completely inconsistent conjectures about them may be ventured with the same probability—just to the contrary. The systematic ambiguity of these explanations has its origins in the following question. Under what conditions is an observable occurrence a consequence of consciousness, and under what conditions is it a consequence of unconscious forces? Especially in mass movements, we can identify innumerable significant, characteristic, purposeful, and also pointless things. But their conscious motivation is quite doubtful.

The entire problem of unconscious mental processes arises in the following way. There are observable actions for which no conscious motivation can be discovered, and these actions are perfectly analogous to actions that are a consequence of conscious deliberation and intention. Therefore we infer that the same motive which is present in the latter case is also present in the former case, only with the following difference: in the former case, the motive is unconscious. The expression "unconscious motivation" is really only an indication that the genuine motive is unknown. It only means that we cannot identify a conscious motive. Therefore we make this negative case, which is not accessible to our knowledge, into something positive. The unknown becomes the unconscious, a certain kind of mental process. This is a surreptitious move. It is only a consequence of our need to insert a motive into the empty causal link in the explanation of human conduct. The life of groups seems to have certain properties which correspond to the instinctual and reflex actions of the individual. An aggressive tendency toward the irresistible and incessant expansion of their borders is ascribed to certain peoples as if it were the consequence of a physical drive. The mysterious attraction of the Germanic peoples for Italy is described as if it were like the instinct of migratory birds—a drive which is totally unconscious and which leads them to fly in certain directions.

Consider the following issue. To what extent does the explanation of human conduct rest on conscious deliberation? To what extent does it rest on a problematical, unconscious teleology? To what extent does it rest on a kind of organic process—parallel to innervation—which has a purely physical cause? This issue will probably always remain a question of personal interpretation. The intermediate zone between conscious and unconscious phenomena is quite variable, lending the same plausibility to mutually inconsistent interpretations. At least one of the reasons for this lies in a peculiar kind of pendulum movement that occurs in intellectual history. Actions which were once conscious gradually become unconscious and are executed in a purely mechanical fashion. Consider, for example, the pianist. At first, he is obliged to concentrate on playing the right note. Later he plays the same note through an established mechanism of association: the image of the note is produced in his mind without any intervening process of consciousness. The opposite process also takes place: actions which were originally mechanical increasingly acquire a conscious status. For example, the blindness of instincts gives way to clear reflections and higher norms. Consider a case in which prudence and necessity have led a group to wage several wars. This can produce a belligerent tendency. In subsequent expressions of this tendency, however, it would be futile to attempt to discover sufficient reasons for making war in the consciousness of the actors. Or consider a case in which the subordination and subservience of one class to another is a result of causes that are fully conscious. Suppose this state of affairs has persisted for some time. Then it would be pointless to seek information about the purpose of a given subservient action in the consciousness of individuals. The action would simply be a reflexive response, the result of stimuli that are formally related to the earlier conscious causes. Consider the naive assumption according to which the meaningful relationship between the actions of an individual or a group are obviously located in conscious mental processes, processes which have a teleological character that is responsible for this relationship. The errors generated by this assumption are obvious.

No examples are needed in order to illustrate the other tendency — in which actions that were originally mechanical increasingly acquire a conscious status. In general, a higher level of culture represents a higher level of consciousness: intention replaces instinct, deliberation replaces acquiescence to mechanical forces, affective responses replace apathetic submission. The development of a single historical content can often be represented as a curve or a function of these two tendencies. Forms of behavior that were originally instinctual rise to the level of clear consciousness. Then they sink back into the level of a purely mechanical exercise. Consider, for example, the praxis of an art. At first, the art is a product of pure instinct. Then it is developed into a conscious technique. After long practice, however, the master employs this technique instinctively and unreflectively.

There is no doubt that both of these tendencies can be identified in the same stage of the development of a group. In consequence, neither the degree of consciousness which the development of the group exhibits nor the aspects of this development which exhibit consciousness can be determined objectively. In many cases, this issue is dependent upon the following question of principle. Can the movements of a group be derived as a composite of individual processes, or are they a consequence of a superindividual total spirit? Are single, dominant personalities the real bearers of action, or do the diffuse masses act on their own impulses? Suppose we take the former view: motivation is individual. Then the consciousness which underpins external events will acquire a more decisive role than would be the case if we regarded totalities as the integral agents responsible for these events. The description of great men as "the consciousness" of their age is an expression of this difference.

Consider, therefore, the following two views concerning the intrinsic properties of an historical event. On one view, they lie in the clear consciousness of individuals. On the other view, they lie in the indifferent, instinctual behavior of the masses. These two views will produce a completely different kind of understanding of the plain facts, different inferences, and different hypotheses. This will also hold when the historical evidence is incomplete. In addition to this distinction between conscious individuality and the unconscious masses, there is another dichotomy that is germane to historical interpretation: the distinction between conscious individuality and the impersonal forces which are implicated in the actions and situations of personalities, sometimes as causes and sometimes as effects. It is obvious that law and morals, language and thought, high culture and forms of social intercourse do not develop independent of the intentional activities of individuals. However the individual actor is not aware of the product of his activities, the development of the social form which embraces these individual materials. In his relationships with others, the individual tries to find the best expression for affection and reserve, indifference and interest. He thereby invents or discovers aspects of the forms of societal intercourse. His religious need is the occasion for words and actions which he regards as the surest bridge to the divine principle. With these materials, he constructs the ediface of a cult. By means of certain rules of prudence in the conduct of business, he attempts to protect himself against defraud, thereby establishing general rules of commerce.

This point might be expressed in the following way. Some contribution to the formation of a social consciousness is precipitated as the *caput mortuum* of every human relationship and every act of self-interest that is not purely self-defeating. This occurs after their products have been extracted from the individual consciousness and distilled through thousands of fine channels. The following point holds especially for the web of social life: no weaver really knows what he weaves. Of course it is true that more advanced social structures can develop only if there is a consciousness of purpose. However their development is—as this might be expressed— *external* to the individual's consciousness of purpose. They are generated by a form that does not lie within the consciousness of the individual. Although they develop in this way, these more advanced structures *affect* the individual. He encounters them as mental constructs which have an ideal existence that lies beyond his consciousness and are independent of him. They make up a preexisting piece of public property. The individual can make use of as many of its parts as he likes. Therefore the following issue turns exclusively on our interpretation of the status of this distinctive historical category: in what sense, if any, are these more advanced structures a product of the consciousness of the individual—the individual on whom they are dependent and who is dependent upon them? These difficulties of choice or decision and these uncertainties concerning the contents of consciousness increase when superpersonal structures appear to acquire their own potential for movement and development.

Consider the theory of the forces of economic production, forces which either mesh with existing forms of production or outgrow and destroy them. This theory subordinates the knowledge and desires of individuals to relationships of a purely objective potency. New forms of society develop in complete independence of the consciousness and the aspirations of their bearers—the individuals who can facilitate or impede this process, even though they can never make it inevitable or impossible. Consider, for example, the transition from slavery to the feudal system and the transformation of feudalism into an economy of wage labor. Suppose that wage labor also "evolves" into socialism. The explanatory causes of these transformations cannot be found in the consciousness of the actors themselves. On the contrary, they lie—as this might be expressed—in the logical consequences of the existing economic technology, the productive forces it generates and the constitution of the society in which these forces are expressed with mechanical necessity. Consciousness, therefore, is completely irrelevant to the identification of these explanatory causes.

In other and more specialized contexts, however, processes of consciousness are interpolated between observable events and constitute a condition for their intelligibility. Existing theories of historiography tend to employ both varieties of interpretation in a rather arbitrary fashion. Even the question of the mere quantum of consciousness that lies behind visible events is completely controversial. In consequence, the principal issue in every historical explanation is left to the instinctive or dogmatic assumptions of the historian, the interpreter. A descriptive theory of historical knowledge, therefore, is obliged to answer the following questions. In which cases and to what extent can consciousness be employed as an explanatory principle? In which cases and to what extent should this principle be replaced by an explanatory principle which rests upon obscure instincts, unconscious purposiveness, or a self-explanatory relationship between purely external events? In what sense are these two explanatory principles consequences of a general world view? Finally, to what extent are standard criteria for historical explanation satisfied—both in principle and in the solution of specific problems—by employing either of these two explanatory principles?

5. *Personal Identity and Group Identity*

There is a difficulty peculiar to the psychological construct that defines our concept of historical personalities. The historian can produce a complete picture of a personality only by reference to its single expressions; however it is possible to classify and interpret these individual expressions correctly only on the basis of a complete construct of the personality. It is obvious how the difficulty posed by this circle is resolved in practice. The investigation begins with a certain interpretation of a single expression of the personality, an interpretation which is chosen on either hypothetical or dogmatic grounds. The investigation progresses by employing this interpretation. It establishes whether all the other individual expressions of the personality can be interpreted in this same way. Either this initial hypothesis is confirmed as being relatively certain, or the necessity for its revision is confirmed. This is a familiar form of reasoning. Initially, the adequacy of an assumption is confirmed by reference to its consequences. Then these consequences are verified by deducing them from the same assumption.

Suppose we consider this problematical relationship between individual conduct—the interpretandum—and the total personality—the interpretans. It is simplified by a certain fact. In practice, the number of possible interpretations of an individual action is not unlimited. Ultimately, each act only provides evidence foi the existence of a specific and finite set of characterological causes—a set which, admittedly, may very well include mutually exclusive members. This same act also provides evidence which would lead us to exclude or reject another, alternative set of characterological causes. Suppose that most of the actions of a given agent provide evidence for the existence of a certain group of motives, motives at least some of which are internally consistent. Ultimately, there will be a single character—a single cast of mind and motivation—that is common to all of these motives and excludes all other possibilities. Although these improvisatory heuristic moves are in fact employed in the praxis of scientific investigation, they are irrelevant to the basic philosophical difficulty. In effect, scientific praxis transcends this difficulty. Its sources lie in the metaphysics of psychology.

There is also a circular relationship between knowledge of observable events and knowledge of unobservable, mental events. All genuine knowledge of observable processes can only be established on the basis of inner, unobservable processes. But all knowledge of inner, unobservable processes can only be established through empirical verification in the observable world. However it is easy to resolve the problem posed by this circular relationship. In every case, a complete and independent definition of the two elements—the observable process and the unobservable process—is available. Knowledge is a consequence of a dialectical relationship between the two processes. The relationship between the human mind or personality as a whole and its individual manifestations is very different from this. We may call this totality whatever we like: character, the nature of the individual, or a basic disposition—it can be identified or defined only by reference to its individual expressions. The moments of mental life exhibit a development that is completely unilinear, very different relationships of resemblance and causation obtaining among them obviously. However there is no single discoverable cause or ontological ground to which they may all be attributed; at least no such cause can be identified by a scientific investigation which proceeds in a rational way. Consider the idea or feeling that there is an integral personal identity which persists beneath or within all mental events—in the same way that a substance endures in spite of destiny or changes in its attributes. This feeling is only a result of subjective, personal experience or the intuition of matters which are ultimately unknowable. In relation to verifiable knowledge, however, the identity of a character is only the inductive product of its individual manifestations. Or, more precisely, it is the collective name for the features that are common or essential to them.

However this cannot serve as an exhaustive analysis of the concept of character. On the contrary, we have the idea that this concept has only one intelligible meaning: it refers to a form of reality that transcends all its individual manifestations, a constant and fundamental human element that cannot be analyzed as a manifold of thoughts and desires. It is a condition for the coherence and the interpretation of these thoughts and desires. The *content* of character, on the other hand, is simply a composite of all these independently identifiable thoughts and desires. Here, therefore, we find that form of circular logic about which so many objections have been raised. A hypothetical causal "force" is inferred from a given collection of phenomena, and these phenomena are, in turn, "explained" by reference to this causal "force." In this case, however, the circle is inescapable. There are innumerable phenomena of mental life which can be understood, classified, and assessed only if they can be ascribed to a certain "character"—i.e. exactly the same character the existence of which is inferred from these individual phenomena. This seems to be one of those fundamental circles the paradoxical features of which have their origins in certain peculiarities of abstract knowledge. The form of reasoning that generates this paradox is, nevertheless, essential to our basic intellectual processes.[4]

From the standpoint of both form and content, the *identity* of a character creates profound problems for the philosophy of history. The existence of personal and group identity is an a priori presupposition of all historical research. In the case of the individual person, this presupposition entails that his actions and ideas seem to be produced by a single integral self, an entity that varies only as a result of organic changes. Such an entity amounts to a mere unknown; nothing further can be said about it. Therefore to say that a person has an identity is to say that his ideas are susceptible to mutual explanation and derivation. If this is possible, there must be certain principles which function in such a way that personal identity is exhibited to us, even though it cannot be directly observed. Suppose we conceive personal identity in the following way. A man whose life is embittered by oppressive unhappiness is disposed to see nothing but suffering and dissonance in the world around him. This same disposition, we say, is responsible for the fact that he is in constant fear of more bad luck and makes life hard for his fellow men. This conception of personal identity is based on our acquaintance with psychological generalizations that seem to legitimate a genetic explanation of any one of these processes in terms of the others. These syntheses are not intelligible because they are homogeneous. Just to the contrary, we see them as homogeneous because they are intelligible to us. They seem to make sense to us only because we are in the habit of observing them. Consider, therefore, the following possibilities. Although a certain person suffers, he tries to make others happy. Or, although he suffers, he also indulges—as a kind of compensation—in a variety of theoretical optimism; this often happens to the physically disabled. These possibilities do not place the identity of the personality in jeopardy. Consider a greedy man. Suppose that there are no conceivable circumstances under which he can be separated from his profits. Or suppose, on the contrary, that he is invariably willing to risk the loss of all that he has whenever he sees the prospects for an exorbitant profit. We ascribe a personal identity to him in both cases. Therefore it is not the content or the intrinsic properties of phenomena that determine whether they constitute an integral entity—just to the contrary. This turns on another issue. Are there generalizations on the basis of which causal relationships can be established between these phenomena?

Consider the foregoing examples. The same disposition or character has antithetical consequences. However this is only a consequence of the extent and the direction of the bearing of this character upon the strata of a given social world. Suppose that we consider conduct as such, independent of its consequences. We shall find that we also ascribe a personal identity to forms of conduct that are logically antithetical or mutually exclusive. Take the case of a person who always remains the same, even in the most diverse situations, someone who—as we might put it—always shows the same face in all of life's changing shades of light and shadow. He is not a more "complete" person than someone who adapts quickly and reacts sensitively, who always seems to change in response to changing demands and stimuli. The behavior of the latter person may be compared to a variable in an equation. Although it always remains the same variable, its value changes as a function of the values of the other factors; in consequence, different results are produced. Consider the conduct of the first sort of person—who always remains the same, even in radically different situations. His identity is no less strictly or rigorously established than the identity of the latter sort of person. However it is obvious that completely different phenomena will be integrated into the "unity" of his personality, and these phenomena will be comprehensible in a very different fashion. Consider, therefore, the following reasoning. Given that a person acts in certain ways, the possibility or impossibility of other modes of action may be inferred. This is never a purely logical inference. On the contrary, it is dependent upon major premises which describe actual psychological experience.

Suppose we consider the bearing of this discussion on the concepts of periods and groups, the construction of historical processes, the interpretation of concrete facts, the interpolation of historical evidence, and also the critical evaluation of this procedure. Then the following point should be kept in mind. Given the "homogeneous nature" of character, there are certain norms which we employ, both for the purposes of description and also as criteria for the evaluation of historical evidence. Once a given fact and its psychological significance have been established, these norms are employed to construct a predictive schema that determines what sort of conduct is probable and what sort is improbable for a personality of this sort. In other words, these norms are employed to answer the following questions. What are the limits within which we consider it possible to provide an explanation for actions that deviate from this predictive scheme? What are the developments and changes that we regard as self-evident, a consequence of the immanent principle of personality? What are the developments and changes that we feel obliged to explain by reference to circumstances that are external to the person? We undoubtedly employ quite definitive principles of this sort: they are implicitly presupposed by both the historian and his reader. But they have not yet been explicitly formulated. The discovery of these principles is the most important task of the philosophy of history.

There are special conditions under which the psychic identity of a *group* becomes a possible subject for scientific discussion. Here I only have in mind the sort of group identity to which historians constantly make reference. It is not my purpose to raise the following thorny question. Is the identity of the group a distinct structure that is independent of the individuals that make it up? Or is it merely the sum of all these individuals? Consider descriptions of the dispositions or passions, moods or tendencies of an entire group. Actually, these psychological data are never observed in *all* the members of the group—on the contrary, they can only be identified and confirmed for certain members. Nevertheless, a homogeneous totality is constructed, and the members of the group to whom these psychological data cannot be ascribed—dissenters, perhaps, or those who modify the general tendency of the group—are somehow included in it. Consider the following random passages chosen from Mommsen's *History of Rome.* "A cry of rage was heard throughout all of Italy" (volume II, p. 145). Marius is described "as a commander who disciplined *the soldier* and nevertheless kept him in a good humor, even to the extent of winning his affection as a comrade" (volume II, p. 192). The aristocracy "did not make the slightest effort to conceal their apprehension and rage" (volume III, p. 190). "The factions breathed a sigh of relief" (volume III, p. 193). Consider also the following passages from Burckhardt's *The Civilization of the Renaissance in Italy.* "Florence had always acknowledged its Guelphic sympathies for the French with a dreadful naivete" (volume I, p. 89). "Here and there in terrifying moments, the passion of medieval repentance was awakened. With loud cries, lashing and flagellation, the anguished people attempted to move Heaven to compassion" (volume II, p. 232).

There are principles that the historian implicitly uses in these cases; the theory of knowledge is obliged to investigate them. Is the psychic identity of a group situated in its leaders, in its average members, or in the majority of its members? What number of possible or actual dissenters may be regarded as a negligible quantity? To what extent do tribulation or frivolity, harsh restrictions or laxity permit or inhibit the functional unity of the group? To what extent may incomplete evidence be regarded as proof of a homogeneous group mind? The above claims about the individual psyche also hold here for the social psyche—if I may express myself in this shorthand fashion. The identity of the social psyche is presupposed. A description of the properties of fragments of the social psyche—for only its fragments can be identified—is supposed to warrant the conclusion that the unknown fragments have the same properties. Quite often the social psyche has the status of a *construct.* This construct makes it possible to infer hypothetical unknown properties from the entity— the social psyche—the existence of which is presupposed. Moreover this construct may not correspond with certainty to any actual historical entity. Macaulay, for example, shows us just how often this may be the case. He claims that his idea of the temper of political and religious parties was not taken from any single work, but from thousands of forgotten tracts, sermons, and satires; in this context, he presents about ten arguments on the basis of which the Whigs decided to adopt a bill. But it is extremely improbable that all these arguments were simultaneously present and equally effective in the mind of any single member of the party. On the contrary, "the party"—the psychic unity of which produces the motive constituted by these arguments—is a mere ideal construct: a fiction that the historian invents in order to produce a synthesis of otherwise diffuse elements. It has the same logical status and origin as the personal "identity" of the individual. The substantive relationship between processes that are correlated by a certain external framework, the functional relations of these processes, and the possibility of classifying them teleologically—all this results in the projection of a certain characteristic identity onto these processes. Subsequently it is the content of this projection which determines whether or not other processes can be identified as part of this same entity.

Consider the pure ideality and the exclusively methodological genesis of this sort of identity. They make it probable that epistemological conditions are partially responsible for its production, conditions that transcend mere psychological observation and the analogy between the social psyche and the ego consciousness of the cognitive subject. The *fact that* this psychological possibility has this particular result is ultimately a consequence of more abstract epistemological requirements. Consider the properties we ascribe to personal identity: the integrity of the self, the open texture of the concept itself, the extrapolation or inference from diverse elements to a single, total construct. Personal identity in this sense is obviously a methodological presupposition of history. Independent of this presupposition, it would be impossible to classify and understand historical data. It has the status of an a priori, a condition for the possibility of history. Consider Kant's view of the apriorities of nature. They are dictates of the intellect that are imposed upon nature. They have no exact counterpart in the given phenomenon itself. However the question of the status of the apriorities of history cannot be resolved so precisely and definitively. Consider the subject matter of history: the ephemeral event as such, the purely objective and atemporal significance of experience, the subjective consciousness of human agents. History as a science encounters this material as a kind of half-formed or proto-product. It is already constituted by a priori forms of comprehension. The categories which constitute this material as history are already present in the material itself, at least in an embryonic or modified form. They cannot be distinguished from this material so absolutely or definitely as we can distinguish the category of causality from the idea of mere temporal succession.

Not that there is any sense—even from the standpoint of principle or theoretical purpose—in which history as a science approximates a reproduction of the event: all of the ensuing will show that this view is mistaken. On the other hand, consider those categories which establish the distinction between history and the mere event as such. We will find a counterpart for these categories in the material of history itself more often than we will find a counterpart for the categories of the intellect in the material of sense perception. Often the theoretical interests of history as a science only oblige us to emphasize, systematize, and—from the standpoint of logic—complete elements that are already present in the object prior to its historical analysis. Consider, therefore, the identity of persons and groups as a methodological form that is employed in order to subject the event to historical analysis. To this extent, the methodological form of identity is—in a transcendental sense—subjective. Compare identity in this sense to psychological identity as an object of real, immediate experience. Quite often—perhaps even invariably—there are transitional or intermediate cases which link these two concepts of identity. This relationship between the categories of history and the unanalyzed data of history is a consequence of the conceptual *import* or *content* of the former. It is the admissible or legitimate consequence of a fact the significance of which is very often misinterpreted: the subject of history and the object of history are the same. Namely, they are both mental entities. But this fact should not deceive us concerning the general distinction between the subject and the object of history. The science of history imposes forms upon its raw material. These forms are a consequence of the intrinsic requirements of history; they are peculiar to the province of history as a science.

6. The Concept of Historical Understanding: Intuitive Recreation

If the events that constitute the subject matter of history presuppose a conscious or unconscious mental basis or foundation, then the question of the identification of its contents poses further epistemological problems. Here too the issue initially concerns a very general presupposition. Are the hypothetical psychological constructs which the historian imposes upon events objectively true? In other words, do they really identify the mental acts of an historical person? This question would hold no interest for us if we could not *understand* the import and the consequences of these processes. Consider any method for verifying these psychological constructs. In some cases, verification does not seem to require psychological reconstruction on the part of the historian: it appears to be immediately given in the utterances and confessions of the historical agents. No matter what method of verification we choose, we would not ascribe what we call truth to these constructs unless we could understand the mental acts which they putatively identify. But what does this sort of understanding amount to, and what are its conditions?[5]

The first condition is obviously the following. We must be able to recreate the mental act of the historical person. As this is sometimes expressed, we must be able to "occupy or inhabit the mind of the other person." The understanding of an utterance entails that the mental processes of the speaker—processes which the words of the utterance express—are also reproduced in the listener by means of the utterance. As soon as an essential difference between the ideas of the speaker and the ideas of the listener arises, then the utterance is either misunderstood or it simply remains incomprehensible. This sort of immediate recreation of mental contents is possible—and it constitutes a sufficient condition for understanding—only if the import in question is purely theoretical. In this case, it is not essential that the mental contents are reproduced as the idea of a specific person. It is only essential that the objective import of the ideas has the same logical form for both speaker and listener. My position in relation to the objective import of knowledge is exactly the same as the position of some other person in relation to this same objective import, a person whose ideas about this import I "understand." He only transmits the content of these ideas to me; then, as we might put it, he disappears. Subsequently, the content of these ideas is included in my thinking in the same way that it is included in his. It is not modified or distorted by the fact that it originated in the ideas of this other person. The following is an appropriate description of this situation. Although I understand the expression, I don't completely understand what is expressed. (Actually, the object of understanding is not the act of speaking, but rather what is spoken.) The situation changes immediately if the speaker's utterance is a consequence of some subjective intention: for example, prejudice, anger, anxiety, or sarcasm. Suppose we identify this *motive* for the expression or utterance. In this case, the sense in which we "understand" the utterance is very different from the sense in which we grasp its import. In this case, understanding is not only concerned with comprehension of what is spoken; it is also concerned with comprehension of the act of speaking.

It is this *latter* form of understanding—and not the former—which is at stake in the project of understanding historical persons. And in this latter form of understanding, "recreation" obviously does not have the same status that it occupies in the former. In other words, there is no sense in which it represents an exact reproduction of the contents of consciousness that we ascribe to the historical person. We believe that we can understand every variety and degree of love and hate, courage and despair, desire and feeling. But we do not believe that the expression of these emotions—on which our idea or image of them is based—grasps or affects us all in the same way. It is obvious that the sort of mental process which we recognize as the comprehension of these phenomena presupposes that they have been psychologically transformed or abbreviated, perhaps even that our image of them has faded. But somehow their content must be retained or recovered.

Suppose, however, that the problem of history is to recover not only what has been known, but also what has been wished for and felt. This latter problem can be resolved only if—by means of some mode of mental transposition or translation—we can will what has been willed and feel what has been felt. If this condition is not satisfied, then we cannot recapture the real experience of these phenomena. And if we cannot do this, then the only conditions under which it could be said that we understand them would not be satisfied. Whoever has never loved will never understand love or the lover. Someone with a passionate disposition will never understand someone who is apathetic. The weakling will never understand the hero, nor will the hero ever understand the weakling. And, conversely, consider the movements, the demeanor, and the actions of another person, all of which are only external symbols of certain emotional states. Our ability to understand the conduct of this person is a function of the frequency with which we have experienced the same emotional states ourselves. Facility or difficulty in understanding varies directly with the extent to which our own immediate mental state is disposed to similar or dissimilar emotions, a disposition which simplifies or complicates the act of psychological reproduction. Consider, therefore, the relationship between the recreation of the mental processes of another person and the understanding of these processes. There is some intimate relationship between the two, some sense in which a transformation or reconstruction of these mental states is a necessary condition for understanding them.

The following is probably the ultimate, definitive principle of this sort of reconstruction of mental processes. Consider the thoughts, feelings, and aspirations which are, in some sense, experienced by the historian, the investigator. They are not represented as his own mental processes, but rather as the mental processes of some other person. In other words, the mental constructs produced by both psychological and historical understanding are detached from the mind of the investigator and attributed to another person. This is a peculiar complication of the following fact: even within the domain of human existence, objects of knowledge are not presented to us as things in themselves, but only as phenomena. Of course the epistemological consequences of this fact have been disputed. We are told that history and nature are accessible to us in completely different respects. The difference between my ego and another ego is completely different from the difference between my ego and nature. Two egos are numerically different, but they are not generically or essentially different. Mind cannot penetrate the inner processes of nature. But consider one mind which can reproduce the contents of another mind with complete adequacy; in this case, the former mind can penetrate the inner processes of the latter. However no bridge across the abyss that separates one ego from another can be constructed upon such insubstantial foundations. Suppose that two minds have the same nature. This does not eliminate the necessity for all sorts of processes of externalization, transposition, and symbolization to mediate between them. A genuine reproduction— the sort of understanding that would be an immediate consequence of the homogeneous nature of the two minds—would either be a form of mind reading or mental telepathy, or it would require a pre-established harmony of minds. Knowledge—even knowledge of a mental process—is a mental process itself. Although it can be generated by stimulation, ultimately it must be produced by the subject himself. However this would only transform a direct correspondence into an indirect one. Ultimately, and in spite of all the requisite detours, it is in principle possible for a mental process which takes place in one mind to be reproduced in another, just as precisely as the words which are telegraphed at one station are reproduced at another. This is in principle possible even though the medium which transmits the mental process is completely different from the mental process itself. The following difficulty, however, is much more profound. The ideas that are produced in this fashion in my mind are not really my own. Even though they are present in my mind and are, in this sense, my ideas, I conceive them historically, as the ideas of another person.

In order to acquire knowledge of another person, the following procedure will also not suffice. First, I recreate his mental processes. Then I say: it is not I, but rather the historical person who has these feelings. This will not work for the following reasons. First, I must in fact have these feelings myself. Consider also the initial content of this feeling and this other mental content—that it is not I, but rather the historical person who has the feeling—which is *subsequently* or *retrospectively* appended to the initial content. The initial content and the latter content do not constitute the same feeling. They remain isolated or autonomous. But if both contents constituted one feeling, the latter should permeate or penetrate the former. It should be directly related to the former, like an exponent. Consider this experience of what I don't actually experience, this recreation of subjective mental states. It is a form of recreation which is really only possible for a subject. Nevertheless, these subjective mental states have an objective status for him. This is the real puzzle of historical knowledge, but thus far, there has scarcely been any attempt to resolve it by employing our logical and psychological categories. It is true that there are two aspects to this sort of knowledge. First, I perform the mental act in question myself, and then I attribute this mental act to an historical person. But this is only a retrospective analysis of historical knowledge into its elements; this distinction is not made within the process of historical knowledge itself. However the issue here does not concern an ex post facto synthesis of elements that existed autonomously prior to this synthesis. On this point, the process of historical knowledge may be compared to the perception of the external world. Sense perception and the perception of space are not logically distinguishable faculties or capacities that are subsequently combined in the perception of the external world. The projection of ideas and feelings onto an historical person is an irreducible, integral act. Nevertheless, one of its necessary conditions is the following: the historian must have experienced the relevant mental processes in his own subjective life. When these mental processes are reproduced as the ideas of another person, however, they acquire a new form. This transformation detaches them from the subjective experience of the historical person, and also from the subjective experience of the historian. Let us even suppose that, in general, there is a correspondence between the subjective experience of the historian and the subjective experience of the historical person. For example, let us suppose that love and hate, thought and desire, pleasure and pain as subjective states have exactly the same essential properties in the minds of both. Even if this were the case, this direct equivalence of subjective states would not constitute historical knowledge. On the contrary, historical knowledge is the mental process of reconstruction or transformation which takes place when the historian's subjective states are projected onto the historical person.

7. The Objectification of Concrete Mental Processes

The mental reconstruction or recreation which provides a psychological foundation for the understanding of observable events is based on a category—it might be called an aggregate state of mind—to which the theory of knowledge has not yet paid sufficient attention. Certain relationships between ideas are associated with the feeling that they are more than accidental and ephemeral phenomena of subjective mental life. We feel that they have the validity of the typical. There is a sense in which one idea provides evidence of its necessary connection with another, and this is independent of the momentary state of mind that is responsible for the realization of this particular interrelationship in a given person or subject. There is no sense in which this is a claim about the truth content of these ideas. It is not a claim that their content is objectively valid, regardless of whether we conceive them or not. *This* sort of subjective necessity, which transcends the domain of the psychological as such, is not at issue here. On the contrary, the present issue concerns a trans-subjectivity or super-subjectivity of psychological structures themselves, structures which are only independent of their realization in any given mind. There are even cases in which a purely mental association of ideas has the same normative character—the same intrinsic necessity, and therefore the same universal validity—as the logical, objective relationships between the cognitive contents of ideas. This point is obviously related to what has been called psychological necessity or psychological nomological regularity. But the relationship is only peripheral; nor is this point affected by the questionable status which the concept of a psychological law must have, given the present sophistication of the science of psychology. On the contrary, the kind of general validity that is at stake here is a psychological property of mental activity itself. It is a feeling immediately given in mental activity, like an overtone or an accent. This quality can accompany very different ideas of the same person, and the ideas with which it is associated may even vary occasionally. As we might put it, this quality is only the expression of an immanent property of mental acts. Therefore the quality itself is not susceptible to either objective confirmation or refutation.

This sort of psychological necessity is linked with the ideas that we use to reconstruct historical personalities. Or rather, historical personalities qualify as reconstructed when this sort of necessity can be ascribed to a construct of their mental states and energies. The content of these ideas may be purely individual and unique. Suppose that, on the basis of their observable conduct, an historian constructs a picture of the character of Themistocles or Moritz of Saxony. Or suppose that he constructs the inner sequence of impulses, ideas, and feelings which is responsible for the coherence and intelligibility of their conduct. The historian feels that there is a sense in which necessity can be ascribed to this psychological construct. Even though—at this point—the mental processes that constitute this reconstruction only transpire in the historian's mind and even though the reconstruction is grounded or legitimated by no objective nomological regularity, the historian makes a rigorous distinction between this sort of construct and other mental relationships, relationships that he acknowledges as mental facts, but which he would never impute to anyone. This feeling of psychological plausibility or appropriateness may only appear after all sorts of possible constructs are tried. In addition, this feeling may not always decide with complete certainty in favor of *one* of the possible mental constellations. However, insofar as it is present at all, it provides the criterion which determines whether a mental construct that has a purely subjective origin is also objectively valid.

In other words, satisfaction of this condition determines whether the construct of the mental states of one person may also represent the mental states of another person. Observation, hypotheses, and psychological generalizations are not sufficient to satisfy this criterion. On the contrary, they only constitute preliminary conditions for the appearance of this feeling, which constitutes the criterion for truth in the domain of mental life. Poems and portraits give us the same feeling. The force with which they convince and persuade us is not a consequence of theoretical knowledge. Theoretical knowledge may be available, and it may even constitute the basis for this feeling, but it can never replace the feeling itself. The feeling remains an independent variable. It is the qualitatively unique point at which—as we might put it—individual mental elements are crystallized in such a way that they produce the unity of a personality, a unity which is determined by the intuitive conviction that these elements must necessarily be connected.

As we noted, the personalities generated in this way may be utterly incomparable and unique. Suppose that we could understand complex and contradictory characters like Themistocles or Moritz of Saxony. We would not do this by identifying their individual characteristics and producing a mechanical composite of them. On the contrary, we feel that the functionally necessary unity of these characteristics constitutes personal identity. Although its constituents may seem to be very different from a logical point of view, this entity has an inner consistency that often cannot be identified in an apparently similar composite of mental elements. The personality acquires a quality of necessity from this inner consistency, a quality that cannot be deduced from its constituent elements, nor from any law. Perhaps it is comparable to the unity that Leonardo discovered in the intellectual and emotional riches of the Gioconda, or to the polar tensions of our emotional potentialities that Goethe expressed in the "*Gesang der Geister über den Wassern.*"

Consider the conditions under which it is possible to construct a mental structure that is associated with the immediate feeling of necessary connection. These are the only conditions under which it is possible to *understand* the historical event that expresses this mental structure. This structure constitutes a completely unique synthesis of the category of the universal and the necessary, on the one hand, and the category of the concrete individual, on the other. Or, more precisely, it transcends this dichotomy, which otherwise requires that every object of knowledge must fall under only one of these two categories. Consider the characteristic relationship of impulses, dispositions, and ideas that constitutes the theoretical construct of an historical personality. This structure is identifiable—in other words, we can ascribe a coherent structure to these elements—only if the elements themselves form a plausible sequence, an entity that is intrinsically intelligible independent of the historical conditions for its realization. Of course the historical personality is unique: it only appears once. But it could not appear—as an intelligible historical personality—at all unless it constituted an atemporal construct: in other words, a construct formed by and understood by reference to the psychological significance of its elements. It is not psychological facts, but rather the psychological as a fact itself that constitutes these elements as an authentic construct, a construct to which we ascribe the property of necessity. This construct is—as we might put it—a consequence of the immanent logic of mental processes. The psychological as a fact is a condition for the representation of this unique phenomenon. The phenomenon itself is, of course, unrepeatable. The dualism of the universal and the concrete individual, therefore, is not germane to the epistemological category that is at stake here.

Consider the possibility of reconstructing the structure of mental values and variables. Consider the validity of these structures, which is independent of each of their individual instances. Given these considerations, they seem to have a universal, law-like status; however this is not actually the case at all. Every mental construct is, by definition, historically unique. And not in the sense that, strictly speaking, physical phenomena may also qualify as unique: the unique as that which is never in reality absolutely repeatable or reproducible. This latter species of uniqueness is only an index of the indefinitely large number of general laws that apply to any given phenomenon. In the case of mental constructs, however, the structure itself is determined by a point of uniqueness that underlies the concept of an *historical personality:* in other words, an entity that is determined with absolute uniqueness—as in a system of coordinates— by its spatio-temporal identification, its nature, and its historical consequences. The ultimate basis of this distinction between the mental and the physical lies in the *identity* or *homogeneity* of the personality.

Consider some unrepeatable physical phenomenon that is a composite of elements. Each of these elements is governed by a general law. We do not conceive a phenomenon of this sort as a purely individual construct; this is because its uniqueness does not lie—as we might put it—in the phenomenon itself. On the contrary, it is only a consequence of the external form that these elements happen to exhibit. But consider the conditions under which a *homogeneous* structure is unique. In this case, uniqueness is not purely formal and relatively accidental; it is an intrinsic *quality* that defines the nature of the structure itself. Only under these conditions do we find the obscurity and intractability of *individuality*. This is the exclusive source of the need to establish a relationship between individuality and some system of totality, intelligibility, and sequence. The intelligibility of all other phenomena, however, is a consequence of the subsumption of the phenomenon under a general law. Individuality seems to be intelligible only as a result of the structure of the traits of the personality. This structure has the property of psychological necessity, the sort of necessity that is exhibited in the empathetic recreation of the personality. This structure—the construct of the personality—acquires, as we might put it, an anonymous validity. It is immanent to the personality and independent of the name of the person himself. Nevertheless, it still has the unmistakable cachet of historical individuality: the mystery of a reality that is absolutely unique.

Consider this category of the objective structure of subjective and personal mental elements, a structure that can be constructed only by means of a subjective, empathetic recreation. This category not only transcends the distinction between the universal and the individual; it is also independent of the distinction between causation and intentionality, cause and reason. Suppose we attempt to identify the real cause responsible for the relationship between two mental phenomena A and B. Either this cause is completely unknowable, or we can discover it only in the form of a general psychological law. For epistemological purposes, we distinguish the content or conceptual import of a mental process from the process itself, conceived as a purely dynamic phenomenon. A mental process is determined by the forces of nature and their causal necessity only if it falls under the latter description. The *content* is the aspect of the process which makes it accessible to our knowledge. It is, as we might put it, only the appearance of the phenomenon itself, the sign or mark by which we identify the process. Therefore radically different processes may very well have the same content. The purpose of psychology is to discover the dynamics of mental processes. For knowledge of this sort, however, only a symbol or sign is accessible to us: the logically expressible content of mental processes. In an ideally complete psychology, the real consequences of mental processes would be deduced from given psychic conditions by the use of general laws.

It is necessary to make an absolutely rigorous distinction between the derivation of ideas from the *causality* of psycho-mechanical events, on the one hand, and the derivation of ideas from *reasons* that are based on the logical relationships of the *contents* of ideas, on the other. We can comprehend that, given certain premises, a conclusion will follow. Given certain ends, pursuit of the means objectively necessary to reach them will follow; given certain organic drives, an emotional interest in objects that satisfy them will follow. In these cases, we do not inquire into the process responsible for the initial factor. This would be the process that produces the subsequent factor, the real bearer of subsequent content, as a consequence of the nomological causality of nature. On the contrary, we are willing to admit that this consequence is not really psychologically necessary—the actual, empirical mental process could produce a different consequence. But *suppose* that the consequence we expect does ensue. We understand this in terms of logical relations which obtain between the contents of mental processes. These logical relations are, as we might put it, atemporal. The necessity which can be ascribed to purely mental acts in virtue of these logical relations is completely different from the nomological necessity of natural processes. Suppose that someone reaches a certain conclusion on the basis of premises known to him. An ideally complete psychology would employ general laws of psychodynamics to explain this as a result of given psychodynamic relationships that obtain within his psyche. Suppose, however, that the conclusion is a reasonable one. Suppose that—given not only the actual psychological conditions, but also the substance of the matter—the conclusion necessarily follows from the premises. We understand this in terms of the conceptual import of the argument itself; it is a consequence of the logical force of the premises that this conclusion, and no other, follows.

Consider now the empathetic reconstruction of an historical, mental event. Considered by itself, this process is completely homogeneous. There are respects in which it both resembles and differs from the two foregoing forms of understanding. Like psychological explanation, it has a content that is utterly indifferent and irrelevant to considerations of logic and rationality. From the standpoint of its conceptual import, a phenomenon that is purely psychological and conceived causally or naturalistically has absolutely no bearing upon the understanding of relationships in terms of their reasonableness, rationality, or intelligibility. A natural process that is purely psychological produces the most reasonable as well as the most absurd consequences—the machinations of a fool as well as the serene logical consistency of legal or mathematical thought—with the same necessity and according to the same dynamics. The mental facts of history exhibit these—from the standpoint of logical necessity—purely arbitrary connections. They are simply *real* psychological processes.

It is necessary to make a rigorous distinction—both empirical and epistemological—between these processes and the logical relationships which obtain between the *meanings* of the contents of these processes. However there is a sense in which our understanding of these psychological and historical processes is also analogous to our understanding of logical relations. We understand mental processes when their content exhibits a coherent logic, when a mental process transpires according to a necessity that only holds for its own content. Intelligibility in this context is not a consequence of a dynamic nomological regularity. On the contrary, it is a consequence of a unique content. In this sense, therefore, mental processes do not resemble psychological *events:* they are not nomological consequences of *laws of nature.* There is also a sense in which they do not resemble the *contents* of psychological events: they are not connected by universally valid relationships of logical necessity. Consider this sort of process. It appears, in its purely historical facticity, as a causal sequence of events that are often completely irrational: their source is in blind instinct, and they cannot be connected in any meaningful or significant fashion. And yet a necessary coherence is ascribed to mental processes, even if this coherence may only hold for a single case.

Consider this entity that produces one mental content as the logical consequence of another and establishes a relationship between the two. With a similar sort of coherent force, it produces a content that, as such, is irrelevant to all logical criteria, and yet the result seems so certain that the entire structure is constructed on the basis of a minimum of given facts. The characteristics of an historical person and the complex of ideas behind an historical act form a coherent and understandable entity. From the standpoint of epistemology, however, neither cause nor reason, neither the real law that governs the event nor the ideal content of the event itself is responsible for this. On the contrary, its source is completely different. The coherence and unity of these purely factual elements is a result of the concrete import and shading of their meaning. This unity is not grounded nomologically, but only empathetically. In consequence, a coherent relationship is established between the contents of each of these facts, but only insofar as this concerns the concrete definition of their content. This is similar to the manner in which logic establishes coherent relations between contents that are conceptually *general* In the domain of historical constructs, we *make inferences* from the properties of one mental element to the properties of another. But an inference of this sort is not a syllogism that is supposed to be universally valid: it is an imaginative synthesis. Within the domain of the purely individual, this synthesis super- imposes the validity of the rational and the logical onto the contin- gency and arbitrariness of the mere event.

Perhaps we find here the solution to the following puzzle: how can a state of mind of one person also be *eo ipso* represented as the state of mind of another person? The mediator between these two persons is the special kind of super-personal validity that can be ascribed to the dynamics and logic of a mental construct. It has the status or *value* of universality even though this universality is not conceptual. Consider the sequences of ideas—and the ideationally represented feelings and aspirations that are associated with them— that are formed in the mind of the observer. They are accompanied— as if by an accent that is peculiar to them—by a feeling that their interconnection is valid. These sequences of ideas are not limited to the mind of the observer. However they do not apply to any form of existence at all, in the fashion of a general law. They only apply to a mental entity of the following sort: historical uniqueness is one of the necessary conditions for its coherence. Suppose we consider this basic difficulty of historical projection. The historian must alienate or distance himself—as we might put it—from the mental process which he recreates and which only exists subjectively in his mind. He must superimpose this process onto the mind of an historical person. This process is only a much more refined and sophisticated form of a process that transpires within the psychology of everyday life.

The problem that arises here is similar to the problem of the naive conception of space: how is it that the perceptual image of the external object, which is produced by our mind, is conceived as representing space, outside the mind? This latter problem is solved in the following way. Extensionality (which includes the idea of what- ever is "external to the mind") is a form of thought or ideation. It is the mode according to which the mind connects sense impressions. The process by which sense impressions acquire extensionality is a purely immanent mental event. Extensionality is a quality of certain ideas. Consider the fact that mental processes assume the form of history: that is, the person who produces them conceives them as the mental processes of another person. This fact cannot be explained simply by the naive idea of "projection." On the contrary, the issue here is to understand the process that this word designates. And this process must surely be an immanent quality of the mental processes themselves, a form of thought. Ideas do not acquire the status of history after they have been produced in a subjective consciousness. On the contrary, history simply *is* the form in which they are constituted, the manner in which they become ideas. This is responsible for their psychological quality: their content has its reality in the mind of another person.

It seems to me that the epistemological explanation of this direct transposition or superimposition lies in the feeling that certain mental constructs and relations are trans-subjectively *valid*—but not in the sense that this applies to external objects. It lies in the consciousness that the mental constructs to which this sort of validity can be ascribed represent the actual relationships of mental contents, independent of the manner in which they are conceived at any given time. In the case of historical knowledge, this trans-subjective or super-personal validity of mental constructs is limited to a single, unique personality. It is the personality that is characterized or defined by these ideas, the personality whose spatio-temporal definition provides the condition for the realization of these ideas.

I am quite aware that my proposed solution to this basic psychological and epistemological problem of historical understanding is only a preliminary effort. Perhaps it can be justified only insofar as it makes the existence of the problem—in all its depth and profundity— clear. Let us leave the special technical interests of the discipline of history, however, and conclude these reflections—like a keystone finishes a building—with some remarks on the bearing of this solution upon the fundamental epistemological problem of history.

8. Historical Realism

In this context, it is most essential to dispose of historical realism. This doctrine has retreated from the theory of the external world to the philosophy of mind. Consider the epistemological realism which explains truth as a correspondence—in the sense of a mirror image—between thought and its object, an object which is necessarily external to its corresponding thought. Insofar as the natural sciences are concerned, this view has been refuted. Moreover it is relatively easy to see that the description of a real event in terms of mathe-matical formulae or atoms, in terms of a mechanism or dynamism, is only a set of symbols, a construct built of mental categories. It is only a system of tokens that represent the object of knowledge. It is easy to see that there is no sense in which this sort of description qualifies as an exact reproduction of the object itself. In the socio-historical sciences, however, the essential identity of knowledge and its object—for both lie within the domain of the mental—still leads us to the same mistaken conclusion: that form of naturalism which holds that knowledge is possible as a simple reproduction of its object and conceives the faithfulness of this reproduction as the criterion for knowledge itself. The task of enabling us to see the event "as it really happened" is still naively imposed upon history. In opposition to this view, it is necessary to make clear that every form of knowledge represents a translation of immediately given data into a new language, a language with its own intrinsic forms, categories, and requirements. In order to qualify as a science, the facts—inner, unobservable facts as well as external, observable facts—must answer certain questions, questions which they never confront in reality and in their form as brute data. In order to qualify as objects of knowledge, certain aspects of the facts are thrown into relief, and others are relegated to the background. Certain specific features are emphasized. Certain immanent relations are established on the basis of ideas and values. All this—as we might put it—transcends reality. The facts as objects of knowledge are formed into new constructs that have their own laws and their own peculiar qualities.

9. *The Transformation of Reality by the Categories of Historical Inquiry*

Consider a province of history like the history of philosophy. Here the immediate reconstruction of the object of knowledge seems to be very easily possible. The history of philosophy even seems to require the sort of account that would qualify as an exact and exhaustive recreation of the object itself. But even in this province, what is at issue is not a mechanical—albeit mental or psychological—reproduction of data. On the contrary, a *forming* or *structuring* of the data is necessary. The intellectual contents which were created and directly experienced by the philosopher must be reconstructed by his historian. It is necessary to provide an interpretation of these data that satisfies the a priori requirements of knowledge. Only under these conditions can the raw material—philosophy—become a new construct—the history of philosophy. Historical truth is not a mere reproduction: it is an intellectual activity. Historical truth produces something new out of its raw material, data that are accessible to intuitive recreation, something that the material itself does not yet constitute. This does not simply amount to an abridged summary of details. On the contrary, history proceeds by posing questions to its raw material and ascribing meaning to singular phenomena. The result is often not what the "heroes" of history meant or intended at all. History reveals meanings and values in its raw material. These meanings and values structure the past in such a way that a new construct is produced, a construct which satisfies the criteria that *we* impose.

Consider a person who views his own life as an historical development. Here the relationship between knowledge and its object seems to be even more intimate. Here it seems even more plausible to suppose that the forms of being and knowledge are simply one and the same melody played in two different keys. In this case, the original data that constitute the object of knowledge are present in immediate consciousness. However this is the very case in which the following point can be made most clearly: knowledge—the synthesis of this original data—is a consequence of a priori forms. Although they hold for this material, they are not deducible from it. Suppose we view our life as a whole. We distinguish our life and all the circumstances and events which—to our knowledge—influenced it from the cosmic process itself. The cosmic process embraces and permeates our life; it determines our life only to the extent that we share a common fate with all other individuals. We also exclude those *inner* factors—intellectuality, basic needs, and self-evident emotional reactions—that constitute the common property of all human beings. Upon closer scrutiny, both sorts of elements are of essential importance to our life as it really was. But suppose that we can discover no obvious connection between these elements and our own individuality. In that case, we regard them as irrelevant for the purpose of self-knowledge, in the same way that we regard the canvas on which it is painted as irrelevant to the viewing of a picture. The main point here, however, is the following: these impersonal, self-evident facts are not like the canvas that lies under the paint. They cannot be regarded in the same way: as located in *one* uniform layer beneath what is really essential. On the contrary, they invariably intersect the really essential factors from the most varied directions and in the most diverse proportions. The result of this intersection is a living entity, a human being.

Therefore the aspects of individual life that we call our history constitute an isolate of personal and differential elements which we distinguish from the conditions of their organic development. The relationship between the elements that are differentiated in this way requires a new construct. In principle, the relationship between this construct and the actual facts of our career is no different from the relationship between an historical drama and its real-life counterpart— events of many years' duration that include thousands of minor plots are transformed into three hours of theater. Moreover, the historical transformation of its raw material is not simply a form of compression or miniaturization, like a small photographic reproduction of a large painting. On the contrary, certain aspects are eliminated completely. But without these aspects, the features that are thrown into relief and transformed could never acquire the form of *reality*, nor would it be possible to represent them in terms of intelligible constructs.

This new form comprehends the elements of life in one theoretical construct. However consider all those forces—unknown or disregarded—without which these elements could not acquire the status of reality; in some way, they must be replaced. This is one function of the historical shift in the emphasis upon significance. The moment of experience itself lends a feeling of importance to individual events that are often completely transformed by the category of reflection. This is not only a consequence of the illusory significance of the present, a result of the fact that the present as such often seems to have a significance that far exceeds its actual objective importance. Certain things may have an importance for life insofar as it is experienced; however they do not have this significance at all when we confront the problem of understanding life. As a result of a single event, certain feelings may be associated with a long epoch of development. Quite often, these feelings attribute a force to this event that obscures the actual intellectual and volitional *content* of the epoch. Suppose we attempt to *understand* this epoch as a whole. In this case it is obvious that the intellectual and volitional content of the epoch constitutes its real motive forces. Ultimately, *they* form its substance and determine its destiny. The feelings in question, on the other hand, only represent the *form* in which the epoch is experienced; from their standpoint, the single event is of principal importance. But from the standpoint of comprehension—the problem of constructing the evolution of the epoch—these objective motive forces are the most significant factors.

This distance between experience and its theoretical construct may appear more clearly in the problem of autobiography. But it is obvious that the distance between any aspect of historical reality and our knowledge of it is, in principle, the same. The decisive point to keep in mind here is the refutation of epistemological naturalism. On this view, knowledge is supposed to be a mirror image of reality. But knowledge is a novel construct, a self-sufficient, autonomous construct that follows its own laws according to its own peculiar categories. Consider the thesis that no science can completely express the complexity and the qualitatively infinite profusion of real existence. There is no sense in which this thesis provides an adequate view of the definitive form of knowledge. This is a purely quantitative viewpoint. Ultimately, it is grounded on the inadequacy of our cognitive faculties, and it is not sufficient to refute naturalism in principle. This thesis fails to recognize that even under these ideal conditions—even if a qualitatively and quantitatively complete description of reality were actually possible—the discipline of history would still be different from a mirror image of reality. Just as a portrait would retain its peculiar nature and value even if color photography could reproduce a phenomenon with absolute accuracy.

Suppose, however, we grant what this viewpoint mistakenly supposes: that the impossibility of a quantitative description of the infinite complexity of real existence poses the definitive problem of knowledge. Even in this case, it would still follow that historical science is obliged to produce a complete *transformation* of concrete existence. Consider the points of concentration and importance, the characteristic tendencies and moments to which historical knowledge reduces the manifold of existence. They must be constituted as *unified entities* that exhibit a continuous process, an intelligible structure, and a character that can be empathetically reconstructed. They must be represented as a collection of phenomena that can be comprehended from their focal point. History weaves a fabric from fragments of material that have been transformed by the process of emphasis and omission. Its threads and categories are very different from those exhibited by concrete reality. Even the quantitative changes involved produce other changes that are formal and purely functional.

Consider, by way of example, the political biography of a ruler. The politically important ideas and activities are distinguished within the continuity of a rich, multifaceted, and expansive life. They make up his political career, the course of which is intrinsically continuous. However it is hardly the case that any moment of his political life transpires in the artificial isolation that this historical construct requires. On the contrary, there are invariably psychological relationships between his political career and mental events that have other sources. Each moment in his political life is also dependent upon the general disposition of his character and transitory moods. His political life is completely intelligible only in relation to his life as a whole. Knowledge of his life as a whole, however, is impossible for any science; so the historian constructs a new, synthetic concept: politics. In view of the generality and abstract precision required by this historical concept, it is possible that politics never enters the consciousness of the ruler. Perhaps, in this sense of politics, he never consciously performs a political act. Consider the following analogy. A single strand is extracted from the multi-threaded web of life. It is unraveled from the other strands—with which, in reality, it is intertwined—and woven into an entirely new fabric. Even this analogy goes too far. It is a poor comparison because there is no continuity in the relationship between fragments of historical thread that are woven together. In history, we find fragments of a fabric that are only partially and discontinuously interwoven. They constitute a "history" only from the perspective of the *historian;* he imposes upon them the problematic which he regards as definitive, the only problematic that will produce a synthesis of these fragments.[6]

I shall clarify the principle that is at stake here with an analogy taken from art. It is not an exact parallel—on the contrary, it is an extreme case. The relationship between history and reality only approximates it. Consider the portrait. From the perspective of our perception, it creates a unity, a set of relations, and a mutually reinforcing interpretation of the elements of an observable phenomenon. All this has nothing to do with the real, ultimate causes of the phenomenon, causes which lie beneath the surface of what can be observed. Of course these physiological and psychological necessities form all the observable characteristics of a person into a coherent entity the various aspects of which are mutually determined. For the purposes of art, however, this is irrelevant: the only purpose of *art* is to interpret traits that are by their nature perceptual. In order to do this, art is only obliged to satisfy the conditions of aesthetic seeing by producing a picture that is complete in itself. In order to make its interpretation of the *phenomenon* satisfying in this sense, the work of art most often changes or rearranges the necessary form of the actual physical traits, the form that is a consequence of real physical causes.

We might express what is involved here in the following way. The work of art represents reality in a medium which has completely new points of refraction. Within this medium, reality is transformed into a world which has its own order, an order that is determined by harmonies and categories that are a consequence of the requirements of perception and only obtain for relationships on the surface of things. This order is independent of the theoretical ideas which represent the relationship between the real substances that underlie these surface phenomena. The exclusive and immediate object of the graphic arts is the phenomenon itself, a construct of surface appearances. Therefore its principles of classification and synthesis retain their distance from the totality of real being. In the classification and structuring of its material, it follows that art gives a kind of free play to individual subjectivity that is not possible in the sciences. However the difference between art and science is only a matter of degree.

Consider the sort of picture sketched by the history of politics, art, religion, or economics. And consider an exhaustive representation of the totality of the event, the only possible object of a history which would describe things "as they really were." In principle, the relationship between the two is no different from the relationship between the portrait or the landscape painting and the complete reality of its subject matter. It is impossible to describe the single event as it really was because it is impossible to describe the event as a whole. A science of the total event is not only impossible for reasons of unmanageable quantity: it is also impossible because it would lack a *point of view* or *problematic*. Such a problematic is necessary in order to produce a construct that would satisfy our criteria for knowledge. A science of the total event would lack the category that is necessary for the identification and coherence of the elements of the event. There is no knowledge as such: knowledge is possible only insofar as it is produced and structured by constitutive concepts that are qualitatively determined. Because these concepts are qualitatively determined, they are inevitably partial and biased. Given a criterion for knowledge that is perfectly general, it would be impossible to identify or distinguish any element of reality. This is the deeper reason why there are only histories, but no history as such. What we call universal history or world history can at best be the simultaneous application of a variety of these differential problematics. Or, on the other hand, it may be the sort of history which throws into relief the aspects of the event which are most *significant* or important from the perspective of our sense of value.

If we are sufficiently careful about how the import of this remark should be understood, we can say that each history—each individual branch of historical science—has its own peculiar criterion of truth; this can be established by comparing two given histories. In the same way that objective differences in their subject matter are identifiable, so we can also identify logical differences between their theoretical ideals or criteria for knowledge. Consider the differences between these problematics. It follows that the kinds of propositions which satisfy abstract criteria for truth within these different branches of historical science will also be different. Therefore it also follows that these propositions cannot possibly be exact mirror images of reality. On the contrary, they are constructs that are formed by a variety of a priori conditions.

Consider, for example, philological history. The distance between the inquiry and its object is quite different from the corresponding distance in the history of morals. The concepts available to philological history can represent the objective reality of the subject matter of this discipline with much more precision than is possible in the history of ethics. This is because the subject matter of philological history simply consists of words and concepts. The subject matter of ethics, however, is an experienced facticity. As an object of knowledge, this experienced facticity can only be represented by a system of symbols that is much more loose and open-textured. Within both branches of history, however, "truth" is ascribed to propositions. But in this empirical sense, truth is a certain relationship between the proposition and its object. It obviously follows that the criteria for truth in these two branches of history—and not merely their special, technical criteria—are completely different. The conditions under which a proposition is true in these two disciplines are simply not the same.

Another kind of difference—but one that is equally important—obtains between the criteria for knowledge that are employed in the history of technology and in the history of internal or domestic politics. The subject matter of the history of technology is defined relatively unambiguously by the concept of technology itself. It is concerned with material objects insofar as they can become tools. The subject matter of the history of technology is thereby defined by a criterion which makes it possible to establish an exact, abstract distinction between these objects and all the other contents of historical experience. Within the complex interrelations of public life, however, where does domestic politics begin and end? The subject matter of domestic politics cannot be defined by a criterion that even approximates the sort of precision that is possible in the history of technology. Economic development, foreign policy, church government, the general level of education, the temperament of political leaders, and public opinion in the broad masses—all these and thousands of other factors form the milieu in which the development of domestic politics is inextricably implicated. Suppose that domestic policy is differentiated from this milieu for historical purposes. It is inevitable that larger or smaller fragments of the threads and fibers of this milieu will adhere—as we might put it—to domestic policy conceived as the subject matter of a history. For the purposes of a history of domestic politics, it is not necessary to develop these fragments fully. It follows that the constructs produced by the history of domestic policy lack the completeness and internal consistency which we find in the history of technology. Absolutely conclusive explanations in the former discipline are not possible in the way that they are in the latter. The totality of essential factors cannot be identified to the same extent that this is possible in the history of technology. It does not follow that the history of domestic politics is simply inferior as history to the history of technology: it only follows that their criteria for historical truth are not the same. These two disciplines impose completely different forms of historical knowledge upon the raw material that constitutes their subject matter. Within each discipline, however, "truth" can be ascribed to the propositions which satisfy *its own* immanent criteria for truth.

A third type of difference in the forms of historical knowledge appears when we compare the history of art with ecclesiastical history. The subject matter of art history is composed of works that are discontinuously related; this is because each work of art is a complete, self-contained entity. The history of art constructs a coherent process from these disconnected works of art. It represents them as if a process of organic evolution joined them together like the annual rings of a tree. Here the relationship between the given raw material of history and the form it assumes as an object of historical knowledge is altogether different from the relationship between the facticity of the life of a religious community and its representation in the form of history. This is because ecclesiastical or religious life really is continuous. The acts of a single religious virtuoso are not only extraordinary moments within religious life: insofar as they occur at all, they almost never have the insularity of works of art. We might say that they are implicated in the homogeneous substance which evolves within the history of religion. The essential point here is the following: in order to write or understand the history of art, a much more spontaneous functioning of personal or subjective synthesis is required than in ecclesiastical history. Consider the conceptual constructs of historical development that are employed in both branches of history. In the history of art, the component of creativity which informs these constructs is much more significant: they are more completely determined by our constitutive, a priori categories; also, continual interpolation is necessary in order to connect the isolated fragments of subject matter into a coherent developmental synthesis. In ecclesiastical history, synthesis is simply an immanent consequence of the objective continuum of the subject matter itself. Nevertheless, historical truth—in the objective sense—can be ascribed to propositions in both branches of history. This is the case even though the process of inquiry in these two branches of history exhibits a completely different relationship— not a difference in degree, but rather a logical difference—between the synthetic, constitutive activity of the historian and the original, given status of his subject matter.

These examples are sufficient to establish the following conclusion: there is no sense in which historical truth qualifies as a mirror image of historical reality. Let us suppose what is not the case: that the constitutive categories that were employed in the foregoing historical constructs were always the same. Let us suppose that the relationship between the synthetic function and the raw material of history were invariably the same. In that case, the kind of historical realism which claims that there is a naive identity between knowledge and its object would not be as defective as it acutally is. This is because the categories would have the status of constant factors. They could simply be ignored. Moreover the universal validity of these categories might lend them the appearance of a direct counterpart of the unity of objective reality. With this in mind, consider the difference between portraits of the same model by different artists. Consider the variations in representations of distance and reserve, from the reproduction of the most direct expression to the most sophisticated stylization, from the accentuation of expressive psychic content to an emphasis upon perceptual form. There is a sense in which each of these portraits could be equally valuable works of art. And there is a sense in which they could all be "alike." These differences between the individual artist's conception of the aesthetic problem—even though different solutions to this problem may be equally valuable—establishes the following point: in the solution of the objective aesthetic problem, it is the personal or subjective factor that is decisive. The same proof also holds for history. In other words, the foregoing establishes *mutatis mutandis* —with the reserve and restraint that the sciences retain in comparison with the subjective or personal freedom of the artist—the *free play* of the constitutive forms of history in their relations to the real event. Our a priori categories are the decisive factors in the determination of these forms.

The issues at stake here may be clarified by the following epistemological reflections. In the foregoing, I distinguished the form which raw material must assume in order to become the subject matter of a science of history from the immediately given reality that actually constitutes this raw material. It would also be possible to conceive immediately given reality as a form which embraces the content of an event. Of course the content of an event may be intrinsically incomprehensible: it may be infinitely complex. In that case, the forms with which we attempt to comprehend the content of an event would only approach that content with varying degrees of proximity. The pure reality which is under discussion here might be compared to the pure content of our concepts. We conceive the latter as ideal, as having a logical validity that transcends the psychological or external conditions for their realization. Nevertheless, simply by virtue of the fact that this pure content is an object of thought, it acquires a psychological status. The human mind has a capacity that is not really logically explicable. It can conceive the content of its ideas—what is *meant* or *intended* by them—*as if* this content were not an object of *thought,* as if it could be divorced from the form of ideation in which it *eo ipso* exists. "Real experience" is an a priori category also. A given mental content may be comprehended by this category, just as it may be comprehended by a cognitive or ethical category. Therefore we could say that the categories of history are exponents of a second power. They can only comprehend material which already falls under the category of direct experience. The relationship here is roughly the same as the following: a given content, in order to be comprehended by the understanding, must first be represented in the form of a possible object of sense perception.[7]

10. The Psychological Presupposition of History and the Historical a priori

The foregoing establishes the logical status of the psychological presuppositions of history within a general epistemological analysis of historical knowledge. In opposition to the usual view of history as a reproduction of what—observably and unobservably—really happened, this essay emphasizes both the proximity and the distance between history and its subject matter. On the one hand, the following is a necessary condition for history: it must be psychologically possible to recreate the mental acts of historical persons. This is a form of recreation that is occasioned by the raw material of history itself. It presupposes that, in some sense, the historical person and the historian have the same nature; unless this condition is satisfied, the observable acts of historical persons would simply be unintelligible motions of physical objects. On the other hand, the mere identity of the content of the historical prototype—the mental act of the historical person—and the content of its copy—the mental act as recreated by the historian—is not sufficient to satisfy this condition. On the contrary, it is necessary to conceive these contents from the perspective of the peculiar category of the historical. This category projects these contents onto a unique personality, a person whose uniqueness is determined by his place in time and space and by the circumstances of his life. This is the point at which the psychological presupposition of history acquires its importance for historical knowledge. There is no sense in which historical knowledge can ever qualify as a copy of the events "as they actually occurred." In history, as opposed to the natural sciences, one *mind* speaks to another. In spite of this, historical knowledge represents a transformation of experienced reality. Like the natural sciences, history is dependent upon the formative purposes of knowledge and the a priori categories which constitute the form or nature of knowledge as a product of our synthetic activities. The complete and conclusive refutation of historical realism depends upon these psychological considerations. The reason for this is as follows. Consider the point at which the congruence between knowledge and its object seems to be most complete, the point at which this equivalence seems to be a self-evident consequence of our demand for empathetic recreation. The foregoing reflections have shown that even in this case, historical knowledge can only be the result of a reconstruction which transcends the simple identity of knowledge and its object.

In view of the foregoing, the following problem of the philosophy of history—insofar as it is epistemology—arises. First, to identify the apriorities of history and then to determine which of the primordial, recreated objects of immediate experience constitute history as a science. There is no sense in which this is simply a question of historical methodology. On the contrary, it is basically an inquiry into the following question: how do the individual methodological tools of history serve the general purposes of knowledge? What are the logical and psychological presuppositions on which a methodology of history rests? Within this complex of problems, I shall only pursue those that lead us to the foregoing conclusion, a conclusion that is quite general: the historian's recreation of a mental event constitutes an interpretation of the observational material of history.

Recall Ranke's intention. He wanted to eliminate his own personality from historical inquiry in order to see things as they really were. The fulfillment of this wish would be self-defeating: if my personal identity is eliminated, then there is nothing left for me to use in order to comprehend whatever lies beyond it. The reason for this is not simply the fact that the self is the seat or bearer of all ideas—not even Ranke denied this. On the contrary, the more idiosyncratic ideas which the historian only acquires through personal experience and which are inseparable from his own personality provide indispensable raw material for the understanding of another person. In their origins, these ideas are possible only as personal and subjective events. Although they have this character, their substantive relationships acquire a definitive, trans-personal necessity. We may, of course, construe this subjective determination of historical knowledge as a defect, a form of incompleteness. However it is one of those imperfections the elimination of which would be self-defeating. We owe to Kant the classical metaphor which expresses what is at issue here. The dove in flight that feels the restraining force of the air might also feel that it could fly much better in empty space. The obstacle that limits or restrains knowledge—the subjectivity of the recreation of experience—is also a condition under which knowledge is possible. Knowledge is possible only insofar as this sort of subjectivity can be limited or reduced. But suppose that this process of reduction were carried to its ultimate logical conclusion, so that the subjectivity of recreation were eliminated altogether. Then historical knowledge would be impossible.

There is a more profound reason for this. The formal factor of individuality, as it is present in the historical person, must also function in the historian. This is a condition which must be satisfied if the historian is to reconstruct and comprehend the historical person. What we call individuality is the peculiar fashion in which ideas—the contents of which are given—are united in one consciousness. It is a form of their coherence which establishes a sense in which complexes of ideas that have completely different contents can become exactly the same. Not only do they have the same general conceptual or intensional status. They are also extensionally identical.

Consider the following questions. Does the peculiar cachet of personal identity embrace all the contents of a given mind? Or could many of these mental contents just as easily be attributed to another person? Is the tempo and rhythm of mental life reproduced in the innumerable sequences of mental contents? To what extent is the energy of mental life concentrated in a single field of force? Does this result in a more pronounced difference between the person in question and everyone else? All these questions concern the *degree* of individuality. That this degree may be the same—or different—in any two persons is completely independent of all other respects in which these persons may resemble or differ from one another. However it seems that the resemblance which one person bears to another in this degree of individuality may be one of the necessary conditions for the historian's ability to recreate historical personalities. A painter who possesses an extraordinarily comprehensive historical knowledge of his art has made the following claim. Only those artists who—from the perspective of the art of painting—have a pronounced individuality and an idiosyncratic technique can paint highly individualized portraits. And it also seems that the only historians who can grasp and represent the real nature of historical individuality have an extremely idiosyncratic intellect.

Therefore consider not simply the elimination of subjectivity, but the elimination of its purest and most extreme form—individuality. This would destroy the possibility of historical knowledge. In other words, the elimination of this most complete form of subjectivity would be *self-defeating.* Here we see the uniqueness of the subject matter of history, as opposed to the subject matter of all those sciences which have mathematics as their paradigm. The recognition that mind is the object of historical knowledge is not sufficient to plumb the depths of this problem: it is necessary to see that the object of historical knowledge is individuality. It cannot be comprehended by means of logical deduction. On the contrary, it can only be psychologically comprehended or *grasped* by another person who has this same property of individuality. The requirements of the norms of methodology are then applied to this psychological comprehension, a form of understanding that is, in a certain sense, inevitably subjective. The result is a concept of historical science.

Consider the relationship between these methodological norms—without which objective knowledge would be impossible—and the peculiar subjectivity on which the subject matter of history is grounded. This is not an indifferent or neutral relationship—just to the contrary. In the case of historical knowledge, these norms allow a kind of objectivity that is more variable, elastic, and less conclusive or definitive than the sort of objectivity required by the natural sciences. Not only the content of historical interpretation, but even the identification of the facts concerning the life of Caesar, Gregory VII or Mirabeau are—given the same intelligence—a function of whether or not the historian is broad-minded or narrow-minded, a function of whether he tends to be more rationalistic or more impulsive. The inevitable differences which arise here are obvious. The background of the historian himself produces differences of the same sort. Consider the question of whether he developed his views on life in provincial, petit-bourgeois surroundings or in an urbane, cosmopolitan atmosphere, in a free society or a political community that was subjugated to another.

And yet in all of these cases, the conclusions which the historian reaches can be accepted as verifiable historical knowledge. The reason for this is as follows. Although specific cases of prejudice and shades of personal opinion are always corrigible, ultimately their revision amounts to the rejection of an incomplete theory in favor of a more complete *theory,* which remains, nevertheless, a theory. The result is an epistemological distinction which should not be confused with the distinction between a correct and an incorrect solution to a problem. In this case, scientific objectivity includes these various forms of subjectivity. Objectivity cannot be detached from its subjective foundation, nor can these elements of subjectivity be eliminated from the results of historical knowledge. On the contrary, they can only be criticized and structured according to standards supplied by methodological and substantive categories.

Consider the act in which the historian empathizes with the motives of another person, with the totality and the individual aspects of his nature, even though only fragmentary expressions of both are available to him—the act of placing himself within the total manifold of a tremendous system of forces, each one of which can be understood only if he reproduces it for himself. This act identifies the real import of the demand that the historian is, and must be, an artist. Consider also the usual conception of this demand. The historian functions as an artist only after all the facts of his investigation have been established and only in his activity of *representing these facts for the benefit of the reader.* This view of the relationship between history and art is completely mistaken. In this sense, it could be said that *every* creation of the intellect ought to be a work of art. In the case of history, however, art is germane not only to the form in which the results of historical inquiry are presented, but also to the content of these results. The significance of this relationship is a consequence of the fact that art also realizes its most profound nature when it transforms the fortuitousness of the individual experience of the artist into an event that has universal significance or validity. Or, more accurately, in art the event that is purely personal is experienced as universally valid.

However the sense in which a work of art has this property of universality is often misunderstood. There is no sense in which its universal validity has an objective significance: the artistic artifact is not a counterpart of the logical concept of universality. This is the logical type, which classifies a number of phenomena by reference to properties that they all have in common. On the contrary, the universality of a work of art is only subjectively valid. It entails that, in principle, the meaning and value of the work of art are somehow accessible to any potential consumer of aesthetic values. It does not entail the unity of many things, but rather the unity of many minds. It does this by activating the capacity to react to the work of art in essentially the same way in all persons capable of aesthetic enjoyment—no matter how different from one another they may be in all other respects. This property of the work of art is also the peculiar feature of the conceptual construct of the historical personality. An entity that is, objectively, totally individual is structured in such a way that it can be intelligible as an object of a general subjective recreation.

The ability to invest a purely individual—even unique—entity with this sort of universality is the aesthetic secret of the historian. It is the point at which the unteachable aspects of his discipline become most decisive. The historian classifies, structures, and interprets the facts in such a way that they amount to a coherent picture of a psychological process. Even here, there is only a difference in degree between history and literature—although the historian does not enjoy the imaginative writer's freedom in structuring his narrative. Suppose that the writer has invented a certain character and has defined his interpersonal relations in a certain way. In this case, the writer is no longer free to do whatever he wants with this character. On the contrary, there can only be a limited margin of deviation between what happens to him and the average psychological experience of men and events of this sort. The literary process begins with free invention. This creative invention must then be structured according to established laws of phenomena. The result is a finished work of art which stands under the following motto. "We are free to make the first move, but we are the servants of the second." History only transposes this motto. In history, the first move is determined by the factual material with which the inquiry begins. In the formation of this material into the totality of an historical process, however, the historian is free. This is because this move is a function of the historian's subjective categories and constructs.

Consider Schopenhauer's view of the nature of artistic activity. The intellect surrenders its own subjectivity in order to become completely objectified in the work of art; every essential distinction between subject and object collapses. The subject completely reproduces the properties of the object. In this moment, therefore, the artist and his artifact are one: the artist as subject is nothing more than this object, the work of art. Actually—if we divest this thesis of its metaphysical trappings—Schopenhauer has also identified what is most decisive for the historian, or for anyone who wants to acquire any kind of historical knowledge. Each time a psychological entity is recreated and understood, this signifies that the interpreter makes this psychological process his own. He immerses himself in knowledge of this process. And—insofar as the person can be identified with his mental states—it can be said that at this moment he really *is* this psychological process.

And here, of course, we must always keep the following in mind. The identity that is at stake here—between the mental states of the historian and the mental states of the historical person—is not a mechanical copy of the primary event. On the contrary, the interpreter comprehends—or shares in—the content or meaning of the event insofar as it is intelligible. The creative artist only intensifies the experience of the consumer of art; his productivity is, as we might put it, a more mature form of the experience of the latter. The creative artist does not become absorbed in the reality of his subject matter—makers of wax figures do this. He immerses himself in what is often called the "idea" of the object: the content of the object insofar as it has a mental form. *This* is the real source of the relationship between the artist and the historian. The historian does not simply let the opaque reality of mental events repeat itself in his own experience. On the contrary, he only understands—or shares in—the meaning or intelligible content of these mental events. This is more or less like Plato's theory of ideas: the idea only includes the aspects of real things insofar as they are objects of knowledge.

11. The Intuitive Recreation of Phenomena that Do not Lie within the Domain of Immediate Experience

Consider the problems of a philosophy of history—which include questions about substantive and methodological norms—as they are set out here. Insofar as these problems concern teleology, they center around psychology. By way of amplification, I shall now pursue one of the central problems in this set of issues somewhat further. The process whereby the immanent aspects of an event are recreated is a condition for all historical understanding. The foregoing discussion of this process stressed the thesis that it is not a naturalistic reproduction, but rather a construct formed as a consequence of the purposes of historical knowledge. However the difficulty peculiar to this sort of recreation has not yet been identified. Independent of any further questions which may be raised concerning the subsequent development of immediately given psychological material, this material itself has a property that is very difficult to understand. We are able to recreate mental contents that have never appeared in our own subjective experience. Given the satisfaction of certain conditions—which are, nevertheless, purely external—we are able to share the mental life of persons who have nothing at all in common with us.

Reconsider the claim that I made above. Anyone who has never loved would never be able to understand the lover; the coward would never be able to understand the hero. This is not strictly true. It only holds within certain limits that were not at issue at that point. Of course we cannot understand another person if this requires a degree of distance or alienation from our own subjective, inner experiences that we find impossible. This is why there is a sense in which we should be skeptical about any claim that we can "understand" the life of ancient Greece and its artifacts, or medieval piety, or—at the other extreme—primitive peoples or the psychology of animals. Nevertheless we are also persuaded that one does not have to be a Caesar in order to really understand Caesar, nor does one have to be another Luther in order to comprehend Luther. Therefore the limits at which our understanding of others becomes problematical or impossible are certainly not determined by a coincidence or congruence between our own personally experienced thoughts, experiences, and feelings and the mental life of the historical person—just to the contrary. Although it is certainly not unlimited, our ability to understand other persons extends beyond this pattern of congruence.[8]

In which case, the following problem arises. What is the source of this intermediate zone in which a reproduction takes place? We produce the ideas of other persons even though none of our own experiences could have been responsible for the production of an analogous mental event. How is this possible? Suppose we explained this as a simple transformation of our own actual experience. First of all, the distinction between form and content is arbitrary. The mere use of the words "form" and "content" only gives this epistemological distinction a name. But it does not make the import of the distinction itself clear. Moreover it would be no less difficult to account for the spontaneous production of a form than to account for the spontaneous creation of a material. Finally, a further issue would still remain problematical. Consider one form in which we comprehend the content of the given experience of another person. Suppose that we have a subjective certainty of its possibility and its reality. There are other forms—just as possible for our imagination as the first and no less accessible to our own experience—in which we cannot comprehend the same experience with the same feeling of certainty. Why?

We call the most striking and unpredictable instances of this sort of ability "genius." The genius seems to create knowledge out of himself, knowledge which the ordinary person can discover only on the basis of experience. On the basis of the slightest hints and allusions, he constructs an internally consistent and convincing picture of the intellectual processes, ideational associations and passions of historical persons, even though the actual examples of this cast of mind disappeared long ago. His imagination interrelates the most disparate fragments and interprets them, no matter how astonishing they may be. In all this, he has access to material that he could not have acquired on the basis of his own experience. It would be a mistake to leave this completely opaque concept of psychological-historical genius unanalyzed. This would be an especially serious error since the real issue does not only concern a small number of extraordinary geniuses. Between the genius and the ordinary person there are innumerable intermediate cases. And it happens often enough that even the ordinary person occasionally exhibits a glimmer of genius himself: the genius's apparently super-empirical ability to recreate mental processes that do not lie within his own experience. The relationship between the genius and the ordinary person becomes even more intimate when we consider that the historical genius can only express his intuitions in words. What he writes may suggest to the ordinary person the mental states which are at stake. This makes it easier for the latter to recreate these states; but, ultimately, this is a process that he must carry out for himself.

At this point, I should like to suggest an explanation for this ability to understand mental processes which do not lie within one's own experience. I am fully aware that this sort of interpretation has been discredited on the most legitimate grounds. However I interpret this phenomenon as a process whereby one becomes conscious of an inheritance that is unconscious or latent. In some form or other, earlier generations have transmitted their organic modifications to later generations; in some obscure fashion, the organic modifications are related to mental processes. In general, however, the later generation is unaware of the immeasurable profusion, the minuteness, and the antithetical character of the individual aspects of this inheritance.

Consider the person in whom this inheritance is so favorably disposed that he can reproduce it easily in clear consciousness and on the basis of a minimum of experience. This is the sort of person that we call a genius. Mental processes that are quite remote from his own individual experience are reproduced in his mind; this is because they are stored in his organism as genetically transmitted recollections. And in exceptional cases, not even the innumerable contrarieties and obscurities of mental processes, which also have the same source, render these genetically transmitted recollections inaccessible to consciousness. Given this hypothesis, we can also understand the occasional flashes of genius on the part of persons who are otherwise not so gifted. This would also account for the possibility that the ordinary person can understand the genius. We can become aware of these genetically transmitted recollections when the genius provides us with clearly expressed and closely related groups of psychological stimuli or suggestions. They function as heuristic devices that make it possible for us to acquire consciousness of this inheritance. In this case, the process of learning really would be only a form of recollection or recognition.

Consider our ability to completely recreate the innermost drives of a person long since dead. Consider our ability to identify his character from the most fragmentary evidence, a character which developed under circumstances totally foreign to us, circumstances we have never been able to observe. It would obviously be a mistake to explain these capacities by reference to the experiences of our own life. For the same reason, it would be a mistake to suppose that the purposiveness of instinctive movements or the direction and correctness of moral impulses could be derived from the same source. Our body retains the acquisitions of many thousands of years of evolution. In some of the more rudimentary organs, even the obvious traces of earlier epochs are preserved. In the same way, our mind preserves the results and traces of earlier mental processes from different stages of the evolution of the species. In this latter case, however, the rudiments which have mental value or significance occasionally function purposefully.

Consider the extent to which we can understand the experiences of our contemporaries, even if they deviate considerably from our own way of thinking and feeling. This may be a consequence of the fact that our inheritance from the evolution of our species includes—in addition to our own basic character—traces of other characters. This makes it possible for us to understand them: that is, to experience the same mental processes these persons experienced.

From our perspective, even physically observable persons only represent incomplete, external or superficial phenomena. On the basis of mere observation alone, every other person is only an automaton for us. Each of his words is nothing but a sound; we can represent this sound as the expression of another mind only on the basis of our own first person experiences. There is only a difference in degree between this process of understanding and historical knowledge. History only encounters a more incomplete and fragmentary body of material and a more uncertain corpus of evidence. Therefore it permits—and actually requires—much more freedom for conjecture.

Consider my hypothesis of evolutionarily transmitted interpretive faculties, a hypothesis which is intended to make sense of concrete mental experience. At the very worst, this hypothesis may be regarded as a methodological fiction. Phenomena occur *as if* this sort of latent correspondence between our minds and the minds of completely different persons really obtained. In this case, the hypothesis may be regarded as a symbolic expression of the as yet unknown energies that are actually responsible for the existence of these phenomena.

12. The Understanding of the Personal and the General

From the standpoint of its objects, recreative understanding has two polar extremes. In spite of the most radical differences between them, both are more or less equally accessible to understanding. The significant difficulties of understanding lie in the intermediate region between these two poles. At one extreme, we find that the mental recreation of individuals who have a sharply defined character is relatively easy. Consider Themistocles and Caesar, Augustine and Kaiser Friedrich II. We think we can understand them more profoundly and unambiguously than we can understand a typical Athenian of the fifth century B.C. or an average Italian before the Renaissance. This point might be expressed in the following way. The complete individual—although he is historically unique—has a universally human nature. When we compare him with the many examples of persons who are only representatives of a given spatio-temporal situation, there is a certain sense in which his nature is timeless. The great historical figure has an identity that is unique and intrinsic; it is independent of the circumstances and surroundings of his life. If he were translated into another epoch, the total person would, of course, be quite different. However the essential core or center of his identity would remain unchanged.

The average man, on the other hand, is spatio-temporally determined. This is because his entire significance is a consequence of the fact that he is representative of a given historical situation. It is necessary for us, as we might put it, to reach out to him. However the great men of history—the unique personalities that are independent of their own historicity—reach out to us. Compared with the average man, they are more accessible to the understanding of other ages. The character of the ordinary person is historically defined. But it is also anonymous. It appears as a mere composite of concomitant and juxtasposed characteristics. In the person with a striking character, however, the form of his identity, which is responsible for the coherence of all its individual expressions—is most prominent. The more pronounced the identity of an historical person, the easier it is for us to understand him. This is because each element of his character sheds light on the other; each is a consequence of his total character. This is the point on which the thesis of naive realism—that knowledge is a product of identity or resemblance—appears to be most defensible. The unity of the intellect, the unity of the mind of the knower, provides the form for the unity of the object of knowledge.

Consider Kant's claim about natural science. "We have knowledge of an object when we have produced a unity in the manifold of its perception." In the most general sense, this thesis also holds true for historical knowledge. The unity of the Kantian "object" is only the unity of an apperception. Apperception is the source of the unity of the multiplicity and heterogeneity of sense perceptions, the ground of their coherence and order. In historical inquiry, the unity of the consciousness of the knowing subject—the historian—is the source of the unity of the historical person—the object of inquiry. In the case of history, however, the content which this form comprehends is more clearly and definitively preformed or prefabricated than is the case in the natural sciences. This is because the basis of the coherence of historical content, or even its origin, is already there—even though it is not immediately accessible—in the historical personality.[9] This is the ultimate source of the coherence of its elements or aspects. Suppose that there is a strong sense in which the data concerning an historical person are invested by this quality of potential unity that is a result of their origin in the ego of the historical person. Then the unity of apperception on the part of the historian will function in a more certain, comprehensive, and profound fashion. This is the reason we are better acquainted with the great individuals of history; this is why we do not feel that they are banished to the inaccessibility of temporal isolation, which is how we see historical persons of very limited individuality. Because of this, it is not so easy for our own faculty of synthetic apperception to "produce a unity."

In this case, it is the *form* of the object which makes it accessible to knowledge. Suppose we now consider the relationship between historical knowledge and its *content*. Then we can identify another type of historical object—the extreme polar opposite of the foregoing—for which historical understanding is also relatively easy. The psychological reconstruction of ordinary historical material proceeds much more certainly and uncontroversially when the historical question concerns the interests and movements of entire groups. This is also the case if these groups provide the basis and ultimate purpose for the action of individual historical persons. In the first place, group relations are—to an extraordinary extent—more simple and unambiguous than individual relations. In dealing with larger masses of people, we are concerned with the primary conditions of existence—general, extensive, and vulgar interests in which large numbers of people are able to concur. It is only on this basis that the more subtle and sophisticated individualization of mental impulses develops. Unlike an individual, a group cannot self-consciously dissemble expressions of its thoughts and desires. For the same reasons, a group is also unable to do this unintentionally; on the contrary, it records its strivings and its mental actions and reactions quite clearly. For the same reasons, the expressions of the simple energies and drives that characterize the mass as a whole are quite clear in comparison with personally differentiated energies and drives of the individual.

At this point, we can see that there is very little contingency or coincidence in the intimate relation between historical materialism and the socialist world view. In principle, nothing can be said against the possibility of a totally individualistic historiography. Individuals would be the exclusive bearers of historical events; the meaning of all history would lie in the acts of its heroes. The interests of public life would be the only ultimately decisive historical causes or motives. Although there may be no empirical psychological evidence at all in support of this thesis, it remains a logically possible speculation. On the other hand, consider a historiography for which mass movements constitute the exclusive subject matter of history. It is extremely plausible that this theory of history would see the masses as driven or determined by motives which could be attributed with certainty to *each* member of the mass in question, these motives being, of course, the production and reproduction of immediate, material life. Does each member of such a mass also have more abstract, sophisticated and highly individualized characteristics? And does each member experience a more individualized fate that is a consequence of these characteristics? These questions are beside the point. The essential point is that these more individualized characteristics constitute *history* only if they are common to all members of the mass, a mass in which all these compounded energies compose a unified force. It is obvious that only the simplest interests—those which are fundamental to the life of every person—fall under this description.

Consider the philosophy of history of classical idealism. It repeats this reduction of the historically given to its most simple or elementary factors, facts that identify what is common to all historical phenomena: their collective character. From the standpoint of substance or content, however, classical idealism has a completely different conceptual basis. It discovered the synthesis of subjective freedom and the objective necessities of reason in the state, the order of law. However the idealists did not appreciate the price they paid for the universal validity and the objective abstraction that their theory achieved for both freedom and reason. The result of idealistic historiography was an abstract schematism, remote from concrete distinctions and interests and indifferent to everything that comprises individual life, the only form of life that offers the possibility of conflicts and deeper levels of experience which cannot be exhaustively subsumed under general concepts. Law has been characterized quite aptly as the "ethical minimum," the ground-zero of ethics. In the same way, the state in general represents the practical minimum of any given cultural situation—the absolutely basic conditions necessary for the existence of this culture: provision for the most general interests and stabilization of the most basic necessities of the culture. The richness of individual life transcends all of this. In principle, the more history is reduced to the history of the state, the more simple and transparent it becomes. The nature and the life of individual personalities is the more complex form of existence, a form of existence that remains inaccessible to immediate expression.

Neither historical materialism nor the concentration of historical interest upon the state takes any account of the problem posed by individuality. Historical materialism remains, as we might put it, within the individual; it is concerned with the mere matter or raw material of life. Idealism, on the other hand, transcends the form of the personality and rises into the region of conceptual generalities. A certain methodological assumption is common to both theories. In both, the immanent recreation of the historical has the following logical status. The structure and nature of personal life is reduced to what is common to every person: the simplest factors. This is the absolute minimum of psychic material necessary to define the historical event. The problematic of individualistic historiography shifts this factor of generality onto the subject or actor. From the standpoint of this problematic, it is the task of history to make the concrete object intelligible and reproducible in a perfectly general fashion. The conditions for the intelligibility and the recreation of the most divergent personalities must all be equally well satisfied. The problematic of historical materialism and idealism, on the other hand, shifts the factor of generality onto the object of historical investigation.

Each of these two theories adopts one of the ambiguous senses of "generality." For historical materialism, the general is the interest that is immanent in every individual in the same way. For idealism—history as history of the state—the general is the unity which *transcends* every individual. Even though all individuals have a part in this unity, it cannot be exhaustively contained in them. For both theories, their substantive and methodological principle is also a vehicle for psychological understanding. The problem of psychological interpretation no longer encounters the incommensurability of the individual and the inevitable subjectivity of any reconstruction of individuality. On the contrary, it confronts the simplicity of the "general." The intelligibility of this element—in other words, the extent to which its corresponding contents are unambiguously confirmed in every mind—is a function of the extent to which these contents are primitive and basic. This is a function of the extent to which they are identifiable in some form as inherited, transmitted, and diffused in every mind. Consider the element of personality and subjectivity which informs the act of empathy in history. We are quite willing to acknowledge its influence when we are dealing with single individuals. However the problematic of idealism and historical materialism can easily conceal its influence. Suppose we make sociopsychological processes the subject matter of our investigation and attempt to reconstruct them empathetically. In this case, we do not have the impression that we are dependent upon our subjectivity and the arbitrariness of our own inner experience. On the contrary, we think that we encounter an entity which has objectively ascertainable properties.

Here again we see both the intimate relationship and the difference between the psychological and the substantive-methodological moments in history. Both historical materialism and idealism attempt to produce a scientific simplification and unification of the subject matter of history. They define and structure the infinitely complex event from the standpoint of a maximally abstract concept. But consider the instrument that both theories actually employ in order to produce this logical construct. It is based on the psychological usefulness or appropriateness of their basic categories, the extent to which their problematic renders the subject matter of history accessible to psychological reconstruction. Ultimately, it can be said that social structures and movements—the legal structure of civil society, the hierarchical relations of groups, any unification for common purposes, the formation of collective life through material or ideal motives—also have the following status. A personal, empathetic reconstruction of these structures and movements is a condition which must be satisfied in order to describe and understand them; moreover it is also a condition for their definition or identification. Even the properties of these movements which we think we can identify by simple observation are really only definable by reference to this mental process. Both the sufficient conditions for psychological understanding and the sufficient conditions for objective-scientific simplicity are united in the simplicity of the "general" which lies within or above the bearers of historical events. This problematic may be quite uncritical about the psychological requirements for the satisfaction of these conditions. Nevertheless, these requirements are a logical consequence of the *psychological* structure that this problematic imposes upon history.

Chapter Two

On Historical Laws

1. The Concept of a Law

No one will deny that the laws that govern the province of historical *knowledge* lie within the domain of philosophical inquiry. But consider the claim that philosophy is obliged to discover the laws of the historical process itself—this task is not infrequently ascribed to the philosophy of history. At first glance, this idea seems to be remarkably bizarre. What would we say if someone told us that scientists in another discipline—physics, astronomy, linguistics—were limited to the collection of facts, the discovery of the laws governing these facts being left to the philosopher? The rationale behind our astonishment on this point can only have its source in the peculiar status that the concept of a law acquires within the province of historical inquiry. The peculiar import of the concept of a law within history can be clarified only if we compare it with the more general import of this concept. The following is a possible, internally consistent definition of the concept of a law that governs an event. It is a proposition which states that, given the satisfaction of a certain set of empirical conditions, the satisfaction of another set of empirical conditions will unconditionally—that is, in every spatio- temporal frame—follow as the consequence. The satisfaction of this second set of conditions will not appear to be definitive if other events also occur within the same spatio-temporal frame. The decisive point is the following. Given conditions of ideal isolation, satisfaction of the initial set of conditions will lead to satisfaction of the second. Suppose that other conditions coexist with this initial set. In other words, suppose that ideal conditions of isolation are not satisfied. Then a result will follow such that—at any given time—the contribution of the initial set of conditions to this result can be deduced without loss of empirical meaning.

2. The Application of the Concept of a Law to the Analysis of Complex and Simple Phenomena

As a matter of fact, these ideal conditions of isolation are never satisfied. Forces of very different direction and origin act concomitantly. The differentiation of a given force or cause within a uniform law governing a sequence of events turns on the following questions. Can the results of this force also be identified in other complexes? And, if this is the case, does the cause in question invariably produce the same result? Suppose we observe that a given complex of facts A leads to another complex of facts B. In this case, we may think that there is a lawlike connection between A and B. Now suppose that we establish that A is composed of the elements a, b, and c and that B is composed of the elements φ, β, and γ. We can establish that φ is a consequence of a when we observe a certain consequence B^1 of A^1 in which A^1 is composed of elements a, d, and e and B^1 is composed of elements φ, λ, and ξ. Suppose we pursued this inquiry further. This would require that a and φ be analyzed into their component processes. These relationships would also be governed by special laws that underlie them. Ultimately, this inquiry would lead to the discovery of the basic elements of all events. In other words, it would reveal the laws which govern the relationships between the most elementary components of events. It is the concomitant and composite effects of these laws which determine or define the properties of complex phenomena as they appear to us.

It is legitimate to speak of a real law governing an event only if the effects of these ultimate, elementary components have been identified. It is a self-evident conclusion that if there is one occasion on which B is produced by A then—given an absolutely identical repetition of the conditions that constitute A—B will always be produced by A. In this sense, it could be said that the following proposition qualifies as a law: A is the cause of B. In this proposition, A includes *all* of the determining conditions of B which occur up to the threshold of the occurrence of B itself. In other words, what is meant by A includes more than the ordinary, weaker, or softer concept of cause. This weaker concept refers to the direct or immediate force which provides the impetus for B. But it does not include the innumerable other concomitant necessary conditions for B in which this immediate force is implicated. It is obvious that the satisfaction of this indefinitely large set of conditions is necessary for the causation of B; however the very self-evidence of this point tends to obscure its absolute indispensability. Even the slightest change in the factors that constitute A would immediately render our knowledge of this law questionable and worthless.

Suppose we only have knowledge of $A(abc)$ and $B(\varphi\beta\gamma)$ insofar as they are totalities. Now suppose that a^1 occurs instead of a. Then our knowledge will not warrant us in drawing any conclusion at all concerning the behavior of B. We can estimate the reason for the variation in B only if we establish the relationship between the component causes and effects—a and φ, b and β, c and γ. Then we could establish that the components β and γ remain unchanged. The relationship between the original and the altered B, therefore, can only be a consequence of a change in φ. As long as our knowledge is limited to collective or gross consequences, we can have no knowledge at all concerning the causal relations of every new complex or composite fact. A given fact may resemble an earlier established fact in as many respects as you like. This is of no significance if the slightest change is sufficient to make any determination of its consequences illusory. Without an analysis of the composite facts into component causes and effects, we will be unable to determine *which* aspect of the earlier observed effect will be changed by an alteration in the cause.

Consider the events which we attempt to correlate in the form of historical laws: it is clear that they have this property of complexity. It is only our conceptual schemes and our sense of value that tend to obscure the manifold of factors that make up each of these events. Our conceptual schemes tend to deceive us because we give single *names* to extremely complex phenomena in order to render them tractable for the praxis of both knowledge and everyday life. Our sense of value tends to confuse us because we stress a single element in one of these complexes as the only aspect that is of essential interest to us. We treat the other elements—which occur concomitantly with this essential aspect and which even constitute a condition for its identification—as irrelevant for our purposes; they are negligible quantities. The propositions which pass for laws of history are generally based on one of these illegitimate oversimplifications of complex phenomena. In consequence, we treat phenomena which are very different—from the standpoint of their immanent or structural properties—as if they were more or less equivalent.

Consider concepts like state and class, religion and culture, the conditions of production and the status of women, civil liberty and individuality, and innumerable other concepts which have the same logical status. Whenever we see that they stand in certain functional relations that are invariably repeated, we conclude that these relations must have a nomological status. But consider all the instances that are supposed to fall under some putative law of history: they are never totally congruent in *all* respects. Therefore the law—which is derived from the observation of *one* situation and its consequence—only holds for this single case: in other words, this case and all of its absolutely identical repetitions. It does not hold for all the other cases which appear to connect cause and effect in the same way only as a result of the suppression of their differences. Because of our ignorance of the causal relations between the elementary components of these totalities, we have no knowledge of the crucial factor. Knowledge of the variations in the value of this factor would make it possible for us to compute a later event as a function of an earlier one. Therefore the putative law is only valid for one case. It has no legitimate application to future cases. Without knowledge of the properties of the basic elements, it is impossible for us to establish whether a certain discrepancy between an earlier and a later instance may concern precisely the factor which is responsible for the fact that a later complex phenomenon is a causal consequence of an earlier complex phenomenon.

3. Remarks on Concrete Causality

In this entire investigation, the idea of a general law is identified with the idea of causal efficacy. However the generally acknowledged equivalence of these two concepts is not immune to logical objections. We are not prepared to acknowledge a causal relationship in the absence of a causal law. In other words, the fact that B follows A

is recognized as the causation of *B* by *A* only if a *law* obtains to the effect that in every case—in other words, invariably—*B* follows whenever *A* occurs. However it seems to me that there is no logically necessary connection between the idea of causation and the idea of a law. I shall not take up the question of whatever difficulties or whatever metaphysics may be implied by the concept of causation. At this point, let us understand the concept of causation in its usual, material sense. In this case, the following possibility seems to me to be logically unobjectionable. At one point in space and time, an event *A* causes an event *B*. At another point in space and time, it causes another event *C.* There is no doubt that we can conceive of a possible world in which *A* invariably—according to timelessly valid laws—produces *C*, just as it produces *B* in the world that in fact exists. For this same reason, there is no logical objection to the possibility of a third world in which the effects of *A* are variable. The essential point is the following. This hypothesis does not replace causation with a relationship of purely arbitrary temporal succession. On the contrary, all the definitive conditions which distinguish causation from the latter—the immanence, efficacy, and necessity of the connection—are retained. There is only one difference. Instead of invariably being fulfilled by the same propositions, they are fulfilled by a varying set of propositions. The conceptual possibility entertained here should not be confused with a thesis once maintained by a logician: that if the law of causality ceased to hold on some distant fixed star, the result would be universal chaos. The consequence of the hypothesis proposed here would be just the contrary: causality would continue to hold in all of its objectivity and strictness. Actually, the domain within which causality obtains would be even more extensive. Instead of being valid for all cases, however, the content of any law would be valid only for one case. The valid content of a causal law would change for each successive case.

The sterility of this hypothesis is based not on logical grounds, but rather on epistemological considerations. Consider an event which has a unique, nonrepeatable content. Consider also the distinction between a genuine causal relationship governing the moments of this event as hypothesized above and a case of arbitrary, purely fortuitous temporal succession. We have no *method* for making this distinction. Granted, causality as a form cannot be derived from experience. Nevertheless, a given law is confirmed only by means of induction, by comparing the repetition of events which agree in content. It is only on the basis of induction that we form a real representation of the category of causality as a "law" which has an established content. Only on these grounds are we justified in claiming that there is a relationship between the observable, temporal sequence of phenomena and causality, which is unobservable and immanent to the event. Without this relationship between the inductively established content of events, there would be no relation between knowledge and its application. Therefore the kind of causation described above—which might be called concrete causality—may be objectively possible. However it is not a possible object of our *knowledge*. We can never have knowledge of causation in this form, but only in the form of a general law which connects a certain event to a certain consequence in such a way that wherever and whenever the same event occurs, the same consequence will also follow.

Nevertheless it is worth taking a hypothetical look at some structural relations in psychology simply as a pure conceptual possibility. Consider the difficulties—heretofore insuperable—encountered in discovering laws of mental life and the astonishing frequency with which the mind produces completely different consequences from what appear to be exactly the same initial conditions. This could be explained on the basis of the hypothesis that mental processes are governed by concrete causality. Since it is impossible to *identify* or *establish* a causal relation independent of a general law, the state of affairs entailed by this hypothesis would seem to be no different from that state of "freedom" which emancipates every moment of mental life from determination by its antecedents. In essence, however, these two views of mental life have nothing at all to do with one another. The causal nexus would be exactly as strict as it is in general laws of nature, the only difference being that the law would not obtain for repeated instances of the same phenomenon. Consider the problem which the theory of freedom has always encountered. How can causality be consistent with the apparently arbitrary changes that take place in our mental life? This problem remains insoluble as long as causality is conceived exclusively in the form of a general law—which is, of course, the only form in which a causal relation is *knowable* or *discoverable*. However let us suppose that these two concepts are logically independent, that concrete causality is at least logically *possible*. In that case, no indeterminist freedom of any sort follows from the nonrepeatability of mental processes. On the contrary, it only follows that the unrestricted validity of the causal content of a natural law is—in an extreme or limiting case—reduced to one unique effect. Ultimately, the subject matter of every history is composed exclusively of mental processes. Therefore the bearing of these reflections on the concept of historical laws is obvious. This hypothesis of concrete causality would make sense of the following state of affairs. Although the concrete individuality of an event cannot be deduced from general laws, it does not follow that the properties of an event that constitute its individuality are arbitrary, indeterminate, and inexplicable.

4. The Causation of Totalities

The foregoing reflections were only concerned with the simultaneous relations which obtain between the motive forces of the individual processes that constitute an historical event. If the obscurity of these relations makes it impossible to establish a genuine historical law, then the difficulties which stand in the way of this concept will become much more severe when these individual forces and processes are regarded as *causes*—causes which are responsible for the production of an event that is an observable phenomenon and, as such, is represented as a factor or variable in a law. We are told, for example, that the following is an historical law. The history of every body politic begins with the intellectual and civil liberty of a minority. From this beginning, it progressively extends to the majority, and eventually to everyone. From this point—the zenith of liberty—a retrogression takes place. Culture, freedom, and power revert to the minority and the individual. However the original confinement of this state of bliss and freedom to the minority is obviously not the sufficient cause of its extension to the majority. And its extension to the majority is not responsible for its subsequent universal enjoyment. Moreover, the fact that it is universally enjoyed is not in itself the real force which is later responsible for its limitation to a minority. The following also passes for a law of historical development. Nations and individuals recapitulate the transition from infancy to youth, maturity, and old age. The intellectual epochs of speculation, faith, reason, and intellectual decadence are said to correspond to these stages of development. But it is obvious that these stages do not identify the real forces which explain the transition from one era to another. Suppose that in a given epoch a nation is devout. This fact certainly does not make comprehensible the necessary connections which are responsible for its transition to an epoch of rational inquiry. The youth of a nation is obviously not the sufficient cause which is responsible for the fact that it later reaches maturity—just to the contrary. Suppose observation verifies that the existence of this putative sequence of stages can be confirmed without exception. This would still not identify the immanent, causal nexus—that is, the law—which explains the relationship between them. On the contrary, it would only identify a heretofore uniform sequence of phenomena.

One final example. Initially, the forms of production in any epoch of economic development correspond to the productive forces of the economy. Within these forms, however, the productive forces grow irresistibly until their forms can no longer contain them. Finally, petrified and obsolete, they are shattered by the new productive forces, which create new forms that correspond to their power. Consider the driving forces which—in accordance with this law—produced the transition from the primitive economy of the clan to a slave economy, the transition from feudalism to liberalism, from the domestic economy to production for the market, from the compulsory labor of the peasant bound to the soil to free wage labor. There is no sense in which this "law" identifies these forces; on the contrary, it only describes the sequence of phenomena as they appear on the surface of historical life. Employing this law, it would be absolutely impossible to deduce the properties of the form of production that will succeed a given form of production. But this is a criterion—the derivation of the effect from the given cause—which must be satisfied by any law of nature.

In these examples, the temporal relations of composite states, the apparent consequences of a large number of single movements and forces, are described, albeit in a dubious and problematical fashion. The fact that one of these states follows another is a result of the functioning of a large number of special laws. But it is not a law itself. It is as if we were told that the following proposition qualifies as a law: organisms are modified in such a way that their organs become progressively adapted to the environmental conditions of their existence. Let us suppose that this process could really be observed without exception. Then it would only be the consequence of innumerable individual functional relations between the organism and its environment; special laws would be responsible for each of these individual functions. The foregoing proposition only describes a result of the concomitant functioning of laws. It is not a premise, but rather a conclusion; it is not an explanans, but rather an explanandum. If a law is really supposed to identify the cause of the individual phenomena we observe, then the description of the temporal relations of complex phenomena like these cannot qualify as a law.

For this reason, the propositions that are called "Kepler's Laws" do not qualify as laws of nature in the strict sense. It cannot be supposed that there is a general force in nature which only operates in such a way that the radius vectors of the planets describe equal areas in equal times. The fact that the planets behave in this fashion is a consequence of certain laws, and the conditions under which they hold are located in a certain preexisting state of matter. But the import of "Kepler's Laws" is not a law itself. The proposition that has this import—the proposition that describes the conditions under which Kepler's Laws obtain—would be Newton's law of universal gravitation. This proposition identifies the primary force of attraction which actually operates between the sun and the planets. The application of this law to the special case of our solar system is relatively inessential and contingent. The motions described by Kepler's Laws are, of course, invariant and lawlike, just as it may be invariable or lawlike that A meets B on the street. However we do not suppose that there is a law of nature which is responsible for this meeting. On the contrary, the source of this regularity is to be found in forces that lie beneath the phenomenon of the encounter, the psychological and physiological impulses and the atomic processes which intersect in such a way that this result is produced. *The fact that* these processes all intersect is not lawlike in the same sense that the processes themselves are. It is a phenomenon of a higher order, a synthesis of elementary sequences that is only produced in the mind, as this might be expressed. Only these elementary sequences contain the cause of the composite effect. Therefore they are also the exclusive source of the nomological status of this cause.

In conclusion, consider an extremely simple example. The laws of growth, as they apply to the palm tree, produce a tree which has a form that is characteristically different from the shape of every other tree. But this would not lead anyone to conclude that there are special natural laws that are peculiar to the growth of palm trees. In the same way, the content of history evolves into characteristic forms that are different from everything else in the universe. But this does not mean that we would be justified in speaking of special laws of historical evolution. Of course it is a lawlike process if freedom and a high standard of living originate in a minority, are progressively enjoyed by everyone, and eventually retrogress to the minority; or if

eras of speculation, faith, and inquiry follow one another succes-
sively. However there is no justification for supposing that there is a
special law which explains why the concatenation of individual
events which lead to these transitions produce precisely this result. In
these cases, there is no higher law that is superior to the lower, more
inferior laws which regulate the motions of individual elements. If
that were the case, individual elements would have two sets of laws,
like the member states of a bund or confederation: this would be an
utterly anthropomorphic conception. Only the motions of the most
elementary factors and the laws that govern them are real causes. If a
collection of these elementary movements constitutes a composite
event, that does not mean that there is a special law governing this
event. The exclusive sufficient cause and explanation of every event
lies in the primary laws that govern the relationship between the
simplest and most elementary processes.

5. The Problematical Status of Simple Elements

If we pursue this inquiry further, we will reach a point at which
its direction reverses. Suppose that the kinematic relations of plan-
etary motion described by Kepler's Laws are simply mere facts,
comparable to the observed succession of composite historical states.
In that case, the proposition that there is an attraction between the
particles of matter which varies inversely with the square of the
distance between them is also nothing but an observation concerning
synchronic and diachronic spatial relations. Suppose we call Newton's law of universal gravitation the true cause of the relative and
contingent fact that Kepler's Laws hold on the following ground.
The former obtains for simple, constitutive elements, and the latter
obtains only for a complex of total phenomena. This transforms a
difference of degree into an absolute dichotomy. As we shall establish very shortly, the analysis of an item into its simple elements and
their relationships is a problematical undertaking. It has often happened that certain elements are regarded as the ultimate constituents
of the universe; their movements are conceived as the immediate,
unanalyzable expressions of the real, fundamental forces of nature.
Subsequently, it is established that these allegedly ultimate constituents are only the products of other forces, structures made up of
other elements that are simpler still. For all we know, someday
universal gravitation may be revealed as a function of different sorts

of conditions and forces. If this were the case, then the cause of universal gravitation would no longer lie in the validity of a special law. On the contrary, it would lie in the following matter of fact: contingent spatio- temporal conditions make it possible for several laws to function in such a way that the complex and quasi-historical phenomenon formulated by Newton's law is the result. Under these circumstances, Newton's law would have the status of an explanandum, not that of an explanans.

6. Personal Identity

Consider the main dichotomy the epistemological significance of which is at stake here. Essentially, it coincides with the distinction between the individual and the societal group. In general, historical laws are concerned with the destiny and the vicissitudes of totalities, the most simple element of which is the individual human being. Therefore let us suppose that nomological knowledge of an event is possible only if its complexity is analytically reduced to the laws which govern its most elementary parts. In that case, the problematical "laws" of individual psychology would be the real laws of history. This is because groups only exist in a secondary sense: their ontological status is of a second order. Groups are only composites of more simple elements; it is these elements alone that have a real, substantial existence. Therefore a genuine nomological status and real causal efficacy can only be ascribed to these elements. In other words, it can be said that molecules of paint, letters of the alphabet and drops of water "exist." But the painting, the book, and the river are only composites of these simple elements, forms that they assume, whether in dynamic relations of functional interdependence or in their concomitant occurrence in consciousness. The following, however, is a logical consequence of this reasoning: it is impossible for logical analysis to concede the status of direct reality to any palpable object.

Consider the so-called elements which I employed in the foregoing examples as illustrations of simple entities, the only items to which real existence can be attributed. Actually, they are composite entities of extreme complexity. In the final analysis, any inquiry into *their* elementary parts can only conclude with the identification of the absolutely elementary atomic parts of the universe. Ultimately, only these basic atoms have the status of reality. In comparison with these ultimate constituents, all observed, empirical elements only have the status of a secondary, purely historical reality. Since they are consequences of these most basic causes, a genuine nomological status cannot be ascribed to them. But this ultimate atom is only an imaginary construct, an heuristic conceptual device which serves as a point of reference for science. Since the process of scientific inquiry is endless, it has no finitely attainable state of completion. It follows that the objective, fundamental entity—the ultimate constituent— simply disappears from the conceptual scheme in which science represents reality. It is replaced by entities that—in the interests of certain theoretical aims—are posited in order to make sense of the phenomena under investigation. For the military strategist, a stand of trees constitutes an entity; together with other elements, it makes up the terrain that is important for his purposes. For the forester, the individual tree is the entity which is of interest to him in the total phenomenon; for the botanist, it is the cell of the individual tree; for the chemist, it is the chemical constituents of the cell.

Simplicity and complexity, therefore, are relative concepts. They do not correspond to the distinction between reality itself and the derivative conceptual constructs of reality. On the contrary, they are both *epistemological* categories in the same sense. The manner in which they apply to phenomena is a consequence of the problematic of the inquiry that is at stake. In a metaphysical sense, therefore, both concepts are subjective, and in an epistemological sense both are objective. Therefore the following thesis is certainly not prima facie self-evident. The composite phenomena of historical life are nomologically comprehensible only if they can be deduced from the established laws of individual psychology. Compare the historian to the forester. The latter knows quite well that in an objective sense the tree—the basic unity of the complex of phenomena he is concerned with—is certainly not an ultimate unity at all. Nevertheless, he pursues his investigation on this basis. He discovers more exact knowledge of the regularities which obtain for this complex and progressively approximates a knowledge of their "laws." For the same reason, the theoretical interests of history could permit the societal group to function as its basic "unit" of inquiry. Or this might be a logically necessary condition peculiar to history, an a priori of history. Suppose that there are no absolutely basic units or entities. Suppose that the definition of the unit of investigation is simply a consequence of the special criteria of each science. If this is the case, then there is no longer any reason in principle why it should be impossible to deduce historical laws from social complexes or other complexes of historical phenomena.

The chief issue, however, is the following. Given its own immanent criteria for knowledge, is it possible or necessary to conclude an historical investigation with knowledge of these complexes? Do the theoretical purposes of history really allow this? Or must the higher-order concepts that are employed in historical laws be reduced to purely individual processes? On the basis of a cursory view of the problem, it would obviously be quite impermissible to waive this reductive analysis. At least in one sense, the irreducible unity or entity that is never identifiable in the external world is accessible to history. It is the individual mind or personal psyche. From the perspective of the modern world view, of course, it does not occupy quite the same status it had from the perspective of a metaphysical belief in the mind or soul as a substance. The mind is a basic unit or entity for this reason: what we call unity or uniformity is possible only as a consequence of the inner, first-person experience of the self. Consider the fact that a certain circumscribed collection of ideas is related to an absolute center or focal point. Consider the fact that a great many statements may be inextricably related in a coherent fashion. Facts of this sort are only given in mental life. Consider observable spatial entities. As such, they are doomed to the status of inalterable functional relations of simultaneity. As components of a *proposition,* however, they acquire a uniformity and coherence for which there is no exact counterpart beyond consciousness. Only on this basis and only by analogy is it possible to apply the concept of unity to nonpersonal or impersonal existence. Therefore it cannot be said that we have an independently identifiable concept of unity which also applies to the individual person. On the contrary, unity is simply the name of the form of life or experience that is peculiar to the mind. It follows that the ascription of unity to the mind is obviously a logically necessary proposition.

The function of human consciousness is to create unity or uniformity in an objective manifold of elements. Therefore it is the only genuinely basic entity that is accessible to us. Consider the complex structures the destiny and forms of which are described by history. It follows that the personal psyche or self is the absolute or ultimate constituent of these complex structures. In this single case, therefore, it would be possible to specify the exact point that the reductive analysis of complexities must reach, the ultimate foundation from which these complexes must be constructed in order to satisfy our criteria for knowledge. Moreover this element is much more concrete or palpable than the putatively absolutely simple physical elements—elements the syntheses of which seem to make possible a complete knowledge of the physical world. Nor does this element, like the latter, lie in the infinite reaches of space and time. In every other inquiry, genuine doubt may remain as to whether the investigation has really identified the ultimate constituents of phenomena, the elements for which the laws of real forces are valid. In comparison with these elements, complex phenomena do not have an independent nomological status. On the contrary, they are only individual consequences and contingent products of these basic constituents. Within the inquiry of history alone, certainty concerning the ultimate constituents of phenomena seems to be possible. The individual mind or the personal self is the basic element of the historical event. It is the ultimate entity of historical analysis; further analysis of this entity into its more simple parts is impossible. It would follow that any composite event—for example, the Battle of Marathon—could be "understood" only if we knew the biography of every Greek and Persian up to the point at which his participation in the battle became psychologically comprehensible as a result of his own complete psychic development. The psychological laws, which constitute a condition for the possibility of this sort of "comprehensibility," would also be laws of history, in the same way that the physiological and chemical laws which make the tree comprehensible as a structure of cells are also laws of botany.

Let us suppose that this imaginary and fantastic condition were fulfilled. Even if this were the case, explanation of the historical event would still remain incomplete. In order to produce a complete explanation, it would be necessary to trace every single mental content back to its psychic and historical origins, origins which lie beyond the consciousness of the individual. Innumerable influences of physical, cultural, and personal milieu—which have countless origins and extend back into infinite reaches of time—must have been brought to bear upon each soldier at Marathon as causes of his participation in the battle. Consider the psychological laws that are responsible for the formation of given mental contents into the results that we call historical. These laws are not sufficient to make historical events comprehensible. On the contrary, for this purpose, cosmic laws are needed, laws that provide a genetic explanation of these individual mental contents and govern the sequences of development in which their appearance only amounts to a link or a stage.

Consider the following inference. The self is the basic, homogeneous entity; therefore the self is the real, definitive constitutive element of history; it follows that psychological laws must also be historical laws. This inference overlooks the following point. The unity which personal mental life creates in the contents of mind is only a formal or functional unity. The explanation of these mental contents would require laws of the total cosmic process, laws which transcend the unity of the psyche. The elements of mental life have different origins. If we inquire into their origin and development, we shall be obliged to identify the entity which is responsible for the fact that all these mental contents appear in a single mind. Suppose, therefore, that in order to discover the laws of history it is necessary to analyze the complex and composite phenomena of history into their basic elements. If this is the case, then the individual psyche—the unity of which seems to provide us with this basic element—does not qualify as the entity that makes the discovery of historical laws possible. It is not psychic unity or the mental entity as such that constitutes the historical event; on the contrary, it is the contents of mind. And there is no sense in which a sufficient explanation for the genesis and development of these contents lies in special laws that are peculiar to them.

7. *Historical Laws as Provisional Speculations*

Therefore suppose that the criterion for "law" employed within the natural sciences is also applied to the subject matter of history. We have reached the following conclusion. Even the reductive analysis of historical phenomena to the simple element of the individual person fails to satisfy this criterion. At this point, there are two paths which might be pursued in order to lend the problem of laws of history some positive significance. The first is a response to the foregoing argument, which claims that no absolute or definite epistemic value can be ascribed to any form of historical law. On the contrary, so this response goes, laws of history can at least have a relative or provisional value. Consider the laws that govern the motion of the fundamental particles of the universe. Only knowledge of these laws would reveal the real motive forces of historical events; in the long run, of course, knowledge of these laws is impossible. On the other hand, suppose that historical laws, putative or established, lie somewhere along the *path* to this impossible goal. In that case, any claim that these laws have exact validity would amount to self-deception, but it would not nullify the intrinsic value of the laws themselves. On the contrary, historical laws would be more or less comparable to philosophical preconceptions or speculations. Even when an inquiry is still quite remote from knowledge of the nature of things, philosophy can provide a provisional hypothesis or a general idea about their properties.

The development of scientific knowledge exhibits the following process. At the outset, general norms and extremely comprehensive principles are set up. A long process of specialized research is required in order for single components of events and processes to be identified as problems. Scientific inquiry begins with broad concepts and general reflections; it becomes more precisely defined to the extent that it becomes more limited. In the beginning, science attempts to comprehend the totality of being with a small number of highly abstract ideas. The analysis of complex concepts and phenomena only begins after innumerable attempts and failures in the domain of abstract thought. At this point, scientific inquiry begins to pursue the individual strands of thread that make up the entire fabric of being—a fabric which primitive science attempted to comprehend as a whole, without knowledge of its structure. Some relationship or other which is observed on the surface or within the superficial aspects of phenomena is raised to the status of a general law—at least this is the case until its cause is identified, and the contingency and coincidence of the relationship itself is established. At that point, this new cause is regarded as the authentically general law. Then it often enough happens that this new, putatively general law suffers the same fate.

On the whole, these stages are aspects of the transition from philosophical knowledge to exact knowledge, the turn from philosophy to science. Metaphysical reflection singles out a phenomenon which it sees as constantly repeated and which becomes the measure or principle of all things. Subsequently this principle is applied directly to the complex relations of the empirical world, the most complex phenomena imaginable. On the whole, metaphysics is content with the general impression that we have as a result of the concomitant action of real, underlying causes. This impression is ascribed to some single, basic, uniform cause. As a rule, metaphysics eschews the analysis of empirical phenomena into their component parts as a contemptible exercise. From this standpoint, therefore, philosophy is a provisional or proto-science; as an initial orientation to phenomena, its more general concepts and norms are useful, at least up to a point. This is the point at which the analysis of phenomena provides us with knowledge of their real elements and exact insight into the causal forces which obtain between them.

The metaphysician, of course, thinks that this provisional hypothesis concerning the surface appearance of things actually identifies their ultimate cause. He misconstrues the distance between his general idea and reality. The metaphysical idea really only identifies superficial aspects of reality; it is an initial, subjective impression. But the metaphysician rotates this subjective impression upon its axis. He mistakenly locates it *behind* reality as its ultimate or absolute ground. As a result, inquiry is petrified at its initial stage. This impedes and infinitely complicates progress to a more exact form of knowledge; that is, a form of knowledge which approximates more closely the real properties of things. Nevertheless, metaphysics represents an initial attempt to make sense of phenomena. It represents the first intellectual conquest of the empirical world. To regard metaphysics as worthless simply because it is a beginning and not an end is only a species of empiricist arrogance.

Let us even admit that philosophy has the following fate: the actual, historically given problems of philosophy will ultimately be resolved or dissolved by the exact sciences. Even under these circumstances, the legitimacy of philosophy remains incontestable until this process of resolution or dissolution is complete. The cosmos is a wild and disorderly process: its changes are implicated in thousands of vortices and axes of intersection. Therefore it should be no surprise that an initial attempt to make sense of the universe is very probably possible only in the following way. A fact which is repeatedly observed in either immediate or in interpreted reality is placed at the center of the cosmos—for example, the flux or the coherence of all things, the relationship between the mental and the physical, or the dependence of the cosmos upon an ultimately inexplicable power. Then the totality of empirical phenomena is explained by reference to this single fact. Perhaps this is only possible by ad hoc devices. Nevertheless, metaphysics makes it possible to draw a first primitive map of the cosmos. As a result, it is possible to find one's way through the confusion of empirical phenomena. Metaphysics has the following formal value: it attempts to produce a complete cosmology according to internally consistent principles. Its value is completely independent of the material or substantive errors of the content of such a theory. Therefore this value remains intact even if our criteria for knowledge are ultimately only satisfiable by inquiries or forms of thought that do not lie within the province of philosophy. Philosophy gives birth to the idea that the universe as a whole is a coherent entity and, as such, is comprehensible. Although we have no knowledge at all of most phenomena, the entire universal compass of phenomena is, nevertheless, commensurable with our concepts—in other words, the universe is completely intelligible. This is an idea that probably would never occur to anyone if it were necessary to wait for a theory that is flawless and substantively complete.

Philosophy, therefore, is a precursor of empirical knowledge, an intellectual apprehension of the world in the large. Given the structure of our mind, philosophy necessarily precedes and prepares the ground for knowledge of the real causal forces of the universe. Inquiry begins with unanalyzed phenomena that are related according to superficial and one-sided similarities. One of these resemblances is putatively identified as the substance and the law of the others. Then a gradual process of specialized research takes place which leads to knowledge of the elements of the cosmos and the primary forces which obtain between them. The uniform, law-like regularity of the universe lies exclusively in these elements and forces.

The evolutionary fate of our knowledge of the cosmos as a whole is reproduced in the various provinces of our knowledge of the cosmos. The properties of the metaphysics of the cosmos are duplicated in the metaphysics of its parts. I believe that the so-called laws of history function as precursors of exact knowledge of historical processes in the same way that metaphysical ideas are precursors of exact knowledge of the cosmos as a whole. Of course laws of history do not represent the climax or conclusion of an inquiry; on the contrary, they represent points of departure or transitional stages. Suppose that the laws which describe the real relations of the ultimate constituents of history—the laws which are responsible for the constitution of historical life—remain unknown. In that case, we must be satisfied with the discovery of certain regularities in the surface properties of historical life. Without attempting to determine what lies beneath these regularities, we describe phenomena in the form of abstract rules or generalizations. In a more profound sense, of course, these generalizations explain nothing. Nevertheless, they provide an initial perspective on the totality of historical life. Through a gradual process of more specialized research, and continued observation and analysis, it is possible to approximate the laws of motion of the basic constituents of history. Philosophical reflections generate provisional, tentative ideas concerning the nature and motion of the stuff of the cosmos, the sequential stages of organic forms and their evolution, the mathematical determination of all being, and much else besides. Then the exact sciences translate these general ideas from the form of speculation and abstraction—the form of observations made with the naked or untutored eye—into knowledge of the real forces which lie beneath the surface phenomena.

Laws of history have the same sort of value. Consider historical laws concerning the differentiation and integration of groups, the material or ideational causes of their changes, the cycles of forms of government, and the rise and decline of their superstructures, artifacts and modes of expression. These laws amount to provisional syntheses of typical historical phenomena; they provide an initial orientation to the mass of individual facts. The above point concerning the value of metaphysics also holds for the laws of history. Subsequent knowledge of the laws of the genuine causal forces of history will surely not contradict them completely. These laws have a permanent formal value insofar as they provide a general orientation and a survey, but they also anticipate the material truth, at least in a partial or fragmentary fashion. Here, therefore, is the explanation of the astonishment with which the present chapter began. How can the problem of the discovery of laws of history lie within the province of philosophy? Laws of history—insofar as they are possible at present—are related to the genuine laws of history, laws that are comparable to laws of nature, in the same way that philosophical knowledge is related to exact scientific knowledge. The speculative form of knowledge or inquiry is a preliminary phase, an intermediate stage between the observation of single, complex facts and the derivation of these facts from the laws that govern their basic elements.

From this point of view, the contradictions between the propositions that now pass for laws of history are not so intolerable. For the same reason, metaphysical principles certainly do not become useless or valueless simply because they are mutually inconsistent. The range of empirical phenomena that provides the raw material for philosophical reflection makes it possible to entertain and confirm the most diverse contradictions imaginable. The flux of all things in the face of their apparent permanence as well as the permanence of all things in the face of their apparent flux, the purposive order of the cosmos as well as its meaningless fortuitousness, the influence of subjectivity as well as the inflexible necessitation of nature: given a sufficiently rich field of observation, each of these theses can be established with the same degree of certitude. And—as a result of our instinctual predisposition for simplicity—each can become the focal point of a cosmology that excludes the others. The fragmentary and partial character of our conceptual schemes has the following consequence. When a given conceptual scheme is applied to the universe as a whole, it must be supplemented by one or more other conceptual schemes. Therefore each conceptual scheme has a relative justification which metaphysics makes absolute.

However this function of metaphysics is not useless to the same degree that it is erroneous. As a rule, the limits of the empirical validity of a principle are established only by the attempt to apply it to all possible cases. The illusion that it is a constitutive law, therefore, has the following empirical value: by employing the principle in an experimental or regulative fashion as an heuristic maxim, the limits within which it obtains are definitely established. For example, suppose that on the basis of a series of observations we believe that we have discovered a certain law of moral progress in history. In that case, it would be quite legitimate to investigate each period of history on the basis of this putative law in order to determine whether the analysis and synthesis of phenomena will confirm it. This procedure is justifiable even if an initial examination of the facts appears to refute the law conclusively. The thesis that moral progress does not take place—that scientific investigation of apparent moral progress will establish a complete invariance in the level of moral values—has exactly the same status. Since each of the two mutually inconsistent principles is employed as if it were absolutely correct, each approaches the limits within which it obtains, limits that are defined by the contrary principle. In consequence, the relative degree of the validity of each principle is established.

These principles are obviously not laws—there are no limits to the validity of a law. However they are proto-forms or preliminary forms of laws. As a result of the reciprocal definition or limitation of the two mutually contradictory maxims, a higher maxim is established. This latter maxim makes it possible to identify the conditions under which these subordinate principles obtain. For example, the principle of the conservation of energy might qualify as one of these higher principles. It functions in such a way that the facts sometimes exhibit a process of moral progress and on other occasions a process of moral stagnation. Then another higher principle is set up in opposition to this one, followed by the search for an even more general law from which both higher principles can be deduced as mere phenomena of changing conditions. In consequence, we approximate more and more closely the ultimately abstract laws which determine the motions of the simplest components of history, laws that constitute the exclusive cause and explanation of the movement of history. Polar oppositions like the "law" of individualism and the "law" of socialism, the efficacy of blind volition and the force of the logical idea, the law of the permanence of things and the law of their constant flux in general function in a complementary fashion. This maximizes free play in the explanation or construction of the single case. Considered solely in terms of its intrinsic content, the law itself provides no clue at all for the construction of the polar counter-principle which defines its limits; a higher principle or a more abstract criterion is required for this purpose. But where could the ultimate source of this criterion lie, if not in the forces and relations of the constituent elements of history? They establish the relative validity of the polar subordinate principles. If these limits of validity are exceeded, these principles become mere reifications of reality.

Laws of history are special cases of laws. They represent the fortunes of an entire province of history as consequences of one unified entity. Laws of history distinguish a given province of history both from its constituent elements and also from the total cosmic process in which it is implicated. Consider any case in which a special force or cause is imputed to a complex phenomenon, a force which is peculiar to the complex itself and can be distinguished from the product of the forces of all its elements. Or—which is only another way of saying the same thing—consider any case in which the properties of the motions of this complex are subordinated to a special, uniform force. We can be sure that any case of this sort is situated at a preliminary or precursory stage of knowledge. Here too, the most abstract norm of psychological and social evolution holds true. A process can be identified which begins with an inclusive and strictly defined construct, a construct that defines its components too narrowly and which is essentially an oversimplification. Following this, the process moves in two directions: on the one hand, toward the dissolution of the narrowly circumscribed complex and its differential analysis into a structure that incorporates as many elements as possible, and on the other, in the direction of the increasing individuation, differentiation, and autonomy of its individual components. The tendency in the direction of maximum universality and the tendency toward maximum individuation coincide. They are both part of the same process which progresses beyond the sort of complex that embraces a number of components—without regard to their individual properties—and claims for itself the definitive status of a totality.[10] The cognitive process which is at issue here exhibits the same form of development. This tiny segment of the cosmos, human history, includes a large number of individual elements. They are comprehended under a uniform concept which represents itself as a special or definitive law.

Knowledge progresses in the following way. The exclusiveness and the apparent completeness of this complex are destroyed: the complex is identified as just one more link in the chain of processes that make up the cosmos. It is to be understood by reference to the general laws of the universe, not according to special laws that are only valid for the complex itself. On the other hand, the analysis of every element of the complex is pursued for its own sake; the forces intrinsic to each element are described. In consequence, the complex is understood as a product of its parts, each of which is independently understood. Obviously it is one and the same process which moves in both of these directions. The laws of the elementary components—the laws which formulate the real, primary forces of the universe—are none other than the laws that govern the total cosmos. These are the only laws that have the certainty of genuinely universal validity—the sort of validity which, as we established in the foregoing, cannot be ascribed to the forms of motion of the complexes. Both tendencies—toward the ultimately abstract and toward the maximally simple—transcend the precursory or preliminary phase of knowledge under discussion here: the stage at which a complex in which a number of elements are comprehended under the same general heading is regarded as a totality with its own special laws.

8. History as a Segment of the Cosmic Process: The Elimination of the Concept of History

We should not overlook the following point. If historical laws are reduced to cosmic laws, then the definitive concept of history becomes completely vacuous. As a matter of fact, this movement toward the dissolution of the concept of history requires a special analysis; it is a tendency that places the entire possibility of laws of history in doubt. All of human history is nothing more than a piece or part of the total cosmos. Therefore the development of each phase of history is dependent upon innumerable conditions. The causes or motive forces of these conditions do not lie within the historical phase itself. They are not limited or defined by the concept of history, nor can they be deduced from this concept. The course of human history is not like a self-contained chapter of a book in which only the beginning and the end are implicated within the general forces of the cosmos that influence them; on the contrary, between the course of history and these cosmic forces there is a perpetual relationship of exosmosis and endosmosis. As a result, history acquires properties which have causes that lie beyond history itself. It follows that these causes cannot be deduced from the most exact knowledge of the course of history.

We certainly do not suppose that the future conduct of a man could be deduced from his past. The reason is as follows. In addition to the motive forces which are stored or accumulated in his past up to the present moment, countless other forces also influence his conduct, and these latter forces modify the direction and intensity of the former. Nor do we suppose that the mental life of an individual is a self-contained causal system; this is because an influx of sensations interrupts the continuity of mental processes. Novel elements, which cannot be deduced from any past state of the mind, also make their appearance in mental life. For the same reasons, we should not suppose that the life of humanity is a self-contained process which develops in such a way that the earlier stages contain all the potential causes of the later; in that case, history would exhibit a purely immanent and self-sufficient causality. However influences that do not have historical causes interrupt the immanent development of history. As a result, historical conditions which seem to be equivalent—and which seem to make knowledge of the future possible—produce unexpectedly different consequences. Each given state of human history would contain within itself the complete conditions for the occurrence of all subsequent states only if human history really were the history of the world. It would be unnecessary to expect extraneous and divergent influences upon each state of human history only if this condition were satisfied.

It is easy to see that this point also holds for the individual provinces of history, even though the point itself is not always appreciated. Consider, for example, a history of art which has the purpose of producing a complete and fundamental understanding of its subject matter. This sort of history could not qualify as an immanent history: in other words, it could not understand one artistic artifact by reference to another or deduce one artistic artifact from another in a nomological fashion. This is because societal relationships, religion, the level of intellectual culture, and individual fate are all codeterminants of future aesthetic phenomena. However these factors cannot be deduced from the aesthetic phenomena of the past. Although it has been supposed that the historical phenomena of economics can, at least in principle, be completely comprehended in terms of natural laws of economics, the same point holds for the economy. The phenomena of economic history may seem to be purely economic, but the energies and motives which produce one economic phenomenon as the consequence of another are certainly not exclusively economic—just to the contrary. Suppose that a given phenomenon of production, ownership, exchange, wages, or speculation "evolves" or "produces" another form of production, ownership, etc. Neither the existence of this new phenomenon nor its quantitative or qualitative properties are exclusively determined by the purely economic forces which the initial given phenomenon sets in motion. Consider relationships in an economy at a very advanced level of development, especially purely monetary transactions. In these relationships, there are some respects in which economic interests lead what might be called an abstract and self-contained existence, but this sort of case is an exception. The purely economic import of a given phenomenon is invariably only *one* of the factors which are causally responsible for the *economic* content of future phenomena. These factors include every imaginable personal, ethical, physical, and cultural determinant.[11]

These remarks on the manner in which individual histories are structured hold without reservation for history as a whole. Genuine laws of history would be possible only under the following conditions. The supervening cosmic (not "historical") factors which have heretofore influenced the development of historical states must remain constant. In this case, they would affect both sides of the equation—the historical law—in the same way. Therefore it would not be necessary to take them into account in order to compute the values of one side of the equation from the values of the other side. In other words, laws of history would be possible only if their contents were total states of the cosmos, and not extremely variable parts or aspects of it. The fate of the cosmos is unconditionally and exhaustively determined by its past. There can be no extrinsic force which brings into play energies or causes that are not grounded in the cosmos itself. For the same reason—given the universal reciprocal causality of all the elements of the cosmos—no single sequence of events can contain intrinsic, sufficient conditions for its own future development. On the contrary, extrinsic forces will always be germane to the future of any such sequence, forces which—seen from within the sequence itself—appear as *dei ex machina*. This point applies in the same way to the career of an individual human being—the individual phases of which we interrelate to form a uniform process—the fate of a given nation, and the destiny of mankind in general.

Therefore suppose that nomological regularity is ascribed to the sort of event that we call "historical." Suppose that the historical event satisfies the conditions for being a necessary consequence of some law. The ultimate result of this supposition is the elimination of a definitive concept of history. We may distinguish a certain class of phenomena and classify them together under a concept that promises to have value for the praxis of knowledge. But this is only a classification of immediate *phenomena;* it does not reveal the more profound elements and forces that underlie them. Suppose that a phenomenon is reduced to its elements, from which its observable or complex properties are deduced. Then the special status of this phenomenon, heretofore justified, collapses. It becomes inextricably implicated in the interplay of cosmic energies. It follows that the class of phenomena defined as "history" cannot supply the causes or laws sufficient to account for its own individual elements. In view of this, consider a thesis which the foregoing reflections granted as possible: that laws of history may qualify as *approximations* of knowledge of real causal connections. At this point, we can see that there is an immanent limit to this process of approximation. The progressive analysis and confirmation of historical *laws* nullifies and transcends their status as laws of *history*. At least it becomes impossible to deduce the historical event from laws that are exclusively historical. Nevertheless, the internal inconsistency implied in the concept of a law of history is only relative. This might be expressed in the following way. The intrinsic import of the concept of the historical is not quantitatively rich enough to fulfill the conditions that the concept of a law requires. However this relative inconsistency is sharpened into an absolute contradiction when we examine the consequences of these two concepts—the concept of the historical and the concept of a law—more closely and from the standpoint of the distinction they are employed to draw within the division of scientific labor.

9. The Definitive Sense in Which History is a Science of Reality

At this point, it is most essential to provide the clearest possible answer to the following question. What are the limits of the determination of existence by laws of nature? Where does the contribution which laws of nature make to knowledge of existence end? In the first place, the very fact that there are laws of nature sets this limit. No law entails that there must be laws, or that these particular laws must obtain: the necessity of a given law could only be proven on the basis of another law. Therefore it would be necessary to presuppose the entity the existence of which is at stake: the law of nature. We can establish proofs on the basis of natural laws only if there are laws of nature. However the fact that there are laws of nature cannot be deduced from any other law of nature. In this respect, laws of nature are comparable to the code of civil law. Legality cannot be ascribed to the latter; on the contrary, it is conduct—which is consistent with the code of civil law and which presupposes its existence—to which legality can be ascribed. The existence of laws of nature, therefore is a brute fact. It cannot be understood by reference to laws of nature. Or, as this might be put: the existence of laws of nature is an historical fact. The same holds for the existence of that substance the formal variations of which are determined by natural laws. *If* a universe exists, then—in virtue of certain logical and empirical laws—certain events must take place within it. However the same necessity does not underlie the fact *that* a universe exists: it is possible to conceive of the nonexistence of all being without contradicting the necessity of any law.

Even these two brute facts, however, do not constitute sufficient presuppositions for the possibility of the universe. A law of nature only states that a given form of matter is transformed into another, so a law of nature invariably presupposes a certain form or structure of matter. In relation to a totally undifferentiated substance or to pure being as such, a law of nature has no possible point of reference. The following, therefore, is a condition for the efficacy of laws of nature in general. Matter must be differentiated. There must be an original, given, primitive form of matter which is not a result of the functioning of any natural law. The reconstruction of the evolution of the cosmos by the use of laws of nature is always terminated by the discovery of a—provisionally—primitive or original state of matter. It is no more possible to deduce this primitive state of matter from a natural law than it is possible to deduce the existence of matter itself or the existence of the natural law. Of course the progress of knowledge can never reach the point at which absolute knowledge of this primitive state of matter is possible. The advance of knowledge can only push this state further and further beyond the horizon of knowledge. This original state of matter is responsible for the fact that a certain law of nature and no other obtains at a given point. Consider the fact that a certain primordial manifold of form exists, a manifold that is comprehended and analyzed by laws of nature, laws which make possible knowledge of the complications and the modifications of the phenomena that constitute this manifold. From the standpoint of the laws of nature, this is simply a random or fortuitous fact—it is a purely historical fact. In this sense, chance or accident cannot be eliminated from our cosmology. This is because the genesis of the cosmos itself is fortuitous and inexplicable. Every subsequent event is only a development of this initial state, a development which is no longer arbitrary or accidental only if the existence of *precisely this initial state is presupposed.*

It follows that laws of nature—including psychological laws—are not sufficiently powerful for the reconstruction of real existence. On the contrary, for this purpose certain given facts are required, and not only facts which pertain to the origin or genesis of all things. The latter would be sufficient only if our knowledge of the facts and our knowledge of the laws were complete. Given an exhaustive system of natural laws, a single fact would be sufficient to produce or deduce the entire universe. This system of laws has a purely ideal character. From this system, as the exclusive point of departure of an investigation, there is no bridge that leads to tangible reality. On the contrary, tangible reality is constituted by a special moment that is independent of this system of laws. Beyond tangible reality, the concept of a law of nature has created an entire universe, the significance of which has been described quite aptly. It is the domain of "validity"—which, of course, does not exhaust the function of the concept of a natural law in our cosmology. A law is "valid"—it holds or functions—regardless of whether the case it describes occurs one time or a million times.

Consider the invariability or universality of a law which has the form "*if A* is the case, then *B* is the case." It has a price. It is quite impossible for a law to establish *whether A* is the case. Criminal law, for example, determines that a certain crime requires a certain punishment. The *validity* of this determination is totally independent of the frequency or infrequency with which it comes into force. We are in the habit of classifying all the contents and the possibilities of our conceptual world in terms of the following dichotomy. Either they *exist,* as objective reality, in either an empirical or a transcendent sense, or they are a product of consciousness and have a psychological existence that is inferential, puzzling, and imaginary. The laws of things, however, constitute a third domain that lies beyond these two. *That* laws obtain or are valid is, of course, a mere fact, an existential proposition, but no existential question is relevant to the question of the content of a law—that is, what it means or signifies. It is true that the content of the law holds for the domain of existence, but existence is not exhausted by laws. Nor is a law to be conceived as a mere object of thought, a product of the psychological subject; on the contrary, it must be rigorously distinguished from every such product. Obviously a law may be conceived by a single person, quite in the same way that it can be realized by a unique combination of existential elements. But neither this psychological form nor this concrete physical form exhausts the meaning of the law. The question of the validity of a law is independent of the question of whether anyone has thought of it; it is also independent of the question of whether our conception of the law is correct or mistaken. From the standpoint of the special category in which it exists as a law, the content of a law may be represented equally well in the form of consciousness and in the form of real existence. But it cannot be exhaustively analyzed into either of these forms, nor into a compound of the two or an intermediate state between the two.

The category of a law is much more closely related to the concepts of thought and being; like these two concepts, it is indefinable. It can only be grasped directly, even if this is not possible with the same routine psychological facility that makes the other two concepts more easily accessible. If the epistemological status of the laws of nature is clear, then it is perfectly obvious that they cannot be constructed exclusively on the basis of history conceived as a history of facts. Nevertheless, laws of nature are *valid* for the facts. Therefore, granting any given factual point of reference, laws of nature make possible the deduction or the comprehension of a subsequent set of facts or the factual content of another spatio-temporal frame to the extent that the laws which obtain for this given factual point of reference have been established.

Suppose that this sort of deduction is not possible. Then knowledge of the facts as such must serve in place of knowledge of laws of nature. In general, what we call an understanding of the facts is a kind of intermediate phenomenon. Our nomological knowledge is not sufficient to construct a coherent framework of facts on the basis of knowledge of a single fact. If, on the other hand, knowledge of facts is historically given, this puts us on the right path to the discovery of laws. By using the map or guide provided by our knowledge of established facts, it is easier for us to discover the laws according to which they function. In consequence, we can at least understand retrospectively why "things must have happened in this way." Without the guide provided by our knowledge of the facts, our nomological knowledge alone would not be sufficient for this discovery. Therefore suppose that the putative laws of history were known. The identification of events that qualify—in the broadest sense—as history would still be essential to historical inquiry; knowledge of historical facts would also be indispensable for the application of laws of history. Suppose that one is inclined to classify these two elements of our conceptual scheme of the universe in the following way. The honorific term "science" is reserved for established laws. It is withheld from the confirmation of facts, without which a conceptual construct of reality would be impossible. This is simply a case of petty jealousy over the use of words. If we have a clear view of the limits of the functioning of laws in relation to reality, then we find that existence poses two different sorts of problems. Our real task is not to christen them, but rather to solve them.

From the standpoint of logic, principle, or methodology, this distinction between laws of nature and matters of fact is absolute. From the standpoint of the praxis of our incomplete knowledge, however, it is quite flexible. The existence of Frederick the Great is not as *calculable* as the existence of Neptune. It is obvious that this is only a consequence of quantitative differences between our psychological-political knowledge and our astronomical knowledge. I have already noted the following point. Suppose that the number of established laws is relatively small. In that case, knowledge of reality is possible only if deductive-nomological explanation is complemented by the confirmation of a relatively large number of facts. Historical reality is the concept which defines the limits of nomological regularity. The reason is as follows. Given an exhaustive system of natural laws, a single historical fact would suffice to produce a complete system of knowledge. In this extreme case, the logical dichotomy of empirical-historical knowledge and nomological knowledge would reach the minimal limit of its extension or application. But this would not deprive the dichotomy of its profound significance. In the absence of a complete system of natural laws, this dichotomy also includes the distinction between historical knowledge—knowledge of actual empirical events—and the knowledge of laws. Laws, of course, are timelessly valid. Therefore they are valid for every event. But because of their abstraction or their distance from reality, they can never take the place which the event occupies in our conceptual scheme. There are innumerable points in our conceptual scheme at which phenomena must be regarded as irreducible, brute facts. Even if our knowledge of the cosmos were complete, the specific content of its spatio-temporal framework would still remain an incommensurable, irreducible fact. Such a fact could not be exhaustively deduced from natural laws; it is deducible only given the presupposition of a prior, equally irreducible and irrational fact.

In the foregoing, we made an absolute distinction between laws—as formulae which describe pure states of energy—and history. History is concerned with complex, existential phenomena. Laws are concerned with the basic elements of these phenomena. Empirical research takes a continuous path from one of these two extremes—which are by definition irreconcilable—to the other. At every stage of empirical research, both concepts are applicable. The relationship between these two concepts is similar in the more radical distinction between historical and nomological knowledge now under discussion. Obviously the temporal reality of history falls under a category that is completely different from the timeless validity of laws. But history never establishes the existence of being as such; it can only confirm a given existential content. Therefore history is on firm grounds in relation to the concrete facts of temporal reality only if this given existential content is a possible object of a law. In this case, we can see the possibility of a curve which increasingly approximates the unattainable ideal of necessity. Reality cannot be ascribed to any putative historical content that falls under no law of observable and unobservable nature. [12] Suppose we summarize Kant's theory in the following paradoxical formula: experience is more than experience. That is to say, in addition to elements of sense perception which give experience its definitive character, it also includes a priori forms. Although experience is dependent upon these a priori forms, they are independent of experience. In the same way, one might say that history is more than history. From the standpoint of its definitive content, of course, history is, by definition, irreducible or incommensurable. It cannot be subsumed under any law. Therefore it will always lie beyond or beneath the ideal domain of laws. But consider the following question. What existential import can be identified within the spatio–temporal framework of history? Given the logical properties of our knowledge, the answer to this question can only be supplied by the laws of nature, laws that are totally indifferent to being itself.

Laws of nature are only valid for simple or constitutive elements. For this reason, therefore, laws of history have an approximate or relative significance. As indicated above, however, a second possible value may also be ascribed to historical laws.

Recall that it is impossible to establish whether any given law really is absolutely valid. It is impossible to establish whether it really has the sort of validity that distinguishes it, as a law, from a mere sequence of matters of fact. Although they are absolutely distinct from the standpoint of methodology, the continuity which exists in practice between laws of history and laws of nature seems to be based on this consideration. However this continuity only moves in *one* direction. Perhaps every proposition that is recognized as a law today is actually only a contingent combination of the genuine nomological regularities that remain undiscovered, regularities that are more profound and fundamental. It is certain, however, that there are many phenomena for which the opposite possibility could not hold. Historical phenomena are *invariably* products of a very large number of concomitant conditions. It follows that there are *no conditions* under which they can be deduced from any single law of nature. Naturally we must consider the simplest form of motion that contemporary science has managed to identify as the real, fundamental type of all motion. The law of this sort of motion must be regarded as the basic causal force. However we must also keep the following possibility in mind. This putatively fundamental motion may someday be revealed as a mere phenomenon, the expression of more basic forces. In that case, these more basic forces would provide the sufficient explanation for all other phenomena. The distance between these laws, the existence of which we entertain as a mere possibility, and laws of history is almost immeasurable.

Suppose we conceded that, in principle, the real effect of a law and its actual force are concealed from us. In that case, we would be dependent upon mere observational consequences. Even under these circumstances, however, the empirical difference between a causal connection and a purely temporal relationship remains. This distinction may be a flexible one. But the class of genuine causes cannot include the most complex of all observed events: these are, of course, the phenomena of human history.

So it appears that laws of history have been condemned in a court of last resort. On the other hand, suppose that we follow some reflections introduced above; then it is possible to acquire a completely different view of laws of history. From the standpoint of these reflections, the historical event is not a composite of more simple, elementary processes, the only processes that are genuinely real. On the contrary, the definitive and autonomous theoretical interests of history concede or require that the original syntheses, collective concepts, and structures in which reality is constituted as history have the status of *entities* or *unities* that require no further analysis. From the perspective of natural science, of course, these constructs do not have this status at all. But they are formed exclusively for the purposes of historical investigation, so the problematic of the natural sciences has no bearing upon their status. Consider what might be called the a priori categories of history, the formative laws that constitute the pretheoretical raw material of reality as a possible object of knowledge. These categories are not concerned with knowledge of the elements which qualify as ultimate from the standpoint of every problematic; the theoretical ideal that leads to this sort of knowledge is differently constituted from the outset. But it does not follow that this ideal is more definitive or legitimate. From this standpoint, it would be possible to follow the problematic of historical inquiry to its ultimate conclusion without ever reaching the elements that are—in the sense of the natural sciences—ultimate. This is because these elements lie at a completely different conceptual level.

10. Empirical Pluralities as Historiographical Entities

In the foregoing, I used an illustration of what would apparently constitute a conclusive or complete "understanding" of an event, a state that is possible only as an ideal. Given this ideal, the Battle of

Marathon would be understood when the psychological and physiological facts concerning the biography of each individual soldier were exhaustively identified and understood. Independent of the foregoing criticism of this ideal, which was ultimately based on the same assumptions as the ideal itself, we can argue that this criterion does not even have the unconditional validity of an ideal. Suppose that this exhaustive factual knowledge concerning the soldiers at Marathon were available. Even under this condition, the questions peculiar to the historical interest would not yet be answered. History is not interested—or at least is not exclusively interested—in the behavior of this or that individual Greek; it is interested in how "the Greeks" conducted themselves. There is no sense in which this new subject is a composite of all the individual Greeks. The characteristics which he has in common with the other Greeks and which make up the total construct of Greek conduct or the Greek character are included in the personality of the individual Greek. These characteristics are also interrelated with other purely personal and idiosyncratic characteristics. The mutual implication of both sorts of characteristics form the total personality of the individual. The relationship between the two is so intimate and so complete that it appears to be impossible to differentiate them in any given case; therefore a synthesis is needed which transcends the atomistic tendency from the very outset and makes possible the constitution of the object that is at stake here. The same sort of conduct in battle can be the result of quite different mental antecedents. These differences are irrelevant to the problematic of history, which is concerned with the cross-section that reveals the aspect of identity within these heterogeneous processes. From the standpoint of the individual, however, the *logical* or genetic significance of this cross-section is no different from the characteristics that differentiate him from everyone else. History, therefore, produces a synthesis of the material which the individualistic problematic of the natural sciences is obliged to reduce to the laws of motion of its most elementary parts. From the standpoint of the categories of the historical problematic, these syntheses function as unified entities. Their formal structural relations may also be called laws; not, of course, laws which satisfy the nomological criteria of the natural sciences, but rather another sort of law. We have not yet given an account of the import of this sort of law.

Consider now a second kind of example of a law of history: the "historical law" of differentiation, which is represented as the definitive determining norm of universal history. In primitive societies, all the activities that must be performed in order to insure the preservation of life are performed by each individual. Progress consists in the fact that a gradual and progressive division of labor takes place: each individual, instead of performing a multiplicity of these activities, only performs a single function that becomes increasingly specialized. Consider the refinement of emotional life; the divergence of interests—interests which, as a result of this very process of divergence, subsequently become organically integrated; the relaxation of violent or compulsory forms of socialization; and the establishment of voluntary associations that have an increasingly objective purposiveness or functionality. All these changes can be subsumed under the concept of differentiation. What produces these individual changes are, of course, special, individual forces. They may be occasioned by necessity or arbitrary constellations, by jealousy or genius. The results of these forces are only summarized retrospectively under the concept of differentiation, which is the product of the functioning of each force. We should not reify it as a collective force or a uniform source of energy that transcends all these single forces, a uniform force which, as a result of chance, is fragmented and dispersed in different real phenomena.

11. The Concept of Truth in History

These real fundamental processes and their individual causes are certainly not the exclusive concern of history. Even when facts of this sort are subsumed under the concept of differentiation, the following questions remain. What are the various stages and forms in which these facts develop? What are the regularities in their appearance? How are they related? What are the elementary processes that are subsumed under concepts that are situated at the same logical level—for example, concepts like freedom, the tempo of development, collective consciousness, the form and content of social change, the solidification of social change into the objective structures of law, morals, and technology. Many other questions also remain unanswered. Naturally what is at stake here is not logical and conceptual relationships and changes, but rather concrete historical events and their regularities, identifiable insofar as they constitute a total phenomenon that can be conceptually represented. What is at issue here is a peculiar class of concepts representing a peculiar kind of analysis and transformation of the basic facts.

We describe historical events or states that are produced by individual causes as differentiation and integration, an increase or decrease in the level of social energies, a hierarchical structure, a social infection, an acceleration or petrification of the life processes of the group. These are not purely general concepts which identify what is common to all the primary data, nor are they mere symbols, a reference system for the primary data which has no substantive relationship to the data itself. On the contrary, there is a certain sense in which they share the properties of both kinds of concept. They classify or comprehend individual historical factors by reference to their effect as a total phenomenon. But the concepts that are employed for this purpose have their own idiosyncratic logical status. They may be nourished from the springs of immediate reality. Like an organism, however, they have transformed this raw material into a new entity. Therefore the exclusive function of these historical concepts and their applications is not the resolution of the problem of the unknowable quantitative and qualitative properties of historical phenomena as a whole. Ultimately, this task only has a negative character. The real problem—of interpreting the function of these concepts within historical science—is a consequence of the fact that they constitute a positive and novel conceptual world.

On this level, the examples of "historical laws" that I criticized above acquire a new significance completely different from the function of describing the causal forces of immediate events. Suppose it is alleged that the following proposition is a "law" of historical development. Every relatively large group passes through the stages of youth, manhood, and senility. In this case, we can certainly reject the claim that this law identifies the causal forces which explain the single facts that are classified in this sequence. Nevertheless, we still have the feeling that some sort of truth content can be ascribed to propositions of this type, assuming that there is no controversy concerning the verification of the individual facts to which they refer. There are innumerable instances in which concepts of this sort are employed to produce a construct of historical development. This is the expression of an epistemological criterion that no longer coincides with knowledge of direct, elementary causality. After concrete, individual events are transformed by these more abstract historical concepts, the *connections* or *relationships* which constitute them as objects of knowledge also change.

Consider the fact that we describe the total character of the constitution of a political group and maintain that the same character is reproduced in the structure of the nuclear family. We note correlations between political decline, on the one hand, and artistic and scientific progress, on the other. We note that an accelerated rate of change in perceptions, fashions, cultural interests, and political tendencies seems to be regularly associated with the economic ascendancy of the middle class. There is no sense in which these correlations identify the network of infinitely complex causal relationships that are responsible for the occurrence of these individual sequences of events. However it can be said that the causal relationships in question are represented in these correlations. Consider the concepts that represent the apparent consequences of these single events. They produce a fabric that has its only legitimate place at this level of abstraction. In general, the relationship between this conceptual fabric and the empirical facts is like the relationship between the great philosophical concepts—being and becoming, mind and metaphysical will, mechanism and vitalism—and reality. These concepts combine and synthesize material from very different sources; as a result, they constitute reality as if "from a distance." In both history and philosophy, this new distance or perspective from which reality is viewed is a product of special epistemological conditions which are not satisfied by the investigation of discrete sequences of reality and their causes. Together with these differences in distance or perspective, this conceptual scheme also entails a difference in style. If this conceptual scheme represents a style, then its criteria for "truth" are immanent; they cannot be derived from completely different requirements that have their source in knowledge of single, direct, empirical relationships.

We must be very careful to avoid confusion here, especially where different forms of knowledge are closely related. This latter form of knowledge—knowledge of single, direct, empirical relationships—invariably remains the raw material of history. The substantive conditions of this sort of knowledge must be satisfied in order to establish the peculiar "truth" of the more abstract historical concepts. This sort of "truth" is, of course, a consequence of completely different epistemological criteria. The relationship between these historical concepts and their raw material occupies what might be called an intermediate level. It lies somewhere between the relationship of causality to temporally given effects of perceptions, on the one hand, and the relationship of the work of art to its observational material, on the other. The logical problem at stake here is to provide a perspicuous view of the constitutive power of knowledge, whose force is easily concealed within the discipline of history. This is because the subject matter of history is "mind." Therefore it is already formed or constituted in some way prior to its historical investigation. The constitutive power of knowledge appears in many different correlated conceptual structures or superstructures. Consistent with the different criteria of knowledge, it remains in force and continues to function, regardless of whether its material has the status of an analyzed or an unanalyzed object from the standpoint of other problematics.

This problem is, of course, a source of mistaken judgments and misplaced requirements which arise in the following way. Abstractions and syntheses which are the products of a given perspective of the basic raw material of reality are set up as norms for other abstractions and syntheses. But the latter have a legitimate relationship to reality that is based on a different perspective. The confusion produced here is comparable to the result of combining different styles in the same work of art. Each style determines the distance or perspective from which the object of immediate perception is viewed. This distance or perspective, which may be as great as you like, is part of what is included in the formation of the work of art. The work of art may only represent the most general elements of reality in imaginary forms. Nevertheless, these forms have their own "truth" insofar as they maintain a constant relationship—even though it may be pale and indistinct and only determined by the sense of this particular style—to the immediacy of existence. Suppose that the different perspectives, which correspond to different forms of works of art, are confused or conflated. In other words, consider a case of what is known as an impure style: a feeling of the falsity of the work of art is the immediate result of this confusion. This is because each standard of distance or perspective represented in this work of art inevitably imposes its own criteria of form upon the whole, criteria which cannot be satisfied by a single work of art. For the same reason, more abstract historical concepts which synthesize singular phenomena into a total impression may become invalid if they are evaluated according to the standards of other synthetic forms—forms that are only valid for singular phenomena and ultimately terminate in the laws of motion of their most elementary parts. To evaluate historical concepts in this way is to impose a false ideal upon them. These concepts can only represent the relations of things as they are reflected in the higher strata of the abstract life of the mind. In order to satisfy the criteria peculiar to this conceptual level, they *cannot* have the precision of direct knowledge of singular facts.

Finally, a third example may serve to characterize another kind of "nomological regularity." It expresses the relationship between elementary processes that have been analytically refined into abstract entities. Since the formal criteria at stake here are also germane to the most exact knowledge of these elementary processes, this example may not be altogether superfluous. Suppose the following is described as a "social law." Among ten thousand cases of death per year, there is a certain number of suicides. This description seems to be quite misleading; each act of suicide is only the result of the social and psychological forces—laws, for example—that govern it. The fact that there are a given number of suicides during a certain year is a result of the application of these laws to a given set of cases, but this fact is not itself a law. Suppose that this yearly ratio between the total number of deaths and the number of suicides is continuously repeated for a considerable period of time. This only shows that the conditions under which these laws function are still satisfied. In other words, this proposition states a matter of fact; it does not identify the cause of this fact. The individual suicide is obviously not concerned with the question of whether a certain number of other people also commit suicide. And it is evident that the following is not one of those natural laws the real consequences of which are ultimately responsible for his act: that in ten thousand cases of death per year, there is a certain number of cases of suicide. The addition of cases is a synthesis undertaken by the observer. The fact that this synthesis produces this particular result is, of course, objectively grounded, but that is only because each of its factors is. Suppose that, conversely, we undertook to deduce the necessary determination of these factors from the necessary determination of the result. This is a fallacious form of circular reasoning. In addition, it represents a species of mystifying teleology.

What is responsible for the fact that this statistical correlation seems to be purely superficial and—as we might put it—without force? It is only the requirement imposed upon it: the statistical correlation should identify the direct causes of social elements. Actually, however, this statistical correlation poses another problem. Suppose that we had a complete and perspicuous knowledge of the elements and causes which determine the individual destinies that constitute this statistical correlation. Even under these conditions, this problem would neither be resolved nor dissolved. By the use of historical and social categories, we construct a societal totality from individual factors and sequences. From the standpoint of the theoretical interests that are at stake here, the components of this societal whole are not real, fundamental, singular processes; on the contrary, they are the surface phenomena produced by these singular processes.

In view of these interests, what we require is knowledge of this new construct, a construct that is produced by scientific synthesis: the numerically constituted group identified as a discrete entity. The fate of the individual suicide, of course, provides the raw material for the question which this new problematic poses, but it does not answer this question. This is because the question itself does not concern the elements of immediate reality. On the contrary, this question is located at the ontological level where our more abstract categories are generated from the elements of immediate reality. The categories of this problematic may be compared to the geometrical description of a crystal and the systematic classification of the forms of crystallization according to geometrical criteria. The forces responsible for the formation of any given crystal are not germane to this geometrical problematic.

Consider the identification of relationships between subjects that are homogeneous component groups of larger structures. The categories that are employed here fall within this new problematic. Consider the following examples. It is regularly observed that the rate of immorality and crime is lower within populations of religious minorities than in the population as a whole. Societies in which there is a large and unmediated social distance between classes are in general more tranquil than societies in which there is more continuity or mobility between social classes. Consider institutions or organizations that satisfy all the social needs of the members of a society and exhaust their entire personality. In the course of societal development, these institutions are replaced by a multiplicity of organizations each of which only fulfills a single objective function. This development, moreover, is correlated with the growth of large, highly centralized organizations of power. In each of these relationships, the inquiry begins with individual sequences the causes of which, however, the inquiry does not attempt to identify. On the contrary, it attempts to identify those more extensive entities which will make it possible to extract knowledge from reality—reality which is, from one standpoint, homogeneous and continuous and, from another standpoint, fragmentary and discontinuous. The relationship between these two problematics—an inquiry into underlying causes and an inquiry into more comprehensive entities—may be compared to the following case. Two lines may be described as parallel even though this fact need not be contained in the description of the formula of either line.[13]

The first question within this problematic of historical science is concerned with a "type." Its properties and its functions cannot be deduced from even the most exact knowledge of its individual cases. On the contrary, it can only be derived from the immanent categories of the type itself. The second question within this problematic is concerned with concepts that are combined and transformed in such a way that the more abstract historical significance of the real, concrete event can be grasped. This is not a result of mere abstraction or generalization. On the contrary, it is similar to a certain kind of mirror image of an object. A mirror with special laws of refraction produces a new image of the object, even though this image is functionally dependent upon the object itself. The third question within this problematic concerns totalities. In this case, knowledge is a result of a synthesis in which single entities are juxtaposed. The relations of such a totality—determined either numerically or by other categories—are only products of the comparative effects or manifestations of the sequences of these single entities. Knowledge of these relations cannot be reduced to any sort of knowledge that is limited to the unique concreteness and causality of individual events and processes. It is important to make the following point clear. We are not discussing an inferior problematic. Lawlike causal necessity is not the only authentic and legitimate aim of science. On the contrary, this problematic has its own distinctive and legitimate theoretical aims and forms. Within the actual pragmatics of inquiry, of course, these aims and forms are inextricably interrelated; they are also intimately related to other theoretical goals and forms. In consequence, they often appear only as fragmentary melodies or refrains. Consider, however, the tortuously complex totality of history, its intersections and interruptions, beginnings and turnings. In order to trace the methodological schema of this totality, the theory of knowledge is obliged to make absolutely rigorous logical distinctions between its various methods and interests. In consequence, a certain misconception is inevitable. From the perspective of methodology, forms of knowledge that seldom appear in practice—and never in a completely self-consistent form, but always combined with other forms of knowledge—are no less legitimate and autonomous than forms of knowledge that are, from the standpoint of pragmatics, incomparably more important. This is because the immanent, conceptual import of a form of knowledge is similar to that of a law of nature. Its systematic value is independent of the frequency or transparency of its individual instances.

The foregoing is an account of the structures which mold the material of history into special theoretical forms, forms which may be *juxtaposed* to the laws of history that are patterned on the laws of the natural sciences. I shall conclude these remarks by employing an analogy taken from art. This example was employed in the first chapter, but for a different purpose. Even if the purpose of a painting is to reproduce its subject matter as realistically as possible, it actually generates a structure, a form, and a dialectical interpretation of the elements of pure perceptuality. There is no relation at all—or only a secondary one—between the structure produced by the painting and the real forces that produce these elements of perceptuality. The painting never follows the individual element to its ultimate causes. On the contrary, the painting only weaves the visible aspects of these elements together with other phenomenological aspects. The result is an image or fabric that has certain principles of unity, certain connecting threads or stitches, which are purely aesthetic and phenomenological. They have absolutely no counterpart in the objective interplay of natural causes, causes that invariably lie below the surface appearances of phenomena. The real natural world interconnects these given phenomena according to constitutive categories that are completely different from those employed in art, categories that are located on a completely different level. The categories of history—in which historical material is structured according to types, concepts, and numerical relations—may be compared to the categories of art. History produces constructs in accordance with abstract criteria or criteria that are only concerned with the phenomenon itself. From the standpoint of history, there is a sense in which knowledge of real causality—which lies in the middle between these two kinds of knowledge—is irrelevant. The singular element, ultimately the object of real causal knowledge, only provides raw material for history. Of course the historical inquiry must have some constant relationship to this raw material. But knowledge of the causes of these singular elements—the sort of knowledge that the natural sciences attempt to establish—is completely irrelevant to the constitutive requirements of historical knowledge. It is equally irrelevant to painting. The portrait does not follow the laws of nature, laws which describe the conditions for the existence of the subject of the portrait. The portrait forms and structures surfaces and appearances in such a way that a new entity is actually produced, an entity that is possible only if the appearances are restructured in a novel form.

At this point, I return to the issue with which this chapter began. In what sense, if any, are laws of history a legitimate concern of philosophy? To what province of scientific inquiry should an inquiry into the laws of history be placed? This is obviously an issue of secondary importance. Suppose that the exaggerated pretensions of historical laws are rejected. Then it is undeniable that there are two possibilities whereby laws of history can acquire a limited justification. These two possibilities represent two parallel paths.

The foregoing account gave sufficient emphasis to the following point. In relation to the development of the exact sciences, philosophical speculation has the role of a precursor. In the form of general ideas or speculative attempts to grope in the direction of what still cannot be proven, in conceptual combinations which lie at the level of observed matters of fact, laws of history constitute theoretical constructs. These contructs are often confirmed and often refuted by the empirical methods of the exact sciences. Even in the latter case, however, the material error is contained in a sketch of the most general theoretical forms and goals. Even if this sketch is refuted and replaced with theories that have a completely different content, it remains as the first fruit of truth, a primitive or protoform of truth. Often such a sketch contains the proper elements; the only remaining problem is to combine them in a more satisfactory way. This is a value that is not really intrinsic to philosophy itself. On the contrary, philosophy has this value only insofar as its results are confirmed by other sciences.

But philosophy has another value that is inherent in the nature of philosophical inquiry itself. Philosophy constructs a world view by employing categories that are irrelevant—or, at least, are not necessarily relevant—to the categories of empirical knowledge. The metaphysical interpretation of the world lies beyond the sort of truth or error that is at stake in the realistic and exact sciences. Suppose that philosophy interprets existence as the phenomenon or observable consequence of the absolute spirit or will. Suppose it interprets moral conduct as the expression of our essential nature, our *noumenon*. Suppose it interprets body and soul as two aspects of one homogeneous substance. These interpretations lie in a conceptual level which contains its own immanent criteria for significance and truth. As reflected in this conceptual mirror, the world is represented in an image or construct that is completely self-sufficient and self-contained. This construct satisfies philosophical criteria, but it does not satisfy criteria that have any other provenance. Philosophical speculation may be rejected in principle or in individual cases. But, in fairness, this cannot be done on the basis of criteria that are employed in the empirical sciences as conditions for significance and truth, criteria which exclude metaphysics from the problematic of these sciences.

Consider these two titles or claims to the legitimacy of philosophical speculation: speculation as intrinsically valuable and speculation as valuable insofar as it is subsequently verified by the exact sciences. They correspond exactly to the speculative value of laws of history. Historical laws may be stages along the immeasurable path where laws of the natural sciences also lie, the path that ultimately leads to the laws of motion of the basic constituents of history and knowledge of their fundamental energies. In this case, laws of history constitute preconceptions or proto-forms of these ultimate laws. Here we can identify the only conditions under which a law of history could be totally false. This would be the case if—as a kind of dogmatic petrification—it represented an ephemeral stage in the evolution of knowledge as the conclusive or ultimate truth. On the other hand, laws of history may construct a universe from the given data of history on the basis of categories which have no place in empirical research and which have no pretensions to any empirical status. They are a consequence of completely autonomous logical criteria, conceptual schemes, and synthetic entities.

In both philosophy and history, each of these two valid forms of historical laws can often be identified in one and the same proposition. Consider the following examples. Historical evolution invariably produces a more abstract and complete differentiation of personalities. Or, on the contrary, it produces a higher degree of collectivization that becomes increasingly rigorous. The development of moral culture is correlated with the development of intellectual culture. Or, on the contrary, moral culture exhibits an independent form of development. From the standpoint of the evolution of intellectual culture, it is purely fortuitous. The development of the social freedom of the individual is correlated with the formation of an objective spirit, a wealth of superpersonal cultural products, scientific, aesthetic, and technological. These propositions and others like them may be regarded as precursors of proto-forms of structures that will eventually be the objects of exact nomological knowledge. But they may also be conceived as conceptual syntheses, self-sufficient and hypothetical projections of the historical event. The abstract or phenomenological categories on the basis of which conceptual questions of this sort are posed do not require more exact answers, nor do they require answers that identify singular realities and causes.

Of course it may happen often enough that these conceptual syntheses are recognized as false, but they can only be replaced by other conceptual syntheses which represent the same kind of knowledge and must satisfy the same criteria. From the standpoint of methodology, therefore, the same distance from the ideal of causality in the natural sciences will invariably be maintained. It follows that these two modes of historical laws represent different intellectual problematics, two aspects which the mind selects from the manifold of its possible theoretical interests. Here, therefore, is a further refutation of historical realism. These aspects are not simply copies or reproductions of reality; on the contrary, they represent an immanent, logical and conceptual structuring of reality. Given the conceptual level from which reality is comprehended, it acquires a special structure that is peculiar to this level of abstraction. This analogy between historical laws and philosophical speculations— which is based on what might be called their reciprocal dialectic— does not in any sense mean that history has the status or competence of philosophy or is in any sense its possible competitor. On the contrary, the analogy only has the following import. In both history and philosophy, quite general theoretical requirements and categories that express our typical relationship to existence produce corresponding or commensurable structures of their raw material.

Chapter Three

On the Meaning
of History

~D~D~D~D~D~D~D~D~D~D~D~D

1. *History as the Subject Matter of Philosophy*

Consider the insignificant interest which the sciences take in epistemological reflections on their research. This may be explained, at least in part, as a consequence of the artificial isolation in which epistemology transposes or displaces methods that are inextricably related in the actual praxis of research. Analysis and synthesis, observation and interpretation, immanence and transcendence—these dichotomies and many others, continually shifting and combining, characterize the rudimentary beginnings of empirical research. From the standpoint of epistemology, this state of affairs reveals total inconsistencies in both the aims and the intrinsic significance of empirical research; this view seems to be directly refuted by the peaceful, even organic, coexistence of its various branches. Actually, the development of the individual sciences often makes a completely harmonious and homogeneous impression. In consequence, the epistemological analysis of these sciences does not seem to be germane to their real structure at all. By reflecting on the process of research, it seems to create its own structure of the sciences, a structure which it projects onto their real form.

And, as a matter of fact, this impression is not entirely false, but this does not establish that the relationship between epistemology and its subject matter is in any sense more problematical than the relationship between any other discipline and its subject matter. No science qualifies as an exact reproduction of the real continuity of its object. Each science represents a projection of this object onto a new plane, a sketch or representation of it. Of course this representation must bear some constant relation to the object itself, but the methods and the categories on which it is based are derived from requirements and conditions that are peculiar to scientific research. In comparison with the immediacy of the object itself, these requirements appear to be either analytic or synthetic.

Consider the thesis that every science has a legitimate right to the autonomous constitution of its subject matter. It is indisputable that the natural sciences have this right. And, as the entire foregoing discussion has established, the same holds for the sociohistorical sciences. The same thesis must hold just as well when knowledge becomes its own object of investigation. Whenever knowledge becomes *an object of knowledge,* the same categories and structural conditions which apply to every object as such also apply to knowledge. These categories establish a distinction between knowledge of the object and the experienced or immanent, real existence of the object. This is why we stressed the necessity of the following strict distinction. Laws of history may be conceived as preconceptions or proto-forms of future laws that will provide precise knowledge of the causation of basic elements. Or they may be conceived as syntheses that are confined to a more abstract conceptual level. We also noted that laws of history in both of these senses may be employed quite naively in the very same proposition. In this same sense, both the empirical praxis of history and historical speculation combine the categories and methods of history discussed in the foregoing with a further category. Its purpose, if we may describe it in a summary fashion, is to identify the meaning of history. From the standpoint of epistemology, however, this category of the meaning of history has a completely different status.

Consider the most highly abstract conceptual forms that history produces: laws of history conceived as abstract, self-sufficient and self-contained syntheses of real, individual facts. From a qualitative perspective, even laws of history have a purely theoretical or intellectual nature. From a quantitative perspective, they represent the individual directions in which the historical event and historical existence develop. Nevertheless, historical laws ultimately refer to concrete observations or experience. Of course there is a considerable distance between a law of history and these observations, and this relationship of reference may obtain with varying degrees of refinement and abstraction. This is why laws of history could be described as analogous to philosophical speculations, but they do not fall within the domain of philosophy itself. Suppose that historical facts become objects of philosophical inquiry: then an entirely novel problematic is introduced.

In the foregoing discussions, knowledge of historical knowledge itself was identified as a task of philosophy. History as an inquiry was identified as the determination of observable data and the psychological interpretation of these data, the description of individual facts and their conceptual synthesis. The general problem of the foregoing account was the following. Within the domain of the scientifically given, how are the real, immediate, brute data of history related to the constitutive categories of historical knowledge? It was possible to discuss the logical properties of this question in the abstract, by employing only a few concrete examples. Now suppose we consider history not as knowledge, but rather as substance or content. Suppose we consider *what* the object of historical knowledge is. From this perspective, we are not interested in history as a function of our mental faculties; we are interested in history insofar as it constitutes an object. In this case, as far as I can see, two different and definitive sets of problems are posed for the philosophy of history.

The first is based on the consideration that history is a composite of concrete empirical facts. Therefore the following question arises. Does this *composite entity* have an intrinsic nature and significance which cannot be inferred from the properties of its components? On the other hand, the following question also arises, a question which may coincide with this first issue. What absolute being or transcendent reality, if any, lies behind the phenomenal character of empirical, historical facts? In addition to these metaphysical—but still purely theoretical—issues, there is a question concerning the structures, the stresses, and the accents which the content of history acquires as a result of the non-theoretical interests of the historical observer. With some reservations that require essential modifications, we may provisionally call this the question of the *valuation* of historical facts. Both forms of reflection upon history—forms of reflection which may bring the historian closer to history or take him further away—are intimately related, often inextricably interrelated, in the actual practice of philosophical speculation. This is one of the typical functional correlations of our mind. An image or construct of the absolute—in view of its content, the construct that is most alien to all subjectivity and personal idiosyncracy—is accessible only by an inquiry that penetrates the most subjective energies of feeling, the frame or state of mind, and the tendencies of the will. Both sets of problems are posed by the same raw material. At this point, we shall attempt to define the relationship between them.

2. The Metaphysical Interpretation of the Meaning of History

Suppose that our knowledge of all the facts of history were exhaustive and absolutely accurate. And suppose that all laws had been discovered which govern every atomic particle and every idea in their relationship to all other particles and ideas. Even under these conditions, it is obvious that the problems at stake here would not be resolved. The reason is as follows. All of this knowledge is confined to a domain which we may call—in the broadest sense of this word and without committing ourselves to any epistemological doctrine—the domain of phenomena. Knowledge of the properties of this domain, therefore, is not germane to the question concerning the absolute reality which lies behind all history—"behind" in very much the same sense that the thing-in-itself lies behind the phenomenon. Is this absolute reality independent of the world of phenomena, but nevertheless in a pantheistic unity with it? Or is it to be conceived theistically, as standing in opposition to the world of phenomena? Or is its very existence to be rejected on materialist grounds? These are more or less material or substantive problems.

From a formal or logical point of view, this series of metaphysical assumptions has the following distinctive feature. Each makes a claim about a relationship which obtains between the whole of history and a principle which in some sense transcends history. Then a metaphysical question is raised concerning the totality of history. Is it really governed by an inner or immanent necessity? Or is it a complex of elements that are ultimately autonomous? Does the composite of all historical changes represent a self-sufficient and self-contained entity? Or is every stage and every fundamental element of history a self-sufficient and self-contained entity? Or can historical changes be represented as forming a meaningful whole only insofar as they are correlated with cosmic changes in general? Can the manifold of historical phenomena be represented as the evolution of an original, homogeneous germ or embryo? Or does its origin lie in the infinite and inaccessible reaches of time and space? Is history a continuous process in which originally discrete elements become more intimately and inextricably related?

Regardless of whether they are accepted or rejected, the logical consequences of these possibilities have no bearing upon the content of the construct of the historical process itself. They could be compared to the symbolic representation of the meaning of a work of art; it does not alter the purely aesthetic relationships of coherence that determine and define each aspect of the work of art unambiguously and with self-sufficient necessity. The most profound religiosity interprets and colors life as a whole, but without altering or interrupting a single moment; it does not ascribe any real content or concrete significance to any moment of life that could not be explained by reference to the immanent conditions and forces of the empirical world. In the same way, metaphysics grasps historical reality as a whole. Its structures and interpretations—as we might put it—only encircle the limits of history. They only touch it at points of extremity. Therefore suppose that there were no metaphysical interpretations of the totality of history. Then it seems that the course of each individual aspect of the historical process would not be altered in the least. The most diverse answers to metaphysical questions have the same logical status in relation to the metaphysical indifference of historical facticity.

Perhaps the logical properties of these questions can be best illustrated by considering the problem of the transcendent purpose, end, or goal of history. Consider the assumption that there is a divine being who will bring the entire cosmic drama to a conclusion, an end which unfolds in a purpose which is either hidden from us or revealed to us. This assumption would only transform the casual sequence of history, which is how we experience it, into a teleological sequence, but it would not alter the contents of history and the laws which connect them in any way at all. History as an inquiry describes the mechanism by means of which this end or purpose is realized. This is very much like the design of a machine which is constructed with certain human purposes in view; the causal forces which are responsible for its functioning cannot be influenced by the purpose of the machine as such. On the contrary, the purpose lies behind the mechanism, or the machine presupposes its purpose.

From the standpoint of science, we can understand the machine as an apparatus, in purely mechanical terms and independent of any volitional moment. Any volitional factor would translate the problem of understanding the machine into the completely different domain of pragmatics or praxis. In the same way, knowledge of the purely mechanical properties of the natural physical world is not necessarily altered by the fact that purposes or goals are imputed to it. Suppose that, like the Darwinians, we attempt to identify the mechanism that is responsible for organic evolution. We could interpret this entire process quite simply as the mechanism or the product of a divine teleological decree, but all of its individual stages could be explained by reference to the forces which produced the earlier stages of the process, stages which evolved or developed according to the laws of the mechanism itself. Suppose we see the meaning or end of all history—the purpose of history without which the motive forces of history simply could not function—as the kingdom of God or the kingdom of the Antichrist, the ultimate and everlasting bliss of all souls or the cleavage of all souls into the saved and the damned, the dissolution of all consciousness in Nirvana or the complete self-consciousness of all existence. From the standpoint of historical research, these issues are irrelevant. The description of the forces of history—as if they enjoyed an independent existence—forms the substance of empirical historical research.

Actually there is a profound relationship between the absolutely complete immanence of all empirical historical knowledge, which is immune to any metaphysical *incursion* or *interference,* and the sanctification of history by a divine teleological decree. This relationship is not simply a consequence of the doctrine so often stressed by theists: that the dignity or perfection of God is a function of the technical perfection of the cosmic mechanism. In that case, no further alterations or interruptions of its functioning are required. In consequence, anyone who sees the "hand of God" more visibly active at one point than at another is convicted of an infantile form of anthropomorphism. The ultimate grounds for this relationship, however, lie in a completely different direction. Suppose that the concrete facts of life as such exhibit no metaphysical significance. Then the need to at least impute a metaphysical significance to life as a whole becomes even more pressing. Therefore the idea of a purely transcendental power that is responsible for the meaning and purpose of the whole becomes even more powerful. This force stands in relief, beyond any obscure confusion or conflation with empirical ideas.[14]

3. The Constitutive Status of Extra-theoretical Interests in History

The foregoing illustration concerning teleology in history leads to the second type of metaphysical problem in the philosophy of history: problems which have their source in the relationship between extra-theoretical interests and the conceptual structure of the objective, historical process. Notice that the transcendental interpretation of the meaning of history as a whole does not *necessarily have to* rest on interests that are any different from the interests of all knowledge in general. What motivates us to engage in theoretical activity cannot be something else that also has a theoretical status. On the contrary, it can only be an impulse of will and a sense or feeling of significance or value. However it quite often happens that we are not clear on the following point. Suppose that the *content* on which these mental energies impinge is purely theoretical. And suppose that we are disposed to explain knowledge as a product of instincts or drives that are ultimately practical or pragmatic. Given these conditions, when does knowledge have its origin in motives that are, from the standpoint of *substance* or *content,* alien to its purely theoretical status? At this point, however, the issue is the following. First, to penetrate the completely indifferent coloration of all historical elements; this is possible only on the basis of a transcendent principle that underpins the totality of history. And then to structure historical sequences on the basis of principles of foreground and background, what is to be accented or emphasized and what is unimportant or insignificant, what is a mere anticipation or precursor and what is an actual accomplishment or fulfillment. Teleological reflection animates the construct of history itself when the following are represented as the purpose or meaning of historical changes: the individualization and individuation of minds or the egalitarian leveling of minds; the domain of objectified mental structures or the domain of moral perfection; an increase in the total quantity of pleasure or happiness or the maximum diminution in the total quantity of pain or suffering.[15]

At this point, it is of principal importance to resolve the following question. Since philosophical speculation is also concerned with the concrete construct of events, it is essential to maintain the detachment and reserve which allows this construct to retain its purely empirical character. In principle, this problem presents no difficulties. A sequence organized, stressed, or accented according to purposes, values, and meanings has exactly the same content as a sequence constructed in terms of theoretical categories. Consider the real forces which make the genesis of every element in this sequence intelligible and the concepts which provide a logical explanation of its contents. They have nothing at all to do with the lights and shadows that the picture of this sequence acquires as soon as it falls within the affective and volitional levels of our consciousness. The simplest example of this duality of problematics is provided by the moral evaluation of conduct, an example so simple that it has become a triviality to emphasize the following point. Our moral judgments may ascribe the highest dignity or the most profound immorality to an action—both are irrelevant to the causal understanding of the necessity of the action. Nor is the domain of imperatives constructed by our moral requirements influenced in any way by the extent to which psychological reality corresponds to it. An event-sequence constituted by reference to moral values has a tempo or rhythm, peaks and profundities, colors and shadings that are utterly different from those the event-sequence acquires if it falls under the category of theoretical history. In both cases, however, the content of the event-sequence is the same. Event-sequences categorized from the standpoint of history and morality lie in two different dimensions. In opposition to these two categories, we may also juxtapose the problematic of aesthetics. Aesthetics, of course, has hardly had any bearing upon human action and the historical totality of human action, but there is no doubt that historical contents can also be structured according to aesthetic values. Harmonies and contrasts, the phenomena of the graceful and the tragic, the scale of values ranging from the beautiful through the aesthetically indifferent to the ugly—these and many other closely related categories also constitute a taxonomy of the world of action. Within this taxonomy, action acquires a meaning that lies beyond both its pure facticity and its ethical value. The projection of the historical event onto this plane produces a completely autochthonous structure. It presents points of emphasis and de-emphasis, connections and disconnections, and sources of animation and stagnation that are not repeated in any other conception of reality. Corresponding possibilities of speculation are also produced. Both ethics and aesthetics generate principles of periodization, stages of evolution, speculative ideas concerning a deeper meaning of the historical event, teleological points of culmination—in short, reflections on history. But there is no sense in which they alter the construct of historical reality, On the contrary, they only express the way in which certain affective or axiological interests are satisfied in this construct.

4. Further Analysis of the Concept of Value in History

Consider the domain of these extra-theoretical interests and emphases. They parallel the theoretical construction of history; their crystallization produces those peculiar constructs that make up the philosophy of history. As far as I can see, the limits of this domain has not yet been identified. Usually these interests and accents are designated as evaluations; however this is not a satisfactory description. On the one hand, "evaluation" may simply be a general concept under which all affective intuitions and extra-theoretical constructs of historical sequences are collected. In this case, the set of problems at stake here has a name, but no solution. On the other hand, "value" might designate the definitive quality which historical contents have insofar as they are categorized according to these extra-theoretical interests. In this case, the category of "value" or "evaluation" certainly does not exhaust the set of constitutive categories at issue here. The ensuing discussion will provide some indication of the extent of this set of categories.

We describe certain phenomena as "significant" or "important" quite independent of the position they occupy in a genuine scale of values. Of course they have such a status, and this could be a reason they are felt to be "significant." However the import of this concept is different from the import of the concept of value; the valuable and the significant imply two different emphases, even if the difference is more a matter of feeling than of precise description. They refer to properties that are purely intrinsic to a phenomenon. And they also refer to properties which a phenomenon acquires by virtue of its effects upon other phenomena and as a result of its comparative relationships with the remainder of historical existence. The significant or important has the systematically ambiguous sense of "good." A given item can be "good" *for something* or someone. Then, however, as a result of an apparently fallacious inference from this relationship, the "good" is ontologically reified; it becomes an immanent quality that can only be ascribed to the ideal of the thing itself. Consider this unique relationship. It is concerned with what a thing *should* be, the idea of its perfection, a picture which is traced out in the thing itself—as if with ideal lines—and awaits or anticipates reproduction by reality. This unique relationship can incorporate into the concept of the good all the other relations that constitute its content.

In some sense, the same holds for the concept of the significant. From a purely logical point of view, the significant must signify *something,* or it must signify or mean something *to someone.* However the qualities of immediate existence—which, as we might put it, transcend immediate existence in producing relative meaning of this sort—can also be felt or experienced for their own sake. In this sense and to this extent, it can be said that a phenomenon is simply "significant" or "important" for us. This predicate designates a property which may be ascribed to persons and events in very different degrees; the result is the possibility of a complete taxonomy of persons and events. But, at least in principle, this taxonomy is not equivalent to a classification of persons and events by reference to the categories of the moral and the immoral, the pleasing and the displeasing, even the strong and the weak. As a matter of fact, these two kinds of classification often coincide. The attribution of morality or immorality, beauty or ugliness can endow the bearer of these predicates with the quality of being "significant" to us. But the latter invariably remains a novel and autonomous category. The same degree of a value which on one occasion is regarded as significant or important may, on another occasion, not fall under this category at all.

At this point, consider another category which affectively structures the objective course of history in terms of differences in the fascination or attraction which historical events hold for us: the concept of the extreme point or position on a given scale of quality. In that case, they acquire an interest that transcends a purely theoretical concern with history. This may hold true for historical phenomena formed by elements that are quite fragmentary; it may be the result of a comparison of phenomena that are otherwise completely heterogeneous. The purely formal fact that we confront one of the extreme limits of human possibilities produces a certain psychological reaction. To a considerable degree, this response is independent of the *content* of this existential extreme. As the customary saying of everyday experience instructs us, "extremes meet" and "opposite poles attract." In the same way, there is an obscure or hidden resemblance between every extremity of the conduct and the existential condition of human beings. This also holds for the feelings by reference to which we distinguish these extremes from the purely causal sequence of events. This is the case even though, from the standpoint of other kinds of feelings, no coherent relationship of this sort can be established. Consider the horror with which we contemplate the monstrosity of certain crimes. Often they have a fascination that we describe as "demonic," a description that implies some sort of exculpation or justification of the crime. This sort of attraction establishes an intimate relationship between acts of this sort and acts which, axiologically, represent their extreme polar antitheses. Logically, the interest in the *typical* character of phenomena is the polar antithesis of this concept. Both concepts have what might be called a quantitative significance. The extreme represents the maximum quantum or measure of a given value; the type designates the number of persons or events that are represented by a given phenomenon. The estimation of the *typical* significance of a single phenomenon also transcends a purely causal problematic. A problematic of types is often obliged to employ as raw material collections of facts that are completely unrelated. It is also obvious that the construction of such a type is irrelevant to any judgment based on any other normative criteria. The interest which a phenomenon acquires simply because it represents a type is quite primary, but it is obvious that the question of whether a phenomenon is more or less interesting from this standpoint is dependent upon the substantive content of the type itself. In their most perfect form, the type as well as the extreme can be objective. In their least perfect form, both are mere projections of our feelings, like the valuable or the significant, or even the merely interesting. On the one hand, we ascribe a *meaning* to historical existence insofar as historical phenomena do not unfold in the monotony and uniformity of mediocre or average qualities, but rather approach extremes of all sorts. On the other hand, we also ascribe meaning to historical phenomena insofar as they are not completely incomparable and qualitatively different from one another, insofar as they possess an ideal structure that transforms individual men, actions, and circumstances into representatives of types of men, actions, and circumstances. A metaphysics of history can find elements of significance and importance in facts of both kinds; they lie, of course, beyond the purely empirical construct of history. From the standpoint of this construct, the extreme phenomena as well as the average, the typical as well as the unique, are produced with the same indifferent, intrinsically homogeneous necessity. Consider the fact that the phenomena discussed here have this function. They transcend history as mere fact. The facts of history provide a point of departure for a more profound picture, a new taxonomy or tendency. This fact is the expression of emotional responses. They paint the theoretical picture of history in colors that cannot be found in the historical process itself; they can only be found in our feelings.

This discussion has been concerned with the issue with which the chapter began. Consider the methodological concepts which the theory of knowledge classifies at completely different conceptual levels. In the actual praxis of investigation, they are generally employed together and interchangeably. The reflections which our speculative and extra-theoretical interests cast on the results of historical investigation are, of course, the elements of a metaphysics of history. The perspective of a metaphysics of history is entirely different from the theoretical description of the historical event itself. The legitimacy of a metaphysics of history—the justification of its existence within the scientific division of labor—is based on a rigorous and absolute distinction between metaphysics and the problematic of theoretical history. On the other hand, pure theory is an ideal that is never completely realized. In fact, metaphysical categories are implicated in theoretical history. For the most part, speculation about history is simply a more exact definition, elucidation, and logical classification of presuppositions and motive forces that are already present in the formation of the raw material of events into history itself. The genesis of historical speculation cannot be fully understood unless we follow its fragmentary beginnings, its partial efficacy, and its development—often hidden—in the more simple and concrete propositions of history itself.

For epistemological purposes, of course, it is necessary to make a rigorous distinction between the metaphysics of history and historical theory. The properties of these constructs are defined by more abstract concepts. From the standpoint of both their substance and value, they are completely independent of the conditions for their historical development. However we can only approximate knowledge of their objective, logical import; knowledge invariably remains tied to its psychological and historical conditions. It follows that insight into the real historical conditions for the development of these constructs provides a foothold or a point of reference for insight into their trans-historical, super-historical, objective meaning.

The same point can be made about religion. There are innumerable circumstances of life in which we find ideas, volitional tendencies, and emotional stimuli which—if they are detached from their singular relationships, intensified until they reach the status of an absolute, and concentrated at one point—can become religion. The conduct of the patriot in relation to his country, the conduct of the devoted child in relation to his parents, the conduct of the enthusiast in relation to his cause, and the conduct of the soldier in relation to his flag—each contains elements of religiosity. Religion is an autonomous form of life with its own intrinsic properties. The feelings associated with the foregoing examples of conduct may be intensified to the point at which they acquire a religious status too—then they become interwoven with the religious form of life. Otherwise they are like sparks or embers that illuminate specific sets of interests. Religion is their point of intersection in infinity; it is the differential and—if this expression is correctly understood—abstract construct in which they are crystallized. The same points hold for both art and the law. In the simpler and more concrete circumstances and contents of life, legal and aesthetic elements always have some sort of function. They serve as indispensable norms or as motive forces of practical processes; in this function, however, they are fragmented and rudimentary, corresponding to the contingency and arbitrariness of these processes. But suppose they are extracted from these everyday processes and placed in relief. In that case, they ultimately develop into ideal structures; they acquire a structure of a higher order that corresponds to their intellectuality. All their fragments and rudimentary elements are combined to form those entities that make up an autonomous art or an independently established system of law.

The same point holds for the relationship between the philosophy of history and theoretical history. The motives with which speculation transcends the theoretically exact construct of history lie within this construct. But they only function as allusions or hints that structure the historical material from a certain distance; they are presuppositions which influence not so much the data itself as the fact that this data is theoretically constituted at all. They often function as unconscious biases which only determine the tone of the whole. In this form, they can neither be confirmed nor disconfirmed. The obscure and fragmentary function of these motives is transformed into a complete, self-contained and self-sufficient system only within the philosophy of history.

The primary metatheoretical fact of history is the interest that originally motivates theory as such. It is obvious that knowledge cannot have its source in knowledge; the necessity of deriving knowledge from non-cognitive or extra-theoretical sources holds just as certainly for the large autonomous provinces of knowledge. It will also not do to characterize the interest in knowledge in general as the self-evident and timelessly valid presupposition of every science. This is a presupposition which no more influences the state of knowledge than, viewed from the opposite perspective, the content of knowledge is altered by the fact that its *existence* is external to thought. There is no sense in which the primary metatheoretical interest can be identified as a diffuse generality of this sort. There are innumerable *possible* objects of knowledge, but the investigation of these objects is not pursued because knowledge of their properties has no value. In many cases, the source of this value lies in knowledge of other objects. Ultimately, however, it is grounded on an evaluation that is not susceptible to rational justification. A "theoretical drive" or an "instinct for knowledge" may indeed exist in the same sense that hunger exists; that is, as a mere feeling defined by its source or *terminus a quo*, a feeling that as such has no relation of any sort to objects in general, and therefore no relation to a particular object. Only very few of the objects in the universe are edible, and among the edible objects, only a very few are available at any given moment. In practice, therefore, hunger is limited to specific objects. This principle of selection, which is a consequence of the specialization of the instinct itself, does not apply to knowledge. A general instinct for knowledge would leave us helpless in the face of an indefinite number of possible theoretical goals. At least this would be true if the following were not the case. From its genesis, our interest in knowledge is differentiated by reference to the special force with which some motives activate this interest much more than others.

5. *The Interest in the Content of Historical Reality*

Historical knowledge is determined by two basic interests. The first is an interest in the content of history. The interweaving of fate and the energies of the individual, the dimensions of desire and fulfillment which set individuals and groups in motion to purposeful or pointless activity, the rhythm of this unfathomable game of profit and loss, the fascination which the comprehensible holds for us as well as the charm of the ambiguous—all of this places us in the following relationship to historical existence. We simply cannot read it off like a book. On the contrary, we are invariably obliged to recreate it anew within ourselves. Consider these interests and the countless other interests without which history as an object of investigation could not possible exist for us. They are only valid for the *content* of history; they would have the same status in relation to a drama with the same content. Our mind has a characteristic and peculiar ability. Emotional reactions are associated with our ideas even though they are conceived purely from the standpoint of their qualitative content and without regard to the question of their reality. This reaction is often weaker, purer, and accented in a completely different fashion if the content in question does not fall under the category of reality. We associate the mere idea of a very noble or a very abhorrent deed, a uniquely complex personality, or a remarkable turn of fate with certain feelings. These feelings are independent of our knowledge that these men and events really existed, persisting even if we discover that they did not exist.

There is an obvious explanation for this phenomenon. These feelings represent associative after-effects of the reactions which the reality of such contents, the objects that actually impinge upon us and affect us, produced in us or would produce in us. It seems to me that this explanation is not as satisfactory as it is obvious. In the first place, it is completely unconfirmed. Let us assume that it is really plausible to suppose that none of the feelings in question could ultimately be caused in any other way except by an *existing* object. This would only prove that these feelings—given their psychological nature and merely from the standpoint of their content—require this more powerful stimulus from perceptual reality as a kind of pace-maker. It would not prove that, subsequent to the fulfillment of this condition, they could not exist autonomously, in such a way that both their extent and their intensity are completely independent of perceptual reality. Mental life is full of relationships of just this sort. In order for two objects to be regarded as totally congruent, very often only the merest suggestion which places one single point of congruence in relief is required. It is not a demonstration which convinces us of the congruence or equivalence in question; on the contrary, we have long since been aware of it, but in an unconscious or latent fashion. It could be said that this explicit evidence of congruence only breaks the ice. Relationships which are completely independent of this evidence now become clear to us. These relationships would not otherwise be clear to us, but the relationships themselves are not produced or determined by this evidence.

Consider the following fallacy: any unobservable mental process can only be a quantitatively weaker after-effect of its real, observable, physical cause or source of stimulation. This fallacy is characteristic of all forms of naturalistic psychology. It does not really represent an instance of the fallacy of *post hoc ergo propter hoc*. There actually is a cause that is produced by external or observable experience, but this cause has the same status as the "causation" of the explosion of gunpowder by a spark. We could even venture the following claim. What the most evident or palpable observable experience produces in our mind is the idea of its logically expressible *content;* this holds for all feelings which experience recalls for us as images or after-effects. The fact that this content is also an *experience*—that is, the fact that it has the form of objective reality— has certain consequences as regards affect or emotion, a point to which I shall return in the ensuing. These emotional consequences may shade, influence, or alter the experience itself, but this certainly does not make it impossible for these purely affective contents to form an autonomous domain. After the disappearance of the cause that actually produced them, they appear and persist with their own characteristic nature. And, most important in the psychological analysis of these contents, they should be distinguished from their causes or existential conditions. *After* contents are given—which may only be possible on the basis of experience—interests develop around them. The same interests could also appear in any other form in which these contents exist or could exist for us.

This mode, therefore, is one element of the historical interest, the mode that ordinary discourse designates as "interesting," in the strict sense of this word. From the standpoint of the logical properties of this interest, it makes no essential difference whether our knowledge of the existence of the process, person, or situation in question is certain or uncertain. Moreover, its temporal location is of importance only insofar as this influences the qualitative definition of its content. Of course this almost always holds true for more advanced historical entities. The definitive import of this interest is the following. Purely fictitious events fall under it no less than real events. This is because the interest only pertains to the category of content, but not to the category of existence. In other words, the event is described insofar as it has a certain content, but not insofar as it does or does not actually take place. This is the point at which the uniqueness of persons who are—from the standpoint of historical potency or productivity—interesting is of most consequence. It is not only important for the identification or definition of the domain of historical inquiry. It is even more essential, although this is not always so clear, when the following issues are at stake in historical inquiry: the problem of condensation or completeness of description, the question of criteria for the emphasis of decisive points, the emotional ardour or indifference of the narration, and the epic or dramatic properties of the narration. If anyone believes that objectivity is possible here, a kind of objectivity that would make it possible to derive structure and emphasis exclusively from reality itself, then he is deceiving himself.

6. *The Concept of Historical Significance or Importance*

In that case, what is "objectively" important? If we limit the application of the concept of importance to the concrete event, or whatever qualifies as the basic element of history, then the following point is immediately obvious. If something is important, then importance must be *"ascribed"* or *"attached"* to it; in other words, it is important because the historian is interested in it. "Intrinsically" an item may be moral or corrupt, gigantic or idyllic, brilliant or profound. It is *important,* in the sense that it is a point of orientation or organization for historical inquiry, exclusively because of the interest that it acquires as a result of the feelings or sentiments of the historical observer. The following seems to be the most plausible method for establishing an objective criterion of historical importance. Importance is not a property of the individual element itself, but rather a property of its *consequences.* But suppose that historical importance cannot be ascribed to these consequences; in that case, it is difficult to see why it should be ascribed to their cause. *Suppose,* however, that they exhibit this property. Then their objective structure would also lend historical importance to their cause. However this would not make the ascription of historical importance any less subjective than it is in the first case. We might also attempt to establish an objective status for historical importance in the following way. It is not the qualitative properties of the consequences which determine historical importance, but only the number of these consequences, which would determine whether importance can be ascribed to their cause. In this case, it is simply the number of the consequences as such that has historical importance. Consider the isolated entity the energies or potencies of which are exhausted in its own production. Suppose that no further consequences can be attributed to it: then it would qualify as insignificant or unimportant. This feeling, of course, will always remain subjective; however this sort of subjectivity would be objectively grounded. As a constant presupposition, it would at least eliminate purely individual or arbitrary differences of interpretation. In any given case, it would be possible to establish, at least in principle, the objective quantity of historical importance. In this case, however, the concept of a "consequence" cannot possibly have the same import it has in the natural or nomological sciences; in this latter sense of "consequence," every event has an infinite number of consequences. But history is only interested in historically important consequences. It obviously follows that we are again confronted with the original question: what is of "objective" historical importance?

Suppose we pursue this inquiry further and in a completely hypothetical and speculative direction. Then it would still be possible to make some progress toward approximating an objective determination of the amount of importance or interest which may be ascribed to the elements of history. We have considered natural or causal consequences. They are indefinitely large in number; therefore only a very small number of these consequences are possible objects of knowledge. We have also considered consequences the historical significance of which is acknowledged. This implies that a selection or discrimination has been made within the domain of possible objects of knowledge. There is a third sort of consequence that we have not yet considered. It constitutes a possible object of knowledge, at least in the sense that it is comprehensible, but it does not fall under the category of historically significant consequences of acts, persons, and states of affairs. Consider the mere quantum—the weight or the number—of these effects as we consciously or unconsciously estimate it. Perhaps this provides the criterion for the feeling of historical interest with which we react to certain causal factors. The causal factors that we designate as "important" are precisely those which have consequences that are, in comparison with "unimportant" events, more observably determinable or quantitatively estimable. In the light of this possibility, reconsider the foregoing requirement: that the effects of a given cause must themselves be historically significant in order to reflect this quality back onto their cause. There are good logical grounds for rejecting this requirement. We would ascribe historical interest only to those knowable sequences of mental events to which a certain quantum of effects can be clearly or intuitively attributed. There is no reason why each of these events must have some intrinsic historical importance. Compare this case to the following. A given composite of kinesthetic sensations produces the feeling of pain, but this does not entail that each individual kinesthetic sensation must be painful by itself. Note that the historical interest gradually shades off and diminishes to a point beyond which phenomena have no affective significance of any sort for us. Or, perhaps they have significance of some sort, but no historical significance. Here it would be legitimate to speak of a *threshold of the historical consciousness,* whose location is determinable by reference to these quanta of effects, reactions, or consequences. It is necessary to emphasize the importance of this concept of a threshold of historical consciousness. It is one of those meta-theoretical assumptions of historical theory that is decisively repudiated by historical realism and naturalism. An independent, abstract analysis of these assumptions provides the material or the form for the metaphysics of history.

7. The Threshold of Historical Consciousness

All of the more abstract strata of the mind exhibit threshold phenomena. Consider aesthetic forms. Many of them, perhaps even all of them, can acquire this status only if they have reached certain minimal dimensions. Objects smaller than this may have reached the threshold of perception or observation, but they have not crossed the threshold of the aesthetic. Many facts that are indifferent or amusing on a small scale cross the threshold of tragic phenomena as soon as they appear in larger or fuller dimensions and are revealed as types of a more universal human experience. The consciousness of justice or legality produces its characteristic reactions only if processes have attained a certain breadth or scope. The theft of a pin is, of course, still theft. It lies within the threshold of this concept, but it lies beyond the point or threshold at which the practical, legal prosecution of a thief would begin. The same point holds invariably. Consider the elements which produce reactions on a given plane of feeling. They have this effect only if they have attained certain minimum dimensions. Beneath this particular threshold, they may very well have crossed the threshold of one or more other energies of consciousness. Consider the fact that there are innumerable events—and not only events that lie in the present experience of immediate personal life—which we can or could identify and which have no historical interest.

Suppose we read in the diary of some otherwise unknown person of the eighteenth century that he has befriended one of his equally unknown contemporaries. Or suppose we find that he was filled with active sympathy for the French Revolution. From a logical or conceptual point of view, these are historical facts, but in the substantively important sense of the concept, they are not. This is because they have no historical interest. If they have no historical interest, this is not because they are lacking in human dignity or interest. Suppose we discovered that both of these facts were motivated by the most profound moral impulses and expressed emotions and a spiritual refinement of the highest order: it would not follow that they fall within the threshold of historical significance. The reason for this might possibly be the following. The number of the consequences of these facts that lies within our grasp or comprehension is simply of insufficient weight or importance. Suppose we learned the same facts about someone whose importance was already known to us as a result of further subsequent events. In that case, they would acquire historical value. This is because we could follow or estimate the extent to which these facts codetermine the further impressions or effects produced by this person, the extent to which they contribute to his causal efficacy in history. In that case, we would see, more or less clearly or obscurely, that many consequences emanate from this sort of friendship or political enthusiasm. From a theoretical standpoint, events that are isolated do not constitute "history." [16] An event qualifies as history to the extent to which we can ascribe effect-sequences to it. These sequences are infinitely diverse, and they intersect at innumerable points; ultimately, they form that compact mass which we call "history."

Consider the feeling or sense of historical significance. There is a definitive difference between it and all other kinds of value or significance. The strength or weakness with which this feeling is associated with a phenomenon is a function of the extent to which its consequences are interwoven into this complex of effect-sequences. The limits of this complex may be imprecise—in many relatively specialized provinces of history, they may even be indeterminate—but its core or center is identifiable in a completely unambiguous fashion. This plurality of identifiable effects does not *constitute* historical significance as an objective property which can be ascribed to the event itself, but insofar as it is the cause or source of a specific mental energy, it *produces* this property in us. It is like all other threshold effects. At a certain point, quantitative changes in the number of causal elements produce a qualitative change in their effects. This may be one reason we feel that persons and events of the recent past lack historical depth or perspective: they have not yet had the opportunity to generate extensive consequences. An effect of great breadth or latitude could, of course, compensate for this lack of depth. In that case, a definitive historical interest or significance could even be ascribed to persons who are our near contemporaries. Suppose we lack this historical perspective on a certain event. Suppose it has an unidentifiable number of effect-sequences. Such an event may have all other possible values and interests for us, but it will have no historical interest until we perceive that the number of its effect-sequences has reached the threshold value of the historical reaction.

A conjecture concerning the nature of aesthetic feelings provides a remote analogy to the concept of the threshold of historical consciousness. These feelings arise when unconscious ideas become associated with a certain smoothness and ease. Under these conditions, an otherwise unattainable profusion of these associations becomes possible within a relatively brief period of time. The same holds for the historical interest. It provides an organization of ideational material. This structure also associates a profusion of ideas with a single idea, an association that is possible only in this fashion. Naturally the mode of association and the corresponding category of feeling that it produces are completely different from the case of aesthetics. At least the following, however, is common to both cases. A single idea is withdrawn from its isolation and placed at the center of an extensive structure of other ideas that are dependent upon it. This is the source of a characteristic impulse or motive which forms this collection of ideas into a definitive province of interests. The purpose of this hypothesis is not so much to argue that the number of identifiable causal functional relations constitutes an adequate objective ground for the subjective historical interest. On the contrary, its purpose is to illuminate the problem itself, the issue I identified as the problem of the historical threshold. Events and persons, relations and organizations may acquire every kind of significance and value, but this does not entail that they have become historically interesting. On the contrary, the historical interest is a specific affective reaction with which we respond to certain taxonomies, summaries, and formal relationships. Only on the basis of the subjective meaning or significance of these elements are they structured and formed to constitute the definitive constructs of history.

8. The Interest in the Reality of Historical Content

However another presupposition may be at stake here, a proposition which the foregoing discussion only considered in passing. Earlier I mentioned two vital interests; as such, they are metatheoretical determinants of historical knowledge. First I emphasized the interest in the *content* of the event. This content would remain the same even if it were constituted by a form different from the form of historical reality. The results of the foregoing analysis are only consequences of the concept of this interest. Ultimately, this analysis produced the concept of a threshold, which concept depends upon a qualitatively and quantitatively distinctive attraction, a result of the interweaving, amplification, and classification of the given elements. The historical consciousness cannot begin to function unless this condition is satisfied. All this only pertains to the contents of ideas. Suppose it were possible to present all these events and their relationships as a mere play, a purely intellectual game or idea that does not correspond to reality. This enterprise would acquire an affective interest that is at least related to the historical interest. However the concept of the historical interest would still remain incomplete. An element is missing, an element which must be added to the interest discussed above in order to produce the full effect of the historical: this is the element that generates the second of the two interests mentioned in the foregoing account. We might call this an interest in *reality* as such.

There are countless things that interest us not because their content has value, significance, or originality, but simply because they are *there*, because they *exist* and have the form of reality. However as a mere idea, no matter how clearly its content may be imagined, things of this sort would arouse no interest. In the foregoing we were concerned with things to which we always respond with the same feelings, even though they are purely imaginary and fall under the category of the mere idea. But there are many other things that immediately lose whatever significance and value they have as soon as we learn that they are "not true." In this context, reality might be compared to an elixir which flows through the mere contents of ideas. When it evaporates, they are left behind as uninteresting and insubstantial shells, all that remains of the identifiable or expressible logical content of such an idea. Consider what holds true in practice. The mere idea of one hundred talers arouses no interest of any sort. On the other hand, the idea of one hundred real talers—although, as Kant noted, it does not contain one penny more—creates an extremely lively interest. The same holds in theory. There is a great deal that is utterly insignificant merely as an idea or an image but which acquires importance and significance as soon as it is conceived as existing.

As everyone knows, metaphysics has established an exhaustive distinction between this interest in being and the interest in content, a distinction so complete that the result is an absolute axiological dichotomy. The "what" of the universe, its substance or content, is as rational and as good as possible; its "that," its being or existence, is meaningless and corrupt. In the work of Spinoza, on the other hand, we feel a passionate but serene joy over the fact of existence, mere existence in which every content, which invariably must be singular and special, represents a restriction or limitation that is insubstantial and trivial. Hegel represents being with the indifference and hauteur of a logician. Simply because it lies beyond every conceptually expressible content, Hegel can only conceive it as a pure nullity. The work of Schopenhauer trembles with horror over the dark and mysterious fate to which things are sentenced. Escape from this gloomy destiny is possible only by flight into the pure ideality of the aesthetic representation or by the repudiation and negation of being as such, not the negation of a single content. The interest in this axiological dichotomy, which varies in its clarity, is universal. Of course it is only philosophical abstraction that takes up each of these two distinctive interests for its own sake and distinguishes it rigorously from the other; elsewhere in theory and practice the two values are always inextricably related, but that does not diminish the profound difference in their meaning.

This existential interest, an interest in facticity that is independent of any metaphysical considerations, is the essential feature of all history. In order to provide a precise account of this interest, I shall offer a profile or cross-section of the world of our ideas. These points were contained implicitly in the previous chapter, but their logical consequences were not set out systematically. In that discussion, the basis for the distinction between the historical sciences and the natural sciences was the difference between the concrete individual phenomenon and the law of nature. The atemporal relationship stated by a law of nature simply correlates two components A and B. But the law cannot determine *whether A* exists. From the standpoint of the natural sciences, the question of existence is insignificant in comparison with the question of substance or content. Natural laws are totally indifferent to the concrete configurations which function *in accordance with* them. Suppose we conceive the totality of the laws of nature as an ideal complex. In this case, there are innumerable different possible worlds that could function according to these laws, in much the same way that the same civil laws can legitimately apply to many different groups. Given the existence of a specific phenomenon, these laws determine its subsequent development. But the laws are utterly irrelevant to the fact that this particular phenomenon *exists;* they are also irrelevant to the fact that it is this *particular* phenomenon that exists. Suppose that a phenomenon with different properties occupied this same spatio-temporal frame. In that case, different laws from the total complex of laws would apply to this particular frame, but this would have absolutely no bearing upon the content and validity of the complex itself. The absolute validity of this complex of laws is only a name for their atemporality. Individual forms and structures, therefore, stand in relief from this complex. It is the qualities of the individual structures that determine *which* laws in the total complex must obtain for them. The identification of these concrete individuals [17] seems to be the task of history. This distinguishes the basic problem of history from the basic problem of natural science. For natural science, it is the law that matters; for history, it is the case to which the law applies. Further, history does not serve as a handmaiden of natural science, providing material which, on the basis of inductive or other grounds, will lead to the knowledge of laws. On the contrary, a given item is located at the focal point of historical interest only insofar as it is individual and singular. And, in contrast to natural science, knowledge of laws is only a tool for the confirmation and analysis of the individual complexes and entities to which these laws apply. Natural science and history, the comprehension of the given by reference to its nomological regularity or in terms of its own intrinsically significant, singular structure, seem to be two different categories for the analysis of the homogeneous manifold of reality. The immediacy and the continuity of this manifold lies beyond the limits of our knowledge. These polar antitheses seem to split our world view in a dichotomous fashion. But consider this dichotomy from the perspective just described: in that case, these polar antitheses appear as the two aspects of *one* conceptual possibility—they both fall under the category of the *content* of things. Both fall under an interest in the *nature* or *constitution* of the cosmic process. Of course it is the *real* world, the world which *exists,* that both history and natural science investigate. From the standpoint of both logical and psychological analysis, however, these two moments—which in reality are invariably concomitant and complementary—may be distinguished. I could, of course, stress the following point: many things that are interesting insofar as they exist become indifferent in the form of mere ideas. However this point alone is not sufficient to make sense of our theoretical aims. From the standpoint of this thesis alone, everything that exists would interest us to the same extent. There is no limit to the number of objects. Therefore the identification of a potential object of knowledge must be a consequence of our interest in its content. And this interest must be logically independent of the question of whether or not that object exists. We discriminate certain objects within this infinite manifold of objects. We investigate the laws that govern them or the unique and individual phenomena that they constitute. In consequence, it is apparent that both of these problematics fall under the common category of an interest in content. The interest in existence may be distinguished from this category. It forms a new constitutive element of historical knowledge.

At this point, we can identify a further sense in which history has a meaning. Consider history as a function of metatheoretical interests, interests that provide a foundation for historical theory. The real world contains many facts which acquire an interest that is completely independent of their intrinsic content. Quite often the significance of everything that we designate as "actuality" is a consequence of an interest of this sort. The present or the contemporary—even though it may have absolutely no bearing upon us personally and cannot possibly have any such bearing—stimulates our interest because of its privileged ontological status. On the other hand, it could be said that both the past and the future are inferior. The reality of the past seems to be less certain; it does not exhibit the immediate, palpable existential properties of the present. This interest in being as such may be associated with items which are indifferent and uninteresting from the standpoint of their content. As I have already indicated, this interest is essential to the historical interest but is not sufficient to constitute it. There is no sense in which everything that exists is historically important. The following is one reason this cannot be the case. If everything that exists were of historical importance, then consider the aspects of historically important reality that constitute possible objects of knowledge: their number would be vanishingly small. These aspects would be so arbitrary and chaotic and so hopelessly fragmentary that "history" would seem to be an utterly childish undertaking. Suppose that reality as such and reality insofar as it is historically important coincide. Then the quantitative discrepancy between historical inquiry and its ideal—knowledge of everything that is historically important—would be immense. Under these conditions, history would not be a worthwhile undertaking.

There is a definitive interest which can be ascribed to certain (but not all) contents of our reality constructs. This interest must be linked with the existential interest in order to identify what is historically important within the infinite manifold of reality. Independent of the category of existence, the interest in content is not sufficient for this purpose. From the perspective of ethics or art, sensuality or logic, there are many things that interest us as mere ideas, but it does not follow from this that they also have an historical interest. In cases of this sort, the interest may often be more lively if the object of the idea *exists.* Or it may be possible for such an interest to arise only if the object exists, but the essential features of the interest itself are logically independent of the existence of the object. This does not hold true for the nature of the historical interest. Both the most exalted and sublime and the most loathsome and detestable phenomena may have immense significance as mere ideas, conceptual constructs, or practical possibilities, but they do not fall within the definitive sphere of the historical interest as soon as it is established that they are not *real.* For the same reason, phenomena which occupy the highest ontological status do not fall within the sphere of historical interest unless a certain importance or significance can be ascribed to their *content.*

In consequence, the threshold of historical consciousness can be grounded on a new basis. This threshold is located where the existential interest intersects with the interest in the significance of content, which has its own peculiar threshold. In the foregoing, I ventured the hypothesis that this threshold is determined by reference to the quantum—the number or weight—of the effects of a given event. Where these two criteria mesh—the existential interest and the interest in content—we find the specific interest in the facticity of certain distinctive sequences of events, persons, circumstances and states that provides the foundation for history.

9. The Interest in Knowledge of Nature

At this point, a further distinction between knowledge of history and knowledge of nature is required. This is necessary insofar as knowledge of nature also has its source in an interest in the facticity of nature and the significance and importance of its content. Perhaps the distinction needed here can be made in the following way. If we look at the matter exactly, the feeling of significance that we have in relation to nature is not ascribed to the natural object, but rather to knowledge of the natural object. On the other hand, the sort of significance that we call "historical" is ascribed to the object itself. No matter how pronounced our interest in the chemical structure of the elements, the relationship between light and electricity, the evolution of organisms, or the composition of atmospheric air, we still know that these phenomena, so fascinatingly mysterious and complex, all obey the same simple, indifferent laws. The same laws hold when we move a piece of furniture or push some object against its base. Suppose we view nature as an objective whole without considering the extremely diverse relationships which our knowledge and our cognitive capacities bear to nature. Then natural objects exhibit no essential differences at all. Without these differences, however, it is impossible for our mode of feeling, which is tied to distinctions and discriminations, to establish an interest. The same point invariably holds for all processes of the transformation of matter and energy to which no meaning or value of any sort can be ascribed. There is a certain property of knowledge of natural processes that often escapes us. In the case of some processes, we have not been aware of this property for a long time; in the case of many, we have only been unaware of it for a short time; and in the case of most, we are completely unaware of it. Some matters are easily accessible to our knowledge, others only with difficulty. Our categories and syntheses distinguish phenomena into the simple and the complex. This fact alone differentiates the monotonous process of a natural event into essential and inessential aspects, those aspects which are interesting and those which are insignificant. The fact that the differential properties of knowledge distribute our interest in nature differently marks the birth of our interest in the singular problem within the natural sciences. In the things themselves, considered objectively, there are no differences that could be responsible for the creation of such an interest.

Within the categories of history, however, distinctions of significance and importance lie in the nature of the phenomenon itself. As we penetrate natural processes more deeply, as the differences of distance between these processes and our cognitive capacities level out, nature becomes all the more abstract. The sense in which it appears to be governed by a formal "equality before the law" is even stronger. The singularity of natural phenomena—which is, of course, disclosed by a more careful investigation of natural processes—is only a property of their form. It only concerns the complications of the conditions under which general laws apply to them. In view of the mutual conversion of forms of energy and the variations in forms of matter, however, it can have no bearing upon their most basic principle. On the contrary, this is a principle that governs all natural objects. In this light, consider phenomena that we call "historical." As we penetrate historical processes more deeply, their individuality becomes more significant. Therefore we approximate all the more closely the mysterious point from which the total quality of the personality emanates. It is a self-contained world of its own that is independent of everything else that exists. Of course the spheres of the general and the particular alternate within the natural sciences as well as in history. In any inquiry, the problem is to identify, through a more refined analysis, the concrete differentia which lie behind every observed regularity. Then the problem becomes the following: how can these concrete differentia be reduced to general laws and types? In other words, we play off one principle against the other in a dialectical and heuristic fashion. The process of inquiry itself has the same properties in both cases, but the directions which inquiry pursues in history and natural science are mutually exclusive. In the case of some phenomena, the inquiry is concluded with the discovery of a general law; in the case of others, the inquiry ends with the discovery of a singular entity. This point holds regardless of whether the inquiry can actually be completed or must remain inconclusive in principle. In many respects, the tempo or rhythm of the inquiry is the same.

As a result of these differences in the definitive theoretical aim or purpose, however, two different inquiries may be distinguished: natural science and history. The feeling of significance or importance—without which we would not find it worth the trouble to acquire knowledge of the content of any idea—has no direct counterpart within the domain of natural objects. Nature as a whole may hold a metaphysical interest for us, and it may arouse our emotions. Consider, on the other hand, individual natural objects. Ultimately, they are totally undifferentiable. Of course individual natural objects might interest us aesthetically because of differences in their perceptual or sensible form. But the individual natural object can acquire a scientific interest only as a result of the distance or perspective that we occupy in relation to the arbitrary and provisional character of our incomplete knowledge. The extreme diversity of natural objects obscures the monotonous uniformity which their objective nature presents in relation to our sense of discrimination. However the kind of substantive significance or importance which motivates the historical interest is a property of the objects themselves. These objects arouse our interest because of their essential and intrinsic existential properties: they are necessarily both extremely diverse and also pre-defined or discriminated.

At this point, we can also see the difference between the historical interest and the psychological interest. The subject matter of history is an *existential* object to which a significance can be directly ascribed. Psychology, on the other hand, is invariably concerned with *abstractions,* the identification of lawlike or quasi-lawlike relationships which invariably obtain whenever their conditions are satisfied—even if, in reality, these conditions are only satisfied on one unique occasion. In the discussion of psychological reality, atemporal psychological constructs are applied to given historical material. In other words, it is no longer simply a purely psychological problem. Consider the definitive and differential significance which is peculiar to the personal and the mental. This is the basis for the distinction between an interest in history and an interest in the natural sciences. This distinction should not be confounded with the difference between the historical interest and the interest in scientific psychology—the latter difference is established by reference to the interest of history in the existential fact. This distinguishes history from the abstract atemporality of psychology; however it is the historical interest in the significance or importance of facts that differentiates it from natural science.

10. *Metaphysical and Empirical Questions in History*

Here, therefore, are the general metatheoretical interests of history. Their dialectical interpenetration and fusion produce the theoretical interest in history. They are not a priori presuppositions in the sense of the Kantian a priori and its variations which were discussed earlier: presuppositions which are immanent to science and which determine its logical structure. On the contrary, they are related to history in much the same way that the earth is related to the roots of a plant. It is true that plants have their own laws of development; however the fact that they have the possibility and the potentiality of developing according to these laws is due to the soil that grounds and nourishes them. Consider the fact that history has any meaning at all for us, both from the standpoint of the substance of history and from the standpoint of historical inquiry. This fact is logically dependent upon the following: the content of the cosmic process and its empirical reality release two currents of interest. When they flow into a certain eddy, it could be said that they form only one interest. These matters lie beneath history as its foundation; they do not influence the actual process of historical inquiry in detail. In the form of metaphysics, they transcend history. As such they preserve—or at least they should preserve—the restraint, reserve, and distance characteristics of metaphysics.

What is it that makes historical inquiry possible in principle? Consider the following facts. Within the chaos of events and the fragmentary data concerning their properties, it is possible to discover a meaning that can be articulated. In the absence of such a meaning—and there is no sense in which this view can be conflated with some sort of atavistic teleology—not even the most realistic and descriptive history would be possible. At least within limited periods of history, it is possible to identify progress, or a balance of constructive and destructive forces, or a decline of all values. The unconscious energies of individuals—which seem to proceed from thousands of different motives—ultimately produce significant results, a single product that is the consequence of their concomitant energies. A value—or a negative value—may be ascribed to the existence of history as a whole. Suppose that all these facts are detached from their function as interests and presuppositions for the structure of historical knowledge. And suppose that they acquire a unified and logically complete structure beyond this function. The result is the metaphysics of history. A given metaphysical theory places exclusive stress upon one of these focal points of interest, which interest is crystallized or reified as the absolute meaning of all historical reality. This may only amount to an intellectual game, a free play of the fantasy that only satisfies its own conditions, but there is a more profound basis for the legitimacy of this undertaking. It lies in the following consideration: the roots of this sort of metaphysics are the interests without which history, knowledge of what has taken place, would not be possible. The metaphysics of history rises above and beyond the structure that rests upon it until it acquires a transcendental status. It is a case of one of those typical turns of intellectual phenomena. The mind is fond of projecting what is most deeply rooted in its own essential nature as far away as possible. For the mind, objectivity lies at what might be called an intermediate distance. Consider, however, what is most intrinsic and essential to the mind, the product of the most subjective levels of mental activity. The mind projects this into an absolute, super-objective or trans-objective sphere. It is as if the mind can regain its equilibrium or emancipate itself from the all too confining isolation and privacy of subjectivity only by means of this leap into the other extreme.[18]

Consider these interests. Insofar as their contents become intellectually crystallized or objectified, they generate the metaphysical meaning of history. In reality, these interests do not have the status of an indifferent, uniform infra-structure or sub-structure, a structure that remains without any definitive influence upon the exact science of history that is constructed upon it—just to the contrary. In addition to the general interests, without which history as a science would be impossible, and pure metaphysics, other special presuppositions can always be identified in the structure of history, presuppositions that transcend all empirical knowledge. They are not the a priori presuppositions which make possible the logical or immanent form of history. On the contrary, they are principles of substantive import, conditions under which it is possible for us to ascribe value to historical knowledge. In relation to nature, these presuppositions—which Kant called "ideas of reason"—remain speculations that lie beyond the structure of empirical facts. But they are immanent to history. In historical research, should we emphasize the publication of primary sources or comprehensive summary descriptions? Should the emphasis fall on profiles of otherwise disparate complexes of phenomena or upon sequences in which some homogeneous entity develops? There is no sense in which these are merely questions of method, technique, and form. On the contrary, insofar as they are concerned with method, technique, and form, they also express certain ideas and sentiments about the nature and significance of the historical facts themselves, even though they do not alter the immediate substantive content of these facts. I shall not pursue all these constitutive, metatheoretical, and metaphysical presuppositions in a systematic fashion. Instead, I shall offer the following by way of a conclusion to these investigations. It is an account of the determination of the construct of history by these presuppositions. At this point, we shall consider their bearing upon the structure of two completely different problems.

11. Illustrations of the Structure of General Historical Problems: The Concept of Progress in History

The first problem concerns the idea of progress in history. At the outset, it is clear that the concept of progress presupposes the idea of a final state. Suppose that some subsequent state of affairs is characterized as relatively more progressive than the present in the following sense: either it approximates this final state more closely than the present, or it realizes the properties of this final state to a higher degree. Such a characterization is logically dependent upon a complete and absolute definition of the properties of this final state. Suppose that we see in history a periodic pendulum movement between epochs that are more individualistic and others that are more collectivistic. One historian might see the individualistic epochs as the genuinely progressive periods. In this case, collectivistic epochs only appear as the occasional obstacles and inevitable moments of decline that are inseparable from every form of progress. Another historian might interpret the collectivistic epochs as the genuinely progressive periods. From his standpoint, only the collectivistic structure of society seems to be of genuine value. Therefore he can identify progress in the natural course of history only insofar as a movement in this direction can be identified. In other words, the question of whether we see some kind of progress in history is dependent upon an ideal. The value of this ideal cannot be identified in the facts of history. Its origins are extraneous to the historical process itself; they are necessarily subjective.

Suppose that we consider the possibility of a purely formal concept of progress, a kind of progress that is independent of any specific substantive final end or state. This would be similar to Kant's attempt to establish a formal ethics, a scheme or a criterion for morality in general. Depending upon the circumstances, this criterion could be satisfied by the most diverse contents imaginable. Such a formal concept of progress, therefore, would be a general concept. Its content would identify the properties common to all the substantively different progressive sequences: the enrichment as well as the annihilation of human life, the intellectualization of the spirit as well as its moral perfection, collectivization as well as individualization. Under these conditions, it would be possible to speak of progress in an objective sense whenever historical events exhibit the required form. This would even be possible when—from the standpoint of material contradictions between different subjectively grounded ascriptions of value—no progress of any sort could be identified. This possibility would be parallel to the following. Suppose that the moral agent is defined by reference to a good will and a consciousness of duty. In that case, it would be possible to ascribe morality to a person's conduct even though, from the perspective of the substance or content of the act, his action is inconsistent with his obligations.

However this hypothesis of a purely formal and objective concept of historical progress is logically objectionable. In the case of the formal moral criterion just considered, there are two logically and psychologically distinguishable elements: the conviction or intention—the *terminus a quo* or motive for the action—and the objective aim or purpose of conduct. Given a single action, therefore, it is possible without contradiction to ascribe a value to one of these elements, but not to the other. But consider the two aspects of the idea of progress: the idea of some sort of change that takes place and the idea that more value can be ascribed to the latter moment of this change than to the earlier moment. The logical properties of this idea are quite different. The latter moment is absolutely variable. The concept of value does not contain any general element which is independent of the subjective ascription of values. Change is actually the property common to all forms of progress. Considered by itself, however, change is not a sufficient criterion for the application of this concept. This is because change is also the property common to all forms of retrogression or decline.

In view of the foregoing, the following move seems to be necessary, and sometimes, of course, this move is actually made. The mere fact of change as such, independent of any eventual end or goal that it may have, constitutes progress. This even holds true for movements of retrogression or decline. Since they represent change, they qualify as progress, even though the value of the complete progressive event may be diminished by the baseness of its content. Given this view of progress, its extreme polar antithesis is not decline. It is inertia or stagnation, a variation in the philosophy of history upon Fichte's view that inertia or laziness is the explanation of radical evil. Considered more exactly, however, this concept of progress only expresses a subjective valuation or a metaphysical dogma. Given the logical and conceptual import of the concept of progress, mere variability or change *cannot* qualify as progress; a change is progressive only if it is also felt to represent a value. This may eventually be the case independent of the content that is realized by the change in question. However there are certain conservative views that regard change itself as an evil: change represents a negative value. These views, moreover, are logically unobjectionable. It follows that, from the standpoint of *logic,* the concept of change is not sufficient to constitute a general, formal concept of progress. Change could qualify as progress only by reference to the ascription of some value that is ultimately grounded upon individual subjectivity.

Consider now the following move, which is quite characteristic of the structure of the concept of progress. As a ground or basis for progress, a metaphysical construct replaces the subjective ascription of a value. In this case, perhaps change could simply qualify as progress on the following grounds: either at the end of all things, or perhaps distributed pro rata throughout every process of change, there is a definitive end or goal to which absolute value can be ascribed. This definitive end of all things is not a possible object of knowledge. We can have no knowledge of *what* its properties are; we can only be certain *that* it will appear. A certain kind of chiliastic religious faith as well as a certain kind of liberal optimism are both representative of this type of concept of progress. On the basis of this sort of thinking, any change at all can qualify as progress, even though—from the perspective of our values—such a change may represent retrogression or decline. From the perspective of the total cosmic process, however, the latter is not possible. Decline or retrogression can be no more than a temporary diminution, in the form of stagnation, in the rate of progress. This view of progress, therefore, transcends the subjectivity of the concept of value, a subjectivity that has its source in the heterogeneity and variability of the contents of values. As a result of this translation or transposition into the anonymity of the absolute, it is logically possible to represent every change as progress. It seems to me that this sort of metaphysical construct is the only possible formal concept of progress, a concept that is independent of the singularity and subjectivity of the ascription of values. Therefore it should be quite clear how far beyond the facts of history it is necessary to extrapolate in order to identify what allegedly constitutes progress.

In addition to the subjectivity or the transcendence of the ideal by reference to which actual historical changes may qualify as progress, there is another possibility. On this view, the problem of historical progress is situated in the deeper layers of the structure of history. Let us even suppose that there is agreement concerning the ideal that constitutes progress. Nevertheless, the question of whether actual empirical realizations of this value should be described as progress still turns on a definition of a concept that is quite variable. For example, it is possible that the historical moments to which value can be ascribed have their origins in some form of spontaneous generation. These moments are not necessarily the product of a gradual process of evolution. The empirical structure that corresponds to these ideals could be the contingent and arbitrary product of forces of nature—forces which, in the next moment, might produce the extreme polar opposite of this structure. Also the realization of these values is not necessarily a consequence of forces that are immanent to history; it could be a result of intervention by transcendent powers. Consider religious views of the world in which the advent of the savior or the idea of a day of final judgment have this status. We cannot speak of progress in history in either of these two cases. Consider especially the first case. It is possible to describe this as an instance of historical progress only if the state of value that history realizes has, in some sense, the property of definitiveness or ultimacy. It is not necessary to guarantee that inertia and counter-movements will not delay or diminish historical progress from time to time, but it is essential to guarantee that the realization of this final, definitive value has what might be called the last word. In particular, reality must not be a dependent variable of some mechanism the operation of which is utterly indifferent to the realization of this value.[19]

The mere fact that there are progressive epochs which are identified by reference to some ideal, is not a sufficient condition for progress in history. On the contrary, it is necessary to suppose that there is an immanent structure that connects the fragmentary and temporally discontinuous realizations of this ideal. This structure must have the following property: in spite of its discontinuity, it persists throughout epochs that have a different tendency. A given partial realization of this ideal must be structured in such a way that its termination leads to a higher realization of the ideal. The claim that there is progress in history presupposes a certain kind of subterranean connection between the periods that are identified by reference to their positive relationship to the ideal. Moreover, this connection must be a consequence of a force that transcends each of its past effects or phenomena, a force sufficiently powerful to ensure that the mechanism of history, in spite of all interferences and deviations, will continue to function in the general direction of the realization of the ideal. The claim that history represents progress definitively rules out the relationship of mere chance or contingency that would otherwise obtain between our ideals and real, mechanical forces. The fact that the forces of nature sometimes function in such a way that our ideals are realized is not sufficient to constitute historical progress. The processes and epochs that develop and culminate as a result of these forces must constitute a homogeneous process of development. The construction and the understanding of later epochs cannot be deduced from knowledge of the immediately preceding external situation and its determining factors. On the contrary, this requires knowledge of their relationship to the earlier stages, perhaps quite remote, of the realization of the ultimate value of history.

There is also another direction from which the concept of progress weaves the metaphysical woof into the warp of the historical event. The concept of progress presupposes that the entity to which progress is ascribed has the status of a homogeneous substance. Consider a number of processes the contents of which exhibit progressive movement in the direction of some ideal. If we discover that this movement proceeds from different, distinguishable substances, we would deny that it qualifies as progress. Consider also what we mean when we say that nature exhibits a form of progress that leads from the lowest and simplest organisms to increasingly complex or higher forms. In this case, we have in mind, often quite vaguely, a certain entity that evolves throughout these developing forms, a certain relationship to a subject—"nature" or "organic life" or something of this sort—to which progress is ascribed, the entity which persists throughout all the sequences of these forms. Even if we consider the matter linguistically, we can see that the unity of a grammatical subject is required—a subject to which progress can be ascribed—in order for it to make sense to say that progress takes place. Consider a sequence of states that increasingly realize some value. We would not ascribe progress to these states if we discovered that they are realized on different stars. In other words, the concept of progress in nature presupposes the synthesis of these dispersed and divergent values in a *Weltgeist* or a concept of nature. The same holds for the concept of progress in history; it presupposes a homogeneous subject to which progress can be ascribed. If this presupposition does not hold, then it would still make sense to say that one state of affairs is better or of more value than another. But it could not be claimed that one state is more progressive than another; this latter claim implies a real relationship between the two states in question, a relationship that can only obtain between two states of one and the same subject.

The only apparent exception to the foregoing claims concerning the concept of historical progress is the development of what is called the objective spirit. This is a seductive and potentially misleading idea. Consider the objective results of historical processes: laws, objects of art, technological advances, and ecclesiastical dogmas, customs of social intercourse and scientific knowledge. They form sequences in which we can identify progress, and not only in the sense that they constitute or signify progress on the part of the group that produces them. As a result of a certain kind of methodological abstraction, we regard these objectifications of evolving group life as purely objective developments. One stage, considering only its objective meaning and totally independent of the motive force that produced it or the entity that bears or represents it, constitutes progress in relation to some earlier stage. Law and art, technology and science simply evolve "themselves" or "on their own." In this case, however, language creates an ideal subject to which discontinuously juxtaposed objects of art—or equally discontinuous fragments of knowledge that have no substantial unity, or other similar objectifications of group life—may be linked as its evolutionary products. Suppose we consider these evolutionary products simply in terms of their objective content. Suppose that their temporal sequence constitutes an objectively or logically progressive series. And suppose also that this series is described as an historical development. Then our criteria for knowledge require that the following a priori condition of historical progress be satisfied: we can identify a homogeneous subject that persists within all the otherwise fragmentary and atomistic moments of history. This is the condition under which these moments constitute a coherent process of *evolution* or *development.* Consider this purely objective sort of progress: evolution in an impersonal, nonhistorical sense. Even this sort of evolution is impossible unless it is conceived as the development of an ideal mind or spirit; for example, a purely rational spirit or a mind to which a personal and psychological identity can be ascribed. Consider, for example, the stages of the history of philosophy as Brentano has described them. They constitute a process of *development* insofar as we have the feeling that one of these phases can be derived *psychologically* from another. Consider the ideal entity that is symbolized in the expression "philosophy evolves" or "philosophy experiences a development." This seems to be the result of a feeling that the subject projects onto philosophy: a feeling of ascent, a continuous, immanent movement that is experienced in the idea of philosophical content. It is the increasing intensity of this feeling and the value associated with it that constitute the temporal sequence of events as a process of development.

Consider, therefore, the objective spirit. It seems to be the most likely candidate for an example of historical development that does not require the ascription of a subject, but it does not constitute a counterexample to the above remarks after all. Such a homogeneous subject is all the more necessary when the issue concerns the concrete totality of historical movements. Any projection of characteristics onto a homogeneous substance as their bearer is admittedly of a transcendental nature. It follows that the inclusion of peoples and individuals in one evolving totality—which is a necessary condition for the identification of progress in history—is really only a subjective synthesis. It acquires a metaphysical status as a result of its projection onto objective reality. Consider the following propositions. Although the persons may change, a homogeneous subject persists throughout history. There is a primeval cell the evolution of which produces the epochs of human history; this cell is the unit by reference to which an epoch qualifies as progressive or regressive. These propositions constitute a metaphysical presupposition without which the concept of progress would not be possible.

12. Historical Materialism

The foregoing problem concerning history in general is defined by reference to the *terminus ad quem* or end of history. In addition to this problem and by way of conclusion, I shall also pose another. This issue centers on the *terminus a quo* or motive force of history. Like the discussion of the foregoing problem, this account will also establish that the empirical facts acquire a coherent historical meaning only as a result of the constitutive power of meta-empirical presuppositions. The problem I should like to pose now concerns so-called historical materialism. According to this theory, the properties of economic life and the structures and processes of group life, which are a function of the production and distribution of the means of existence, determine the whole of historical life: both domestic and foreign policy, religion and art, law and technology. To what extent has this principle been applied to the facts of history with some plausibility? To what extent is it possible to produce a temporal and substantive schematization of events and states which establishes that they can all be causally reduced to relations of the productive process? These questions are irrelevant to the present discussion: our exclusive interest is in the epistemological structure of the theory and the various kinds of epistemic assumptions that bear upon it.

What the theory seems to offer is a unified psychological interpretation of history. Marx, of course, stresses the point that hunger alone is not sufficient to make history. However the relations of the production and exchange of material goods would also lack the power to make history if hunger did not cause pain. Hunger, therefore, is the motive force behind these relations. It follows that the description of this theory as "materialist" is misleading. It is obvious that the theory has nothing to do with any sort of metaphysical materialism. On the contrary, it is consistent with any monistic or dualistic view of the nature of mental processes. In this context, perhaps "materialism" could simply signify that history is ultimately dependent upon nonmental forces or energies; however this view is inconsistent with the content of the theory itself. According to historical materialism, there is an important sense in which history is psychologically motivated. It is evident that variations in historical content must be dependent upon factors other than hunger. Since hunger is always present as a constant and invariable factor, it cannot explain these variations; hunger is, as we might put it, the steam that drives the engines of history, even though the construction of these engines may be extremely diverse. The greatness of the theory lies in the following source. It attempts to discover the ultimate motive force that lies concealed within the contradictions and transformations of history, a force of elemental simplicity that can reveal unity within the infinite complexity of the mechanisms of historical life. Historical materialism is simply a psychological hypothesis like those discussed in the first chapter. Mental processes lie behind the external, observable behavior of human beings. In the final analysis, these mental processes may be traced to the interest in the "production and reproduction of material life." A certain property of the theory is responsible for the fact that its hypothetical character is easily concealed. The mental impulse from which the theory derives events in the human world has the indubitable status of a matter of fact. The undeniably empirical status of this basic impulse seems to imply that the structure based on this foundation also has an empirical status.

This is the first of several points concerning the special significance of historical materialism for the fundamental problem of this book: the refutation of historical realism. It is precisely this theory, historical materialism, that represents itself as the most literal reproduction of reality. And yet here too we can prove, step by step, that the structuring of the empirically given data is determined by the theoretical and metatheoretical presuppositions and requirements of the autonomous intellect. However this particular error concerning the epistemological significance of the method of historical materialism does not diminish the substantial contribution it has made—as a result of the discovery of new causal relationships—to the actual praxis of historical research.

The foregoing is a point of principle or logic. Historical materialism does not have the certainty to which it pretends, the certainty of a physiological fact; it only has the hypothetical value of a psychological reconstruction. But this does not diminish the importance of the theory—just to the contrary. Consider now another issue: the problem of the *selection* or *choice* which historical materialism has made from the range of possible ultimate motives or causes of history. As regards its actual empirical appearance, human life presents a bewildering complexity of sequential series of interests. Like strands of different thread in a fabric, they are interwoven through consciousness, the relations of power, and the external phenomenon itself. Each interest, considered independent of all the others, is homogeneous and continuous, but only limited aspects of any given interest appear on the actual surface of life. The interest functions at a deeper level, beneath the aspects that intermittently appear on the surface. On the level of human life as it is actually experienced, no interest is independently identifiable. Religion and the economy, individual life and the constitution of the state, art and law, sciences and forms of marriage—all are inextricably interwoven. This is the source of what we call history. Its moments are continuous, and each moment is identifiable in all of the others. These moments exhibit the following variation. At different points in space and time and at different levels of consciousness, a given moment may acquire a dominant interest. This explains a possibility mentioned above. Although there are only partial and specialized histories, but no history as such, there is, nevertheless, an "idea" of "history in general" that transcends all these fragmentary histories. This idea provides a synthesis of the spatio- temporal interrelations of all these sequences. "History as such" is a unified entity that we cannot grasp directly; however the idea of this entity prevents our construct of history from collapsing into incoherent splinters and fragments.

We owe to historical materialism a novel and partial realization and a cogent demonstration of this a priori, ideal entity. Historical materialism has made it plausible to suppose that the evolution of the economy and the development of ideal values, which seem to be utterly unrelated, are intimately connected, at least at many points. Suppose we think that this intimate functional interconnection, which holds for both facts and laws, is revealed throughout the entire course of history. Then it follows that we could conceive all historical contents as a function of economic development. Given the laws that govern this correlation, it could be established that all historical states and events are functions of economic phenomena. In other words, the history of the economy is the symbol of history in general. Any approximation to this theoretical possibility may, of course, be very significant. However this possibility entails the following presupposition. The role of the ultimate explanans of the totality of history may be ascribed with equal legitimacy to every historical moment. In this respect, the economy is no different from all the other sequences that make up history. Consider the history of forms of government or customs of social intercourse, intellectual

cultivation or criminal law. There is a complete continuity of relationship between each of these histories and every other history,
even though this relationship may be indirect and more or less
remote. Therefore each of these histories could function as the
ultimate epistemic basis for a complete or universal history. Historical materialism, of course, claims that economic processes constitute
both the epistemic ground and the ontological ground of all other
phenomena. From the standpoint of this theory, economic processes
constitute the motive force or cause of all other historical phenomena. Ultimately, however, the different categories of events and
processes are indistinguishable. Therefore this particular thesis of
historical materialism seems to be a premature and dogmatic fore-
shortening of our ontological perspective.

Consider the following example. We are told that large-scale
industry—as a consequence of its supplies of raw material and the
markets for its products—does not require a plurality of small nation-
states; therefore *large-scale industry* produced the large, unified
nation-states of the recent era, namely Italy and Germany. Suppose
that this particular causal relationship could be demonstrated. What
about France and England? Their national status can hardly be
explained as a consequence of large-scale industry. Perhaps these
nation-states might be represented as the products of other economic
causes that prevailed during this earlier period. Once in existence,
however, they favor the origin of large-scale industry. In other words,
the functional relationship that obtains in other cases—the large
nation-state as a consequence of large-scale industry—is inverted. But
in these other cases, the large nation-state, once in existence, creates
innumerable large industries. In other words, the reciprocal relations
at stake here are infinitely complex. From the standpoint of our
possibilities of knowledge, the process whereby these relations
develop has no identifiable origin. Therefore the moment with which
we terminate an historical explanation—the moment to which we
ascribe the ultimate cause of all subsequent historical phenomena—is
quite arbitrary. *Each* moment that bears upon a given historical
sequence is obviously a condition for the development of ensuing
sequences.

Consider another example from the literature on Marxism.
Calvin's theory of predestination is represented as nothing more than
the expression of a certain fact. In the commercial world of competition, success or bankruptcy is not determined by the industry and
ingenuity of the entrepreneur. It is a consequence of unknown,

supremely powerful forces. This fact is alleged to have a special validity for that particular period of economic turmoil and revolution. Let us suppose that this thesis is more than an intellectual joke. To take this view at all seriously is to admit that the inverse relationship might just as well hold. Consider a community that has become fatalistic for purely religious reasons. Such a community would also be disposed to fatalistic convictions in all other human relations. Therefore this community would have a disposition in favor of a laissez-faire economy—a result of the conviction that all foresight and precaution, all human teleology and planning are utterly pointless.

Suppose, therefore, we see history as an interwoven fabric in which qualitatively different kinds of event-sequences are interconnected. Given this picture of history, we must admit that historical materialism has achieved a hitherto unattained synthesis of the totality of historical data. In a reduction of extraordinary simplicity, the whole of history is tuned to a single key-note. But consider the claim that historical materialism provides a naturalistic reproduction of reality. This is a methodological error of the first class. It confuses the conceptual construct of the event—a product of our theoretical interests—with the immediacy of the actual, empirical occurrence of the event itself. It also confuses a principle that has an heuristic import, and should always be employed in an exploratory fashion, with a constitutive principle, an assumption from which the facts of history are derived. Consider the claim that the economic motive is the self-conscious cause of human consciousness; even the non-economic contents of consciousness are a function of the economic motive. No one would maintain this. No one knows what transpires in the unconscious and what kinds of causal relations obtain within this medium. Therefore only one possible sense remains as the import of the thesis of historical materialism: events occur *as if* the economic motive governed human behavior. On the other hand, consider the relationship between the external observable contents of history and its inner, unobservable contents, the sort of connection that historical materialism has emphasized so forcefully. Suppose we also consider the variations in which first one motive and then another alternatively dominate consciousness. These considerations include the following possibility: every other conceivable interest may also function as an heuristic principle. In this light, consider the great achievement of historical materialism. From the standpoint of their intrinsic content and value, our interests are polar antitheses. In the process of their historical realization, however, historical materialism has established that there is an intimate relationship between these interests. Precisely this achievement deprives the basic economic motive of its privileged status. It is only an heuristic principle from which facts of other categories can be *explained* or *derived,* facts which could also be explained or derived from other principles. Of course the methodological utility of this particular illusion lies in the following consideration. The extent and the limits within which a principle legitimately holds can be established with certainty only if the principle is applied in an absolutely radical fashion. The dogmatic exploitation of the consequences of this kind of illusion are ruled out as soon as these principles are transformed into heuristic maxims. But consider the elimination of the naturalistic conception of these principles and its replacement by a more prudent view, a view according to which the principle is only an heuristic device. The formation of the raw material of history by means of our *epistemic* requirements is most emphatically not a realistic reproduction of objects by the mind. On the contrary, the mind constitutes these items as the objects of a scientific investigation.

Suppose history is viewed as an interwoven and constantly interweaving fabric spun from many closely coordinated pieces of cloth. Materialism is obviously not in agreement with this view. For historical materialism, the economy, which is located in the most basic historical stratum, is the permanent and self-sufficient condition for all other developments. It is an undercurrent which does not alternate with the currents of other developments. It is the source from which they flow. In relation to other historical phenomena, the economy might be called the historical thing-in-itself. Historical materialism is possible as a constitutive principle only under the conditions entailed by this structure; given this structure, however, the construct of history becomes problematical.

This particular difficulty arises insofar as historical materialism is conceived as a metaphysics. Let us suppose that the development of morals and law, religion and art, etc. follow the curve of economic development without influencing economic changes in any essential way. In that case, I simply do not see how the transformations of economic life itself can be explained. We are told that the invention of firearms, the discovery of America, and the intellectual fertility that distinguished the close of the Middle Ages do not provide the cause of the transition from feudal and natural forms of economy to the economic forms of the modern era. On the contrary, the economic changes in question demand and produce these intellectual, technological, and territorial expansions. But why do human beings not remain permanently satisfied with a natural or feudal economy? At least originally, there was supposed to be an absolute correspondence between every form of production and its age, but "the age" in which any form of production is located is defined exclusively by reference to the form of production itself. Therefore it is not at all clear how subsequent contradictions—between the forces of production and the forms of production—could develop from this initial state of correspondence. Facts of other categories are supposed to have no role in producing changes in the form of production. It follows that every stage of economic development must contain the forces responsible for its own transformation—a self-generating process. It takes place without cross-fertilization of any sort, a kind of parthenogenesis of the economy. The pure immanence of this process is reflected in expressions of the following sort. The forms of production in a given epoch are said to have become "outdated" or "antiquated"; new forces of production are said to have "developed"; new societal forms are said to be in a state of "evolution." These expressions are only empty phrases, not much better than an explanation of these changes by reference to the "force of time." It is almost as if an initial quantity of vital energy were granted to every economic epoch, a quantity that gradually exhausts itself. But suppose that *reciprocal causal relationships* between all historical factors are excluded in principle. Then *what* can be responsible for the exhaustion of one form of production, the increasing tensions and contradictions, and the birth of new economic forms? It seems that this question can be answered only on the basis of an obscure metaphysics, a metaphysics in which the concept of the "autonomous movement of the idea" still survives.

However it is not our purpose to engage in a fruitless polemic against historical materialism. On the contrary, we want to learn what contribution this "realistic" theory of history can make to the refutation of realism. Perhaps the rigorous internal consistency which is the hallmark of historical materialism only exhibits with a peculiar clarity the metaphysics implied in every other theory of history. It is impossible for us to gain a perspicuous view of the reciprocal causal relations of *all* historical factors; however this reciprocal causal nexus is the only genuinely unified entity in history. It follows that any coherent construct of the total historical process is possible only as a result of an artificial, one-sided partiality or bias. Of course we can inquire into the individual developmental sequences of a great historical epoch and follow their development into another epoch. If we examine this matter exactly, however, we can see that the total character of each epoch is invariably only a presupposition on which the inquiry rests. As I emphasized above, a given stage of a sequence is never the complete cause of the next stage; on the contrary, any subsequent stage can only be a result of all the simultaneous consequences of all other sequences. In view of the conditions under which historical knowledge is possible, however, it is absolutely necessary to construct individual sequences as if they were self-sufficient and self-contained. The result is inevitable: the immanent self-development of the sequence in question. In innumerable cases we replace the causes which produce a new stage of development—causes which proceed from the totality of the cosmic process—with purely inner or immanent droves which may be compared to occult qualities. In the same way that more or less mysterious "evolutionary instincts" have been ascribed to organisms, certain transformations and developments appear in historical inquiry as if their growth were self-evident—at least this holds true for historical inquiries that supplement the genuinely explanatory reciprocal causation of historical elements. It is as if a certain rhythm of growth and decline, self-perpetuation and aberration were inherent from the beginning in the self-contained unity of historical subjects. In specific cases, this metaphysics is difficult to identify. This is because it appears very irregularly and in a very rudimentary fashion; also it is an aspect of the naive mode of historical thought. It could be said that historical materialism places this metaphysics in relief. Historical materialism ascribes an autonomous evolution to one sequence of events. This sequence influences the other sequences without being influenced by them. Therefore the individual historical forms of this sequence are purely immanent products of the sequence itself. Their evolution is the product of an initial, given, developmental tendency.

At this point, however, historical materialism exhibits a property that is related to the methodological principle defended in this book. The foregoing criticisms are only directed against the illusory idea that it is possible to construct a realistic reproduction of history. Actually, historical constructs are creations of the requirements of our *epistemic* or *theoretical categories.* One historical materialist seems to agree with this criticism: he stresses that his theory is justified by the consideration that *historical development is not the same as the totality of human life.* There is no sense in which everything that we experience falls within the domain of history, which only includes items that evolve or develop. However human life includes many constant factors that have no "history": for example, procreation, child-bearing, digestion, etc. It is obvious that this distinction imposes an extremely important conceptual dichotomy upon existence. In each moment, both the constant and the variable components of existence form an indivisible unity. Consider the invariable elements of the corporeal and the logical, desires and feelings, sense impressions and inter-individual relationships. From our epistemic standpoint, they have no "history." They constitute the substance—or the accidental qualities—of the variable elements; the interrelationship of both elements constitutes the single historical moment. From the standpoint of the single moment, a given element may be experienced as constant and unambiguous, even though its properties vary before and after that moment. On the other hand, elements that have an invariably recurrent content are experienced as surprises, absolutely unrepeatable in their combinations and consequences. When the materialist claims that history is only concerned with the variable elements of existence, he acknowledges that history amounts to a process of selection. Inevitably, it is a novel synthesis of the elements of reality. The constant factors—which, together with the variable factors, constitute absolute reality as it is actually experienced—are excluded from history. The remaining variable elements, therefore, must be placed in novel relationships that are peculiar to them. In this respect, history is comparable to a work of art that only comprehends the impressions of *one* sense; such a work of art can give these impressions a form only by means of relationships that are peculiar to *this* sense. However the actual counterpart of the object of art exists as an entity only as a result of many other relational forms.

Consider this distinction between history and the totality of all events, the view according to which history is constituted exclusively from the variable elements of events. This view amounts to an absolutely unequivocal rejection of naive realism. It is a declaration of the sovereign independence of the category over the raw material of history. Moreover, this view has other logical consequences that are worth considering. "We are told that the economic conception of history does not pretend to explain the following facts and derive them exhaustively from economic conditions: that Caesar had no children and adopted Octavian, that Antony fell in love with Cleopatra, that Lepidus was a weakling. However the theory does claim that it can explain the collapse of the Roman Republic and the rise of Caesarism." Notice that these latter historical concepts are clearly comprehensive. Their real referents are plain, individual, concretely determinable facts, facts which the first proposition in this quotation acknowledges are historically inexplicable. Therefore it seems that individual events and processes do not qualify as history. They become history only insofar as they fall under developmental concepts that make it possible to identify the "variability" of a given sequence, conditions comparable to those prerequisite to the existence of space. Sense impressions—which, as such, do not have the property of extensionality—are the objects of a synthesis produced by the conceptual form of extensionality. In the same way, singular facts acquire the import which qualifies them as history insofar as they fall under the special category of variability, which itself is not a property inherent in any individual fact; on the contrary, it is a consequence of the relationships, the comparisons, and the developmental units that the historian imposes upon the facts.

Here as elsewhere, however, historical materialism limits the logical significance of its own methodology. This is a consequence of the one-sidedness of the theoretical aim to which its methodology is restricted. The variable element, the only element that qualifies as history, is the economy. All other elements are essentially constant; they change only as a result of variations in the economy. This thesis makes it perfectly clear how arbitrarily the economy usurps the dominant position in relation to its correlates, all other historical phenomena. For this reason, the thesis seems to require not so much a substantive or logical analysis, but rather a psychological analysis. Put another way, in order to elucidate this thesis, it is necessary to identify the nontheoretical motive that historical materialism expresses.

Among previous advocates of historical materialism, the politics of socialism is the motive that explains why the psychological, metaphysical, and methodological forms of their theory of history have the economy as their content. The immediate and most obvious grounds on which this move is based were discussed earlier. For a political program that concentrates on the large masses, the economic interest must be decisive—no other interest can be identified with the same certainty in every member of the mass. This is the reason, from the perspective of historical materialism, the economy seems to be the genuine variable of history. It is obvious that an absolutely rigorous distinction must be made between the invariance of the economy as a general factor in human life and the variability of concrete economic structures. Perhaps there is no other interest in which the tension between the conceptual uniformity of its typical existence and the extreme diversity of its forms and contents is so pronounced.[20] Moreover, it is not difficult to understand why an historical construct oriented to volitional and emotional tendencies will appear most convincing—and, so to say, with the best conscience—when the nature and the content of these tendencies are related to the interests of the *large masses.* An interest characteristic of an individual seems to be more determined by differential spatio-temporal circumstances. But suppose that the definitive import and significance of an interest is a consequence of the fact that it is the focal point for the interests of the masses in general. In this case, such an interest can easily appear to lie beyond all considerations of temporality and individuality, at a level of abstraction in which the interpretation of the past and the regulation of the future only appear to be two forms or aspects of the same axiological substance. There may be all sorts of differences among individuals; nevertheless, an economic interest of some sort is identifiable for everyone.

Therefore a moral and political program oriented to the large masses will—if it is not based on religious considerations—focus upon material values. The economic interest is common to both the past and the future. Consider, therefore, a political program concerned with the future and its economic structure. In order to achieve unity or simplicity, the same interest will dominate the theory of history, the theory that is concerned with the past. From the viewpoint of democratic—socialist convictions, therefore, only the economic perspective can constitute history. Assume that the individualization of the individual is complete. The universality and inevitability of the material interest is still the point at which the practical interest centering around "the masses" confronts the economic structure of history as the structure of a uniform entity and a totality.

This relationship is open to a further level of analysis. The apparent intention or purpose of any interest that focuses on the masses is egalitarian. Modern socialism may decisively repudiate a mechanical form of reductive equality. Nevertheless, the elimination of unearned privileges and differential values of the same quantity of labor that are a result of birth, competition, concentration of capital, etc. can only produce—in comparison with the present—the most radical leveling of statuses imaginable. Even if all the necessary reservations are made, this process of leveling remains a factor of principal importance for socialism, both as a propaganda technique and as an expression of one of the most fundamental axiological convictions. There will always be certain kinds of people for whom equality is a self-evident, self-justifying ideal, an axiological absolute, and there will always be other persons for whom social distance and differentiation are ultimate values. Neither view can be demonstrated or refuted, because the desire to realize either of these values is an existential quality of the personality.

The decisive point in this context is the following. It is reasonable to suppose that the sort of leveling which produces equality is possible only within the economic domain. Consider other perspectives from which equality might seem to be possible: religion and politics. In the former case, equality is not possible through institutional changes, and in the latter case, equality is impossible, even under socialism, because of the necessity of leadership. Consider other perspectives: morality or aesthetics, the energy and perfection of the individual, fate as determined by purely personal luck, temperament, and intelligence. From the standpoint of all these perspectives, the attempt to level all differential personal qualities can only appear ludicrous. The idea of such an egalitarian reduction is conceivable only within the domain of economic production and consumption. Egalitarianism in production could be achieved by the socialization of the means of production and the evaluation of all products exclusively by reference to the quantity of labor time required for their production. Equality of consumption could be achieved by a communistic program for the distribution of these products. In the most profound sense, socialism may concern much more than an economic problem. It may concern the entire man, and not simply one individual, substantive content of experience. Nevertheless, both in principle and in practice, its egalitarian tendency must be restricted to the domain of material interests. This is why the politics of socialism is biased in favor of a materialistic- economic view of life. For a socialist politics, the development of socialism is the meaning of history. For this reason, the substance of history, the real nature of history, can only be *the exclusive* complex of interests that makes this process of social leveling conceivable and possible: namely, economic interests.

At this point we can see how far historical materialism transcends a crude and purely sensual sense of the concept of materialism. Historical materialism is a logical articulation of an interpretation of history based exclusively on a final and ultimate meaning. The sense in which all of history is grounded on this meaning is radical and complete. It is so radical that this meaning—through the mediation of economism, which has become intimately associated with it as a result of actual empirical relationships—is the sole determinant of what in general falls within the domain of "history." From the same perspective, the illusion that historical materialism creates is no less radical: the view of historical materialism as a realistic conception of history, completely independent of all nonobjective factors. We are told that the materialist conception of history necessarily leads to socialism; socialism, the future of society, can be derived from this conception of history. This claim is only the consequence or the mirror image of the fact that the politics of socialism necessarily leads to this conception of history. It is the sovereignty of an *axiological* idea which, on the basis of the relationships just explained, determines what qualifies as history. From the perspective of socialism, therefore, we can understand why history can only be the realization of this value.

Of course there is a certain sense in which historical materialism is a completely realistic conception of history. Historical materialism represents itself as the absolute polar antithesis of all "idealistic" conceptions of history. These latter theories regard certain "ideas" as the causal forces of history: freedom or happiness, the cultivation of the individual or the race, religious ideals or the rationalization of life, the dialectical process or the moral order of the world. From the standpoint of this sort of metaphysics of history, historical events roll off like the pictures on the rotating reel of a film projector. Observable causality is nothing more than the relationship in the succession of the scenes of these pictures. Within this sequence, the appearance of the content of each *picture* seems to be determined by the content of the immediately preceding picture. However this relationship, which is only valid for the phenomenon, is superficial. The real driving force is the invisible reel, the motive force responsible for the appearance of every picture. It is an idea that harnesses reality with reins that are different from those of causality. In an absolute sense, it could be said that causality is impotent. Like every individual picture in the sequence, it is also incapable of actually producing the appearance of the succeeding picture by itself. This motive force is the absolute and unconditional cause of history. Individual forces only serve as mere technical means for its operation or forms that document its efficacy. From the perspective of historical materialism, precisely the contrary of this relationship obtains.

Suppose that the facts really held to a course that corresponds to one of these ideas. This would only amount to a purely external arrangement of scenes; in no sense has the ideal content of this arrangement the power to determine the content and the position of each individual scene—this is an illusion. It mistakes the conceptual content of a construct for its motive force; the idea is mistaken for the cause. The purpose of historical materialism is to destroy this illusion by unveiling the real causes of history. Ideology mistakes the effect for the cause. It ascribes properties to the cause that can only hold for the superficial *appearance* of the real event. Suppose, for example, that history really were the progressive realization of freedom. This would only be the contingent *result* in which the actual, empirical processes of history culminate, or the concept which makes them comprehensible. But historical processes themselves are the effects of much more palpable and tangible forces.

This may indeed be a useful rejoinder to certain metaphysical errors, especially those pernicious metaphysical theories that are interwoven with factual accounts as if they were precise descriptions also. Here too, however, a significant and important principle is applied in a mistaken fashion. Let us suppose that the idea as an entity or a source of metaphysical energy has no causal efficacy in history. This proposition does not exclude the possibility that an idea may have causal efficacy as a psychological event. And there is certainly no sense in which it follows from this proposition that the actual concrete motive forces of history must be materialistic and economic. The conception of the Kingdom of God as the ultimate end of history may indeed be an illusion. As a religious idea in the minds of men, however, it can have eminently real consequences. Consider the distinction between the metaphysical idea as the ultimate motive force of history and individual, empirical, historical processes as causes of other individual, empirical, historical processes. Historical materialism confuses this distinction with another: the distinction between ideal interests and material interests as the driving forces of history. The idea that the economy is ultimately the only motive force of history is the result of a *quaternio terminorum*. From the proposition that historical understanding is confined to concrete, empirical relationships of cause and effect, historical materialism fallaciously derives the proposition that these relationships are restricted to a single province of interests. This move is made because there is a sense in which both propositions deny that the "idea" has a causal efficacy in history. The first proposition only denies this status to ideas as metaphysical abstractions, but the latter proposition also denies it to ideas insofar as they have concrete, psychological meaning.

If this account describes the justifiability and the legitimate limits of historical materialism from the standpoint of its content, then a similar relationship follows as regards the methodological status of the theory. Independent of its illegitimate restriction of historical causes to the economic motive, historical materialism attempts to refute historical idealism in principle. The epistemological idealism defended in this book has the same purpose. The distinction between historical idealism and epistemological idealism is no less radical than the distinction between historical idealism and historical materialism. Actually, historical idealism is a form of epistemological realism. It does not conceive the science of history as a distinctive intellectual construct of reality determined by constitutive, epistemic categories; on the contrary, it regards history as a reproduction of the event as it really happened. From the perspective of historical idealism, however, what is "real" is a metaphysical idea. Consider the form of ideology or idealism which claims that ideas as they are reflected in our thinking are the actual empirical factors of history. This form of idealism is actually a species of materialism. Its view of the content of history is different from the view of historical materialism; however its methodological principle is no different from the image that historical materialism projects of itself.

Historical materialism is not actually the naturalistic theory it pretends to be. Consider the following consequences of historical materialism. History is distinguished from the totality of human life. The possibility of *historical* explanation is limited to complexes of events that fall under more abstract concepts. Given the privileged axiological status of economic interests, economic events are distinguished as the primary sequences within the inextricably related event-sequences of reality; there is a sense in which all other event-sequences are only products of the economy. All this represents a structuring and an organization of concrete existence. Regardless of whether it is substantively complete and internally consistent, a structure of this sort is necessary in order to form the chaos of interwoven elements into the distinctive construct of history. Historical materialism is a form of epistemological idealism. This holds true in spite of the fact—or, actually, because of the fact—that historical materialism is an attempt to refute an ontological idealism, an idealism of the event. Historical materialism is an attempt to discover the meaning that history must have in order to conform to our epistemic categories that are based on the idea that existence has a meaning. In the absence of a pre-established harmony, however, it is *possible* for history to have such a meaning only insofar as these categories constitute the pre-historical raw material of events as history. As the *content* of the meaning of history, historical material- ism has selected material interests—a choice that is, in a certain sense, utterly unidealistic. But historical materialism fails to recognize that even material interests motivate history only as mental values. This is an obstacle to the recognition that the idea is the *form* of history. Historical materialism is disposed to conceive this form in a realistic fashion too, a conception that is inconsistent with the actual content of the theory.

13. *Historical Skepticism and Idealism*

In taking a general view of the foregoing inquiry, there is a temptation to conclude that its principal tendency is skeptical. At the outset, "history" was restricted to items that are not accessible to any kind of direct verification: namely, mental processes. This essential symmetry between the subject and the object of history does not entail a realistic congruence between this object and the contents of knowledge. On the contrary, it entails that there is absolutely no mechanical correspondence between knowledge and its object. Instead, a complex and dialectical *process* of mediation can be identified, a process in which knowledge stands in a variety of different relationships to its object; this holds true whether or not the object of knowledge is the mind itself. This sort of substantial uniformity of knowledge and its object is actually only an index of the functional autonomy and legitimacy of knowledge. Also recall the following point. The types and concepts in which every form of history is obliged to fix the real event, the syntheses of event- sequences into more abstract total phenomena—all this amounts to the construction of a world of knowledge. Its definitive features cannot be replaced by any knowledge, no matter how exact, of the real causal relations of individual events. In the innumerable prob- lems which these considerations pose, history becomes quite remote from reality as it is directly experienced or immediately given, what we are disposed to designate as reality as such. Consider the fact that the conceptual apparatus of history does not qualify as a representation of directly experienced reality. This does not denigrate the explanatory power of history, nor is it a mark of the impotence of history as an inquiry. History simply does not have this purpose; it pursues a radically different aim. From raw material constituted by reality that is grasped in its concrete immediacy, history produces a structure with different dimensions and another style. Finally, the entire organization of the construct of history seems to be dependent upon ideas and metatheoretical interests. The meaning of history, without which we would not find it worthwhile to produce a construct of history, is determined by presuppositions that establish a qualitative distinction between history and "the brute facts." In the same way, the necessity for making a selection from the manifold of objectively homogeneous events also implies a qualitative distinction between history and "the mere facts."

Suppose that all this is interpreted as a form of resignation or defeat. This would be no more intelligent than the criticism of art on the grounds that it cannot achieve a reproduction of reality. Actually, the entire *raison d'etre* of art lies in the distance which separates the object of art from reality. This distance does not signify some negative incapacity or defect of art; it is the mark of a positive structure the values of which are measured by standards that are intrinsic to art. They are not determined by the distance or proximity between the object of art and reality. Suppose that we impose the following self-contradictory requirement upon history: it must describe the event "as it actually happened." This requirement is certainly not equivalent to a criterion for *truth;* a criterion for truth is a functional *relationship.* But this requirement demands a mechanical congruence. The point of view defended here can be represented as skepticism only if we insist upon this requirement. This is the same kind of misconception that represents Kantian idealism as a form of skepticism. Transcendental realism, of course, ultimately leads to skepticism, because it poses a problem the resolution of which contradicts the very essence of knowledge itself. But suppose that the objects of knowledge are a priori determined by our epistemic forms. Than any discussion of the unbridgeable discrepancy between subject and object—the basis of skepticism—becomes pointless. History is a construct built from the raw material of the immediately given. Its form is exclusively a consequence of epistemic conditions and requirements. Consider the skeptical objection that we cannot grasp the full reality and totality of historical existence. This complaint can retain its illegitimate force only because it confuses historical truth with experienced reality. The criterion for historical truth, however, must be an immanent property of historical inquiry itself.

Notes

1.   [The third edition, pp. 4–5, adds the following material]

Before further discussion of the sense in which psychological facticity constitutes the substance of history, it is necessary to establish, at least provisionally, the methodological relationship between psychology and history. In the usual sense of "historical interest," it is undeniable that all processes that interest us historically are mental processes. Even material processes—for example, the construction of St. Peter's Cathedral or the boring of the St. Gotthard Tunnel—interest the historian exclusively from the standpoint of the mental processes that are immanent to them. In other words, they are interesting insofar as they are the repositories of volitional, intellectual, or affective processes; however the interest in a mental process is not necessarily a psychological interest. For psychology, a mental process is significant simply because it is mental. There is no psychological interest as such in the *content* or *import* that psychic energy contains. Naturally we can acquire knowledge of mental processes only on the basis of mental contents that are or were present in consciousness, but the psychologist is only interested in the dynamics of the process itself. The contents of these processes would be completely uninteresting to him if they could be detached from the conditions under which they are produced by psychic energies. This distinction—between mental contents and the psychodynamic conditions for their production—can be made within logic, the sciences, and metaphysics. That is why these disciplines stand in polar opposition to psychology.

History is not so much interested in the *development* of psychological contents as in the psychological development of *contents.* For history, each content is fixed within a definite temporal frame. Therefore it is obvious that the question of greatest historical significance is the following: what is the process by which a given content appears in a given temporal frame and becomes comprehensible within it? The process itself has no intrinsic importance for history. On the contrary, the process is important only because it is the vehicle for the realization of historical content: the objective import of practical, intellectual, religious, or aesthetic consciousness that makes up an historical sequence. There is a certain sense in which history lies between a purely logical or substantive conception of mental contents and psychology, a purely dynamic conception. Psychology is interested in the dynamics and the development of psychic contents.

Consider the unity of psychic being and becoming. It can be directly experienced, but it can never be directly grasped or comprehended. Every science investigates this entity in its own characteristic fashion and with its own peculiar emphases. In order to investigate this entity scientifically, we analyze it into process and content. Psychology is a product of this division of scientific labor; its purpose is to describe this process and—in whatever sense this exists—its nomological regularity. This division of labor also generates logic and the sciences of substantive concepts. They investigate the import or meaning of mental phenomena in abstraction from the psychic conditions for the occurrence of these phenomena. Now consider history. In the ensuing, we shall show that its subject matter can be defined only by reference to some sort of intrinsic or objective significance. History is concerned with a content or import that is identified by reference to its essential significance; history investigates the psychic process in which this sort of content or import is realized.

2. Of course the a priori also has another epistemological function that is quite different from this. It lies beyond the limits of all being and becoming; it is the ideal norm of our knowledge, conceived purely from the standpoint of its content. However this is not the sense of "a priori" that is at issue in the present discussion.

3. In order to explain these phenomena, it is worth emphasizing at least one element in the structure of knowledge. Knowledge is inevitably based on the following assumption. In every individual case, a given constellation of causes necessarily produces its effect. Suppose it seems that the recurrence of the same constellation produces a different result. This can only be a consequence of the fact that the presence of different causal conditions has escaped our attention, the reason being as follows. Consider the truly individual properties of mental causes, their nuances, their increments, and their reciprocal causal efficacy. Either we are completely unable to identify and understand them, or we are able to do this only in a very incomplete fashion. Consider general concepts like love and hate, the sensation of power and depression, intelligence and will power, egoism and resignation, and many other concepts of this sort. We use the same concept to describe phenomena which are in fact utterly different, and we do this in a very crude fashion. In the further development of the constellation, these empirically heterogeneous phenomena then acquire an obvious causal efficacy.

One of the simplest illustrations of this point is the completely different—even directly antithetical—effect which the same mental energy has, depending upon the intensity of its activity. We know that love is sometimes extinguished by separation from its object, but we also know that separation from the object sometimes generates the most impetuous passions. There can only be one reason for this difference: in the first case, the emotional energy is much weaker than in the second case. In the quantitative scale of emotional energy, there is probably a threshold of the following sort: when it is reached, one effect of separation is transformed into its polar extreme. This would correspond to thresholds in our sense perception. Purely quantitative changes in stimuli make the difference between pleasure and pain; however we do not even have an approximate measure and expression for the determination of these degrees of affect. We are limited to general concepts that cannot be used to make these quantitative discriminations. In consequence, we inevitably use the same name to describe phenomena which have very different real properties and causal force. This is responsible for the following apparent fact: it must be the same causes which produce effects that are so very different. As regards the quantitative properties of these phenomena and their individual accents, tones, and fluctuations, our knowledge is incomplete.

Perhaps this incompleteness is not without some deeper basis. Perhaps it means that the purely individual aspects of mental processes are simply not accessible to the conceptual scheme of scientific knowledge. Perhaps we can provide a scientifically comprehensible reproduction of the mental only insofar as we can establish that something generally (or at least relatively generally) human gives it life: namely, that which is common to both the knowing subject and the object of his knowledge. Given the nature of knowledge, this limitation to the general concept, which cannot comprehend any concrete, individual manifold, would be a formal and completely adequate expression of the limits of the content of knowledge.

4. For the argument in support of this thesis, see my *The Philosophy of Money,* Chapter 1, section III.

5. [The third edition, pp. 28–29, adds the following note] Historicism remains unclear about the presuppositions of historical constructs that transcend every historical process; this lack of clarity is one of the epistemological sources of historicism. The doctrine is most seriously in need of revision in the following sort of case. Not only does the historical fact *constitute* a mental content—in the final analysis, this holds true for all historical facts. In addition, the historical fact also *has* a mental content. This is the case in the history of the sciences, religion, and the arts. Consider the understanding of the spatio-temporal development of these historical facts. This sort of understanding is completely dependent upon an understanding of the import of these facts and their objective, logical relationships, which latter are independent of the temporal conditions for their realization.

The following claim, for example, has been made about Kant: to understand Kant is to deduce him historically. Let us suppose that the import of pre-Kantian theories and their relationship to the work of Kant were not understood logically or psychologically, or in any other purely objective fashion. In other words, let us suppose that this relationship did not constitute a sequence that can be *understood* independent of its historical realization. In that case, the relationship of historical succession which obtains between the philosophy of Kant and the philosophy of his predecessors would amount to a discontinuity of purely temporal significance. The "historical deduction" of the work of Kant would be nothing more than the "understanding" of this discontinuity. Contrary to the historicist position, the "historical deduction" of Kant would be possible only under the following conditions. First, it would be necessary to "understand" Kant and the other relevant philosophers logically or substantively. In order to do this, it would not only be necessary to understand each individual philosophical theory; it would also be necessary to understand the objective relations between them, relations which are completely independent of any considerations of "dates."

The same holds true in the history of art. Consider the development of all the elements of art: the movement and tangibility of bodies, juxtaposition and perspective in space, a sense of color, and an understanding of form. The history of art may make clear the sequence of artists within which the progressive development of these elements takes place. However this reconstruction could never have the continuity and coherence of a unified historical sequence unless we had knowledge of the *substantive* or *objective* contributions of each artist, a form of knowledge which is completely independent of knowledge of their historical relationships.

It would be necessary to construct an ideal sequence of these artists, a sequence which may be compared—*cum grano salis*—to a syllogism: major premise, minor premise, and conclusion. From a psychological standpoint, of course, the elements of a syllogism do constitute a temporal sequence. But the temporal relationship between these elements would lack coherence and a definitive content unless it were possible to establish that they are related by an atemporal structure of *meaning,* a structure that is independent of all considerations of antecedence and consequence. Consider the following view of the history of art. The woodenness of Byzantine and Gothic groupings is followed by the individualistic disorder of the quattrocento. The latter receives a unified synthesis in the lawlike harmonies of the High Renaissance. From the end of the cinquecento, these harmonies begin to collapse, either into a shallow formalism or into a chaos of wild confusion. It is the intrinsic relationships of these aesthetic constructs—which we must understand in terms of their purely substantive significance and from the standpoint of the logic of art—that makes it possible to form them into an "historical" sequence of real, temporally related phenomena. Independent of these relationships, they would simply amount to an incoherent succession of phenomena. The conditions under which it is logically possible to constitute them as *one* coherent sequence— and, therefore, the conditions under which it is possible to identify this sequence within the infinite manifold of events—would not be satisfied.

Upon reflection, all of this is obvious. The following, however, remains the view of empiricist historicism: the mere observation of "historical reality" is sufficient to establish coherent historical relationships. But actually, coherence is a presupposition of history, a necessary condition which must be satisfied in order for reality to become history.

6.   [The third edition, pp. 47–48, adds the following material) Here again, we see the difference between history and psychology. A political decision is obviously an event that is produced by psychological causes. The following are necessary conditions for the understanding of such an event: all the actual conditions that exist in the mind of the actor, conditions that comprehend his entire life, including all of its extra-political aspects. Suppose that the actor had not experienced all the joys and sorrows of his life, all its ethical and aesthetic passions, all of the respects in which he had lived in harmony and in conflict with his surroundings. Without these experiences, the political decision in question might have been made in a completely different way. All of these considerations are irrelevant to the political historian. For his purposes, he produces a hypothetical construct: the political actor. This construct disregards the existential continuity between political activity and all other circumstances of life: it is as if they did not even exist. The political historian conceives his hero as if he were an exclusively political animal; he focuses upon the political aspects of conduct. In reality, of course, political activity only takes place within the psychological context of the extra-political factors just mentioned, but the political historian ignores this context. Suppose that he explains one political decision by reference to another; then he is obviously thinking in psychological terms. But this is a peculiarly hypothetical kind of psychology—it falls under the category of politics. It is an abstract sort of psychology in which the mental event is only represented as a mental construct of the consequences of contents insofar as they are understood in terms of the logic of politics. Mental phenomena that are conceived in this way function according to their own immanent laws. In empirical psychology, however, every mental event is understood as a consequence of the total structure of the personality.

The same sort of logic is employed when the biography of a scholar is represented as the history of his scholarly work. In this case, the various aspects of his mental life are of importance only insofar as they are oriented to an objective, cognitive or theoretical idea. Obviously the ideas that make up his work must have originated in his mind; conceived as mental events, however, they are connected and implicated with innumerable other ideas that have no bearing upon his scholarly work, which is why they are irrelevant to a history of this sort. Such a biography, therefore, is not an account of what the historical person actually experienced. The category by reference to which coherent aspects of his experience are identified and relationships of coherence are established lies beyond the origin of these aspects in his mental life. In lies in an objective idea, even though the mental life of the historical person is the ground of these relationships of coherence. Independent of his mental life, these relationships would not constitute "history."

7. [The third edition, pp. 56–58, adds the following material] In the foregoing, I made reference to a "subjective factor." Here we must keep in mind the distance and detachment which any science requires, in contrast to the free play of the artistic imagination. In addition, however, and completely independent of the question of more or less, there is no sense in which this "subjective factor" represents a purely variable moment of caprice and fortuitousness. One of the most profound and universal limiting conditions of our conceptual scheme rules out this possibility. The following point may be quite correct. It is one and the same complex of contents that we comprehend under the great forms of mental life: the forms of the empirical and the religious, the aesthetic and the practical, the conceptual and the emotional. But a form has certain specifications. It is never absolutely comprehensive; it is always historically determined and subject to historical variations. It follows that certain contents seem to have a predisposition for a certain form; other contents fall under this form only with difficulty or in a fragmentary fashion, and some contents simply do not fall under it at all. Not every arbitrarily chosen content of reality can be made into a work of art. Some contents do not occupy a position in our scale of emotions. Religious significance cannot be ascribed to every content. And it seems that there are contents that cannot be represented in certain stages of the conceptual apparatus of the sciences. Any form only comprehends reality in an incomplete fashion.

    If this point holds for the relationship between the universal forms of the mind and the raw material that they constitute, then it is obvious that it holds for more limited constitutive concepts which structure one domain of ideas. Suppose that the historian confronts an existential totality. Its properties appear differently, as if they were reflected by different mirrors, each with its own characteristic angle of refraction: politics, artistic accomplishment, religiosity, and epochs of specific types provide examples of these differences in perspective. In relation to the totality of real life, each of the images produced in this way is subjective. Each is determined by the purpose of historical knowledge. But the purpose of historical knowledge cannot be derived from reality; nevertheless, certain aspects of reality tend to fall under some forms but not others. The historical perspective is only applicable to certain aspects of reality; it only applies to certain modes of classifying these aspects. The objective properties of the elements of reality are not, as such, historical. It does not follow from this that history is capricious. However it does follow that the concept of the "history" of a personality is essentially different from the real personality or the reality of the personality. The concept of "history" has its source in a single, definitive category, and no other.

These points apply less obviously to the nuances of the principal categories. The concept of "politics" may be represented as one of the definitive angles of historical refraction. From the perspective of politics, the totality of the life of individuals or groups—a totality which is historically incomprehensible—is transformed by historical synthesis. But consider also the following questions, which in this context could either be stressed or disregarded. What subsidiary phenomena are relevant to political history for the purposes of confirmation, supplementation, or delimitation? In the temporal sequence of event-complexes, where are the causal lines to be drawn? These questions are dependent upon formative concepts that cannot be identified in the material of reality. If objectivity is ascribed to this material, then these concepts could be called subjective. But the general epistemological perspective of these concepts is certainly not always uniform and of the same invariable value. On the contrary, from the perspective of the general theoretical idea of history, we clearly judge that certain of these constitutive concepts apply to given cases, but not to others. In some cases, they reveal the significance of an event with absolute clarity; in other cases, they do not.

Therefore the "subjectivity" of history as a form does not entail that historical concepts are employed in an arbitrary fashion—just to the contrary. As a consequence of the ideal or—as it might be put—teleological relationship between history as a form and the heterogeneity of reality as it is actually experienced, this "subjectivity" is located within a latitude that has definite limits. The ambiguity of the concept of "objectivity" has created misunderstanding in this context also. Consider the belief that objectivity—in the sense of a categorically certain criterion that transcends contingency and caprice—can only be achieved by establishing some sort of necessary connection with the "object." In other words, there must be some sense in which it is necessary to provide an exact reproduction of the objective reality which can be distinguished from a priori subjectivity. However there is no sense in which satisfaction of criteria for certainty and significance requires a mechanical reproduction of "what really happened." Each of the functional relations between both—relations that are subject to innumerable modifications—can acquire certainty and necessity from the perspective of our concepts and purposes. From this perspective, the distinctions between the certain, the less certain, or the absolutely false remain secure. The value of "objectivity" is not a consequence of a reproduction of the intrinsic properties of the object.

8.   [The third edition, pp. 65–66, adds the following note] Certain historical constructs which have their own definitive properties and values are a result of the fact that there are general and irreconcilable differences between the

character of the person who produces them and the character of the historical person who is represented in the construct. The image of Italy in the mind of the Northerner is utterly different from the Italian's own mental picture of Italy. The character of the Italian is intimately related to his country. But this does not mean that the Northerner's image is "false." The same relationship holds for a man's description of femininity. Consider the portrayal of women in the works of Shakespeare and Goethe in comparison with the more exact conceptual construct which women have of themselves and of other women. This sort of representation is completely original and idiosyncratic. The issue at stake here does not concern the usual dependence of a picture upon the conception of the person who produces it, a dependence which makes it impossible to represent properties that are intrinsic to the object itself. The issue is not an epistemological problem, but rather a psychological problem within epistemology. Actually, this problem presupposes an objective, immediately given image of the object, the image which a subject, who has the same essential nature as this object, projects. It also presupposes an image of the object which can only be produced if there is an essential difference between subject and object. Such an image of the object has its own special "truth." The criteria for this sort of truth are based on this latter special presupposition. Even if we assume that there is an essential difference between the person who produces this construct and the person whom it represents, the distinction between conclusive truth and falsification or misrepresentation can still be made.

9. Strictly interpreted, the following Kantian claim also holds for history: constitutive unity is never "given in the object." On the contrary, "it can only be produced by the subject."

10. There is an extensive discussion of this process in my *Investigations into Social Differentiation*, Chapter 3.

11. In reality, each moment of economic history is codetermined by an influx of factors from every other imaginable province of existence. Consider, on the other hand, the tendency to see economic events as a unilateral or unidimensional sequence of causal relations. Extreme historical materialism exaggerates this tendency even more than the above remarks indicate. In the same way that mere freedom is invariably transformed into the struggle for domination, so, from the standpoint of extreme historical materialism, the independence of economic factors in relation to the totality of historical existence is transformed into the domination of the latter by the former. Historical materialism, therefore, is the exact polar antithesis of the principle emphasized above. Every single historical sequence is implicated in all other sequences. Therefore every moment in every sequence is a product of history as a whole. But historical materialism denies this: history as a whole is a product of the evolution of one of its individual sequences.

12. In this essay, I shall not take up the following difficulty, which belongs to the theory of knowledge in general. To what extent can laws, which provide us with knowledge of reality, be deduced from reality itself? Actually, this seems to be one of those paradoxes which has its basis in the relativistic character of knowledge. In any case, the above claims are independent of any solution to this basic problem.

13. Here we should note the following point, which will shortly be given a general interpretation in the text of the essay. Consider the structures which are, so to speak, produced on the surface of historical phenomena. In practice they are continuously related to the deeper, more profound structures that constitute historical causes. Quite often the correlation of individual sequences of phenomena, each of which contains its own imma- nent and sufficient causes, is based on a reciprocal form of sociological causation. This may be a result of the fact that the discrete sequences influence and modify one another to the point that they become similar. Or it may be a result of the fact that they produce or encounter an independent variable that acquires the status of a predominant, auton- omous causal structure, a structure the influence of which tends to eliminate the differences between these discrete sequences. Even the invari- ance in the purely quantitative values of the surface relations of these phenomena allows an inference which, if pursued, would lead to the discovery of their underlying causal laws.

    Suppose that among m cases of death—say about ten thousand—a certain number of suicides n remains constant. This fact could be explained by reference to the law of large numbers. The variety of influences which determines the conduct of each individual within his own milieu is can- celled. It becomes statistically insignificant *for observation* whenever a very large number of individuals—in this case, ten thousand—is considered. Suppose that in another sample of ten thousand cases of death a number of individuals deviate significantly from the norm. It is also probable that a corresponding number of individuals will deviate from the norm in the other direction. Therefore the average number of suicides, which corres- ponds to the value n, will again be produced. In this case, the question is analyzed as a mere problem of probability. Its factors are isolated indi- viduals, and their various differences are generalized in the computation.

    However the question can be analyzed in another way. Suppose that society is conceived as some sort of homogeneous totality or entity. Suppose that the immanent forces of this entity are a function of the number of its members. On this analysis, the collective social life of about ten thousand people would generate conditions which—given the further assumption of observed characterological differences—would in fact drive n number of these people to suicide. We know that purely quantitative changes in a group can produce qualitative modifications in its structures and its fortunes. It might very well be the case that m and its corresponding multiples are exactly the number of persons necessary to create the social relations that will dispose n number of persons to commit suicide.

The issue concerns two assumptions, both of which are only crudely sketched here. (1) As a result of differences in the original endowment of energy, intelligence, luck, etc., collective life generates relations of competition, oppression, and disappointment. Moreover the extent of these consequences is a function of the dimensions of the social totality that produces them. (2) In any given human population, there is a certain proportion of people who have a choleric, sanguine, phlegmatic, etc., disposition. The concomitance of these two empirical facts produces the following result. In a given social unity of a certain size, a certain number of individuals will be driven to suicide. Therefore let us suppose that from the standpoint of methodology the number m not only designates a composite of a certain number of individuals. Suppose it also identifies the inherent nature of the social entity, an entity the specific properties of which are functionally dependent upon its size. In this case, the proposition that among m persons in a given set of cultural conditions a certain number n will commit suicide is obviously not a genuine "law." But perhaps it is an approximation or a proto-form of a law, an example of what we noted in the foregoing as the *first* ground for the justification of historical or societal laws.

14. Consider the possibility that the segment of the cosmic process which we call history bears, as a homogeneous whole, a metaphysical import of this sort. This could be represented as a consequence of some sort of privileged relationship between the divine principle and one single ontological province, a consequence of the privileged and exceptional position of humanity that transcends the symmetry of the domain of the natural and the real. In this case, the restricted legitimacy of metaphysics, which is a consequence of its indifferent or symmetrical distance from reality, would be eliminated. As a matter of fact, a theistic metaphysics of history can be entertained as a logical possibility only insofar as it is implicated in a metaphysics of nature in general. However the following possibility also remains. The teleological chain, which begins with the lowest, most insignificant and insensate form of existence, has its ultimate or final link in the human race. In this case, human history leads directly to the ultimate or absolute purposes of the universe. For any teleological theory, in contrast to a causal theory, only a continuous relationship to its *ultimate* point is required. Therefore it follows quite obviously that a theistic teleology which is restricted to human history does not commit the error just criticized. There is no sense in which it denies the same metaphysical foundation to nature in general; it only employs the following legitimate principle. The teleological chain, which begins at the highest or most abstract point, may be broken off at any given point for the purposes of this metaphysical theory. The causal

chain, which begins with the lowest or least abstract point and proceeds in the direction of generality and abstraction, has the same legitimate claim to the use of this principle.

15. Suppose that the end of history is not identified as the purpose of some transcendent power that produces the drama of history and its denouement for reasons of its own. In that case, the use of this concept encounters serious difficulties. The reason is the following. Suppose that certain moments of history are said to be ends or purposes for which the remainder of history serves as an instrument or means. Unless these purposes can be ascribed to a subject, a subject which at least bears some sort of analogy to the human consciousness, this thesis appears to be incomprehensible. Consider the Kantian maxim concerning the teleology of nature. Certain natural processes transpire *as if* they were guided by a purpose. In the present case, this Kantian maxim is applicable only in a very different and aberrant sense. This is because the present issue does *not* concern a criterion for knowledge of reality—a criterion which, in any case, is already available—nor an epistemological claim, but rather a metaphysical thesis.

Suppose that great men are identified as the ends or purposes of history, and the existence of the masses is only an instrument for these purposes. Or suppose that the same status is ascribed to the following: the ethical acts that are consummated within the domain of historical phenomena, or the breakthrough of justice from the contingency and violence of events. In order to distinguish the teleological event from the merely causal event in these cases, it seems that a *nature, essence,* or *entity* which forms these purposes is necessary. If the structure of things is viewed from the standpoint of its meaning, however, this sort of reification is superfluous. Compared with the historian, the metaphysician of history views the course of events in a new light and from the standpoint of a novel problematic. He perceives or feels the dichotomy of means and ends as an immanent quality of the contents of history. From his perspective, it is unnecessary to suppose that there is a subject to whom this purpose can be ascribed, a subject that would classify events in terms of means and ends. It is unnecessary for the same reason that the order of things that corresponds to the norms of logic does not require the existence of a creative spirit which structured all things in accordance with these norms.

Consider historical events simply as empirical facts. They produce—depending upon the stratum of categories that they react with—the idea of a logical or a teleological structure. As a result of the famous transcendental axial revolution, the consciousness of subjectivity in a certain epistemological or metaphysical sense—the origin of the idea of a logical or teleological structure—has led to the absolute spirit. The rational or the teleological order of things emanates from the absolute spirit in such a way that we can read off or deduce this order from the things themselves. Logic has transcended this stage. Logical intelligibility simply represents an unmediated or direct definition of the conceptual object. In the same way, teleology can be represented as a quality that is immanent to things insofar as they are conceived from the perspective of metaphysics. This idea could be expressed in the following way. The course of history transpires *as if* a mind or spirit had constituted certain of its moments as ends for which all its other moments serve as means. From the standpoint of the requirements of metaphysics, however, this is either too much or too little. Either this absolute force that institutes the purposes of history will have the metaphysical status of an authentic, existential reality. Or—since there will be no need for this force to function as an heuristic principle—purposiveness will be felt as the metaphysical meaning of the historical event itself. No person or quasi-person of any sort who is extrinsic to this meaning and provides its basis or foundation will be required.

We should not suppose that a teleological view of history and a valuative or axiological view are interchangeable. Quite often both views coincide, and it often happens that the inner animation which history acquires as a result of its organization by reference to purposes is intimately related to the development of an axiological perspective. Nevertheless, the logical structure of the concepts of purpose and value is completely different. Moreover the import which these two concepts have for the philosophy of history need not be equivalent. It is certainly logically possible to suppose that the objective cosmic process culminates in some sort of purpose which an immanent or transcendent power has imputed to it without ascribing a value to the purpose itself. Value could be ascribed to some stage along the path to it: there are innumerable moments in history with which a feeling or sense of value is associated. Countless times this feeling tells us that for the sake of a certain deed or a certain sentiment it would actually be worthwhile to set the entire apparatus of history in motion, with all of its suffering and negative values. Yet we are also convinced that the mechanism of history does not function for the sake of these moments, but rather in the interest of other, future, or more comprehensive purposes. In addition, it would be possible to ascribe an objective purposiveness to the process of history and deny that it has any value at all. For example, we might suppose that, from a relative standpoint, the world is as good and as purposive as it can be. From an absolute standpoint, however, it could be ordered as badly as possible, so badly that it lies beneath the zero-point of value. Finally, we could deny that history exhibits any purposiveness at all and still ascribe value to it; for example, we could ascribe value to one of its aspects or to history as a whole.

16. Obviously these facts also acquire historical interest as soon as they function as exemplars of important types. The same holds if they represent

examples of more general states or stages that constitute necessary transitional points in a total process of development.

17. In order to avoid misunderstanding, "historical individuality" in this purely methodological sense is obviously not restricted to individual persons. On the contrary, it refers to all unique and qualitatively determined singular constructs. Therefore groups and situations, states and complete processes of evolution and development, as well as the existence and career of persons are all historical individuals.

18. At this point, the extent and limits of the problems of the philosophy of history appear quite clearly. Consider any subject. There is a sense in which a philosophical inquiry into this subject lies both beneath and beyond an investigation of the same subject by the exact sciences. Philosophy investigates the presuppositions and norms that provide a foundation and a direction for the exact sciences. These are the "conditions for the possibility" of the sciences. Therefore they cannot be located within the exact sciences themselves. Philosophy also brings the content of empirical knowledge—which is invariably fragmentary—to conceptual completion. It follows the various strands of knowledge—which in empirical reality are always confused and fragmented—beyond empirical reality until they can be woven together into a complete and self-contained conceptual fabric of being. The exact sciences are dependent upon the receptivity of the intellect to the given material of the cosmos; however it is obvious that both epistemology and metaphysics focus on the sovereignty of the intellect. As a result of the status of philosophy, it may happen that the a priori concepts which constitute conditions for the possibility of experience provide the warp for the metaphysical fabric which is woven into the absolute from the woof of the fragmentary contents of the cosmos and human life.

19. It is obvious that the form of progress in history which is at stake here would not be ruled out by the destruction of the human race. Suppose that this occurs. And suppose that the forces of the cosmos—which produced history in the form of the human race—develop completely different modes of expression. The form of progress with which we are concerned here is only progress within history. Its culmination at a certain point is not rendered illusory even if history as a whole does not have this property of ultimacy or finality.

20. On this point, sexual relations could provide, at most, only an analogy. Sexual relations also exhibit an incomprehensible diversity of psychological combinations that develop from the same invariably uniform foundation. But the number of actual palpable historical forms in which the possibilities of sexual relations are realized cannot be compared with the number of historical forms of economic life.

Index

Index

Aesthetic realism, vii, 20-21

A priori:
    concept of, 42-46, 78, 203n. 2,
      214n. 18
    Kantian, 42-43, 132-33, 176

Apriorities of history, viii, 6, 17-18,
    24-25, 28-29, 35n. 12, 42-43, 47,
    62-63, 83-87, 114, 134, 176-77,
    187

Apriorities of nature, 6, 17-18, 24,
    42-43, 62-63

Art:
    and history, 30, 33n. 6, 34n. 9, 70,
      78-79, 81-82, 86, 89, 91-92,
      138-39, 143-44, 151, 154-55,
      167-68, 193, 201, 205-206n. 5
    and philosophy, 23, 29
    and science, 82
    as a form, 20-22, 82
    the portrait as, 12-14, 33n. 6,
      80-82, 85-86, 143-44

Autobiography, 25, 78-80

Axiology:
    and the interests of historical
      knowledge, 36n. 15, 155
    and the presuppositions of history,
      29, 36n. 15, 197

Causation:
    concept of and the concept of a
      law, 104-109, 112
    concrete, 106-109
    mental, 43, 49, 51, 72-73,
      203-204n. 3
    physical, 43

Experience:
    as a form, 25-26, 35n. 12, 79-80,
      86-87
    historical, 1-2, 17
    human, 7-10, 79-80

217